About the

Gail Thibert grew up in Morden and attended a convent school in Wimbledon, where she was expected to be a 'good Catholic girl'. But then punk happened. Aged 15, she rebelled by dyeing her hair bright blue and started to design and make her own clothes.

After holding down a variety of jobs, Gail found she excelled at reading tarot cards. She is now known as one of the UK's top psychics and has made many appearances in magazines and on TV, notably giving readings to the cast of *The Only Way is Essex* and on Sky cable TV.

Gail is still in love with punk music and with playing in bands, and currently sings with Sarah Pink's Gravediggers and Flowers in the Dustbin. She lives with her teenage son near Epping Forest, where she works as a clairvoyant and medium.

Singing with Adventures in Colour. Photo by Andy Fennesy

SOAP THE STAMPS, JUMP THE TUBE

SOAP THE STAMPS, JUMP THE TUBE

GAIL THIBERT

Unbound

This edition first published in 2018

Unbound

6th Floor Mutual House, 70 Conduit Street, London W1S 2GF

www.unbound.com

All rights reserved

© Gail Thibert, 2018

The right of Gail Thibert to be identified as the author of this work has been asserted in accordance with Section 77 of the Copyright, Designs and Patents Act 1988. No part of this publication may be copied, reproduced, stored in a retrieval system, or transmitted, in any form or by any means without the prior permission of the publisher, nor be otherwise circulated in any form of binding or cover other than that in which it is published and without a similar condition being imposed on the subsequent purchaser.

The author and publisher are grateful to the following for kind permission to use copyright material: Adventures in Colour for lines from 'Adventures in Colour'; Steve Battershill from the Lost Cherrees for lines from 'The Rape Goes On'; Marianne Elliott and Maxwood Music for lines from 'I Can't Do Anything' written by Marianne Elliott; and Dave Hughes for extracts from his letters.

While the events in this memoir are true, some names and identifying details have been changed to protect the privacy of those involved.

ISBN (eBook): 978-1-912618-19-4

ISBN (Paperback): 978-1-912618-18-7

Design by Mecob

Cover images: Courtesy of the author

Printed in Great Britain by Clays Ltd, St Ives Plc

Dear Reader,

The book you are holding came about in a rather different way to most others. It was funded directly by readers through a new website: Unbound.

Unbound is the creation of three writers. We started the company because we believed there had to be a better deal for both writers and readers. On the Unbound website, authors share the ideas for the books they want to write directly with readers. If enough of you support the book by pledging for it in advance, we produce a beautifully bound special subscribers' edition and distribute a regular edition and e-book wherever books are sold, in shops and online.

This new way of publishing is actually a very old idea (Samuel Johnson funded his dictionary this way). We're just using the internet to build each writer a network of patrons. Here, at the back of this book, you'll find the names of all the people who made it happen.

Publishing in this way means readers are no longer just passive consumers of the books they buy, and authors are free to write the books they really want. They get a much fairer return too – half the profits their books generate, rather than a tiny percentage of the cover price.

If you're not yet a subscriber, we hope that you'll want to join our publishing revolution and have your name listed in one of our books in the future. To get you started, here is a £5 discount on your first pledge. Just visit unbound.com, make your pledge and type GAIL18 in the promo code box when you check out.

Thank you for your support,

Dan, Justin and John
Founders, Unbound

With grateful thanks to Des Connolly, who helped to make this book happen.

Super Patrons

Terry Anderson
Mary Angelo
Beatriz Arruti
Nina Ashby
Joanna Avalon
David Ball
Richard Barber
Sue Barber
Mickey 'Penguin' Baxter
Paul Beck
Linda Biesemans
David Bignell
Penny Bigwood
Mat Blackshaw
Nick Bliss
Steve Bonallie
Michelle Brigandage
Sharon Brown
Donald Brown
Sharon Brown
Cathy Burns
Paola Camacho
Wendy Cartledge
Andy Cavendish
Charlie Chainsaw
Elaine Chambers
Keith Chapman
Beth Charley
Pink Charlotte
Jo Clairvoyant
Simon Collins
Sue Hughes, Sandra Kenealy & Simon Collins

Gayle Colyer
Des Connolly
Dave Cooke
Sascha Cooper
Mark Cooper
Jed Cordner
Steve Cotton
Sean Cregan
Richard Cruttwell
Debs Dade
Andi Dalton
Hardcore Dave
Dai Davies
Donna-Marie Delaney
Mike Dines
James Dodds
Alastair Doggett
Vanessa Doidge
Sinclair Dowey
Tony Drayton
Jake Dyer
Michele Edwards
Corin Engdahl
Rachel Evans
Sian Evans
Pete Fender
Dave Fennessy
Mary Flannery
Anne Flannery
Sean Forbes
Margaret Forman
Felicity Fowkes
Aldo Framingo
Mark Fraser
Marc Freeman
Alan Galaxy

Suzan Galip
Jenny Gallagher
Tony Garton
Benedikt Manuel Gfeller
Nigel Griffin
Lal Hardy
Tony Harris
Gail Hart
Ashley Headbutt
Angela Hodgetts
Tony Holton
Nic Inparticular
Christine Ives
Andrea Jamieson
Ronni Jayn
Clare Jones
Brendan Judge
Kaffo Kaff
Dan Kieran
Pete King
Michele Knight
Linda Krawecke
Jmz Kross
Jon Lamb
Sam Lambert
Sunny Lazic
Wilf Lebois
Scott Lindsay
Dave Lusby
Maxine Lynch
Gerry Lyons
Pete Lyons
Bill Mahony
Maria Malo
Hazel Manuel
Gary Mccrindle

James McPhie
Fiona Ní Mhuirri
Zillah Minx
John Mitchinson
Lucy Moffatt
Gary Morgan
Bruce Moxham
Marge von Munchingindahausen
Stephen Myhill
Glenn Noble
Andy Norrie-Rolfe
Catherine O'Brien
Mark Oliff
Steven Pegrum
Monica Pelle
Helen Pilavakis
Sarah Pink
Claire Piper
Kieran Plunkett
Justin Pollard
Paul Pugh
Mike Pugh
Sue Punkette
Frederick Pyott
Yasmin Rahman
Robert Ramsay
Paul Redfern
Pete Relph
Mimsy Riccio
Lucy Robinson
Nina Rosser
Mick (Nick R) Rousseau
Marion Rowsell
Jennie Russell-smith
Warren Samuels
Paul Schofield

Hermann Schultebeyring
Anne-Marie Shevlin
Sara Shevlin
Simon Simon
Ania Skarżyńska
Lynne Skevington
Graham Smokey Smith
Jesse Smith
Martin Smyth
Peter Sode
Pete Spence
Bridget Stark
Phil Starr
Al Stevenson
Albert Tatlock
Sarah Taylor
Lily ThePink
Dawn Thibert
Lorna Tiefholz
Mel & Sonny Tyler
Tricia Venables
Rachel Vickers
Rich Walker
Gareth Waltrip
Steve Watson
Ian Weavers
AR Webber
Stuart White
George Willey
Ken Wilson
Mark Wilson
Priscilla Wong
Dave Wood
Julie Woolmore
Steve Worrall
Mareike Wunderlich

Sachiko Yamamoto
John Youens
Marina Young

Prologue

I was a good little Catholic girl born of conservative, right-wing parents, growing up in a quiet London suburb. I went to school, studied hard, did my homework and never, ever rocked the boat. And then, when I was aged 13, in 1977, punk happened.

The following journey encompasses the punk scene as it exploded in the UK in the late 1970s. Never before or since has teenage rebellion been so loud and so colourful, begging for its discontentment to be heard by Thatcher's Britain.

The following story also includes a wee bit of witchcraft (without a pointy hat in sight), big shiny motorbikes (vroom vroom) and a giant cast of kaleidoscopic individuals I have encountered along my merry way through this thing called 'life'.

Some people we encounter have a very positive impact on our lives, and some a negative, the latter often leaving us with permanent scars to prove it – this is life. I have altered some people's names to protect both the innocent and the guilty.

The following story documents my experiences as a young woman growing up in the London suburbs during the late '70s and beyond. Like most people, the passing of time has led to my viewpoint altering drastically along the way. Now in my early fifties (where the fuck did the time go?), I am kinder now and (slightly) less cynical. I have tried to remain as faithful as possible to events as I recall them and as they actually happened.

If you grew up in or around London, or perhaps in another UK city, between the late '70s and early '80s, maybe you can relate to what you are about to read. Perhaps we even met along the way? Regardless, I hope my story (so far) will serve as a true representation of what it was like to come of age during this era…

Down the King's Road with, from left to right, Pus, Hardcore Dave, me and Jenny

Chapter 1

Sounds

**BORED LONDON PUNKETTE (18)
SEEKS WEIRD OR INTERESTING PEOPLE
FOR FRIENDSHIP AND GIGS
REPLY TO BOX NO 13561**

I placed the above advert in *Sounds*, a weekly music newspaper that ran between 1970 and 1991. It really does have a lot to answer for. For a start, it was partly responsible for me joining and performing in post-punk synth bands – Adventures in Colour and, later, the Lost Cherrees.

I unwittingly placed the personal advert myself, with the sole purpose of finding some like-minded friends in a world as yet unchanged by the Internet and social media. I realise now that, ignorantly, I advertised for weird people to write to me – meaning a bit unusual, a bit left-field, y'know. I'd been a punk since I was 14 and, at 16, I had bravely dyed my hair peacock blue, much to the disbelief of my conservative parents, with whom I lived in Morden in Surrey (a shithole south-west of London, whose only claim to fame is that it has no claim to fame and that it is a shithole in South-West London).

Up to the point a couple of years earlier when my hair turned blue, when I was aged just 16, my life had been that of a typical suburban teenager – i.e. pretty boring. Many of the things we take for granted today – DVD players, mobile phones, smartphones, the Internet, social media, 24-hour television, satellite TV, digital cameras and Justin Bieber – hadn't even been invented. Many weren't even a twinkle in their inventors' eyes in the '80s. A home generally had a TV (approximately the size of a tank and weighing slightly more than Saturn, but with an inexplicably small screen) with three channels and a landline phone if you were posh or decadent enough.

My conventional parents had foolishly hoped that I would go to school, get a steady job, marry a steady man and have some steady kids and that I would not, at any point, have blue hair. I, however, wanted adventure, punk rock, cider in copious amounts, to not live in Morden, to go to gigs and to have blue hair. Once people become parents they seem to forget all of a sudden exactly what it was like to be a teenager, and my parents were no different. They wilfully failed to appreciate my teenage urge to express myself and to embrace anarchy with my middle fingers raised to the sky. And they *really* didn't like peacock blue. Morden was, and still is in my opinion, the utter pits. I know there are much worse places in the world but, when I was a teenager, Morden for me was akin to hell. Absolutely nothing goes on in Morden. And at that time there were only three pubs in the whole damn town and you wouldn't actually have wanted to set foot in any of them, unless you were a bloated darts player or over 50. Or both. I know this might blow any chances I ever had of working for the Morden Marketing Board, but Morden is a shithole.

It didn't take much then for me to quickly establish myself as a rebel. Wearing a cardigan that wasn't beige or leaving the top button provocatively undone was considered an act of rebellion in Morden in the late '70s and early '80s. I exaggerate, but only a little.

I'd had the same long, chestnut brown hair for as long as I could remember, but the dreariness of my surroundings and the simultaneous birth of punk made me want to stand up, stand out and be goddamn noticed. I'd been inspired by the discordant styles of Lene Lovich, Toyah Wilcox, Hazel O'Connor and the high priestess of gothic alt-rock, Siouxsie Sioux, all of whom had gained exposure during the late '70s and early '80s, and so blue hair just seemed like the obvious way to express my burgeoning creativity. Despite trying to fit in with my school colleagues and with girls the same age as me, it had quickly become apparent that I really didn't fit in with them and never would. And nor did they want me to. I didn't fit into the suburban norm. And I was beginning to realise that I didn't want to fit in either. I was desperate for a change and for some excitement to chase

CHAPTER 1

away the dismalness of Morden in the '80s and, anyway, I had always liked the colour blue.

With the help of a friend, several bottles of bleach and many tedious hours, I rinsed my hair to find a colour I can only describe as straw yellow with toothpaste white roots. It was already getting late and so, running out of time, I swiftly emptied the blue Crazy-Color dye all over my yellow-and-white head and waited, somehow expecting my hair to suddenly transform into a cascade of beautiful blue locks, like I had envisaged. Imagine my surprise when…

I got home that night and scuttled up the stairs like a panicked rodent, terrified of what kind of extreme weather conditions my parents' anger might herald upon seeing my new 'look'.

'I'm really not feeling well!' I told my mum as she came running upstairs after me, wondering if everything was OK with her formerly chestnut brown-haired and fairly normal-acting daughter.

It was only with the cold and terrifying light of morning, and the natural light it brought with it, that the reality really hit me. The blue hair dye had chemically reacted with the straw yellow, turning it a kind of tropical sea green. That's fine, you might be thinking. Not what you were after but at least it's a colour. Loved blue with a passion. Hated green with a vengeance. And what's more, although the roots were a pleasant shade of electric blue, it wasn't exactly the look I had been aiming for.

There was really no way of hiding this hideous do other than decapitation and we didn't have any sharp-enough knives in the house. I therefore knew that I must summon up all my bravery in order to face my folks which, at the age of 16, was a hugely terrifying prospect akin to admitting one's part in the murder of a member of the royal family.

'My hair's gone green!' I exclaimed innocently to my mother, as if the transformation had inexplicably occurred without any assistance from myself or half a litre of primary-colour hair dye and a friend. My mother pivoted on an axis, stopping mid-toothclean and staring in rabid disbelief at the general greeny-bluey-ness of her formerly chestnut brown-haired child.

'Ang agger guy gold goo gok goo!' she said. She spat the mouthful of toothpaste spume into the sink and then repeated, somewhat more articulately, 'And after I told you not to!' She slowly took in the full carnage of her teenage daughter's do in a state of quiet, yet minty, disbelief.

It was true. I had previously expressed an interest in a more experimental hair colour than chestnut brown. And her response had been an unequivocal no. Having had my original request for blue hair negated, I had run through the rainbow of possible hair colours that she might find more acceptable, but every shade from blue and purple to yellow and pink had met with parental disapproval. Disapproving is what parents do best.

I had therefore decided that I would make my own decisions about my appearance, regardless. It was my hair after all. I was 16 years old and therefore a very mature adult. What right had my parents to tell me how to dress? I didn't ask to be born etc, etc.

My mother did finally regain the use of her limbs after what seemed like several hours of staring in shock at the top fifth of my body.

As Mum and I usually took the same bus into Morden (her on her way to work and me on my way to college) I decided the day after I had turned blue-green to give her several additional minutes of enjoying life with a normal daughter by taking a later bus. However, I realised this plan had backfired as I approached the bus stop and saw that my mum was still there, waiting, and surrounded by her bus-stop cronies.

'Look at that girl with the green... the blue... the greenish... bluish...!' uttered one of the women, as her jaw dropped open, ever so slightly wider than the Blackwall Tunnel.

'That,' said my mother, 'is my daughter.'

My mum later told me that this woman was a bitch (I've paraphrased her slightly there for dramatic effect) and so I was never sure whether her statement relating to ownership was born of reluctance or perhaps the tiniest amount of pride. I like to think it was the latter. It was probably the former.

Gradually my family became used to my daring hair colour and, in fact, my mum even bought me some pink dye one day. I suppose, in her mind, pink was most definitely the lesser of two evils. Pink

Chapter 1

was at least feminine. And my dad only stopped speaking to me for two weeks, which meant a whole fortnight without having to listen to terrible dad jokes, which was great. Dawn, my sister, of course outdid me by managing to avoid dad jokes for an entire two-year period, after she came star-jumping out of the closet a few years later to inform my parents that she was a lesbian.

Unnatural hair colours were a new concept. It wasn't like today, when even mainstream pop stars like Katy Perry and Lady Gaga sport brightly coloured hair. Hair of any colour other than natural shades was extremely rare. Cyndi Lauper hadn't appeared on the world stage yet. Toyah Wilcox (who had a few hits in the early '80s) was more famous for having outrageous bright pink-and-orange hair than for her musical output, and it was she who really paved the way for a generation of neon-topped girls and boys.

So, anyway, there I was, aged 18 and bored in Morden with less bluey-green hair and now a peroxide crimped barnet, looking for some like-minded friends to go to punk gigs with and to hang out with, being all anarchic-like. Morden at the time was full of soul boys and girls. Soul boys wore Farahs, a brand of smart trousers that I found revolting, with ghastly argyle-patterned Pringle jumpers (that's right, there was a time when golfing attire was willingly worn by teenagers). Soul girls wore polyester A-line skirts with stilettos and no tights, which were fine in the English summer, which could sometimes last for up to a week, but the rest of the year the cold made their legs look blotchy, like slabs of leg-shaped corned beef. Both sexes had bleached-blonde wedge haircuts and, inexplicably, wore sheepskin jackets (the go-to fashion item for used-car dealers). They listened to Luther Vandross (more like utter dross!) and Lionel Richie. I was most definitely not a soul girl.

Whilst the soul boys and girls were stealing fashion hints from Del Boy, I was studying for my exams and listening to the legendary Radio 1 DJ John Peel, whose regular radio show featured eclectic musical styles from progressive rock to punk to death metal to you name it. His was the holy grail of radio shows for anyone interested in the alternative scene in the '80s and '90s.

From the late '60s until his sad and untimely death in 2004, if you had ever played a note on a guitar or sung in front of the bathroom mirror with a hairbrush microphone (at one time more popular and definitely more affordable than the industry-standard SM58), then you had probably dreamt of your band being played by the legend that was/is John Peel. I really never had the remotest idea that, just a year later, I would be playing in one of the bands featured by Peel on his radio show.

Meanwhile, inspired by the dramatic punk fashions, I had taught myself to sew. Punk attire was characterised by rips and zips and buckles and graphic imagery and crude slogans. It was the antithesis of fashion. Punk clothing meant anything goes. Clothes were handmade, shabby, fucked up and unique. I started making my own clothes and soon had a few commissions to make clothes for other people. I wanted to be a fashion designer like my heroine Zandra Rhodes. Her clothes were as crazy and colourful as she was. She had shocking pink hair and a wild, larger-than-life personality to match.

As I may have mentioned before, Morden (or Snoreden) was a bit of a quiet place full of soul girls and boys. I was very much the only punk in the village. And punks get lonely too, you know. So in order to alleviate the boredom, I decided to put that ad in the classifieds section of *Sounds* inviting weird or interesting people to contact me. I tentatively placed the ad in an envelope with a cheque to cover the cost of advertising, dropped it into the postbox and went back home to wait for all the weird and interesting people to come and find me.

A week later I received my first reply. In retrospect, 'weird' was probably not the best choice of word I could have used in that situation. Meet Malcolm. Henceforth known as Malcolm the Foot Fetishist.

Malcolm described himself as 'tall, thin, with dark-brown hair and a moustache.' A description that, I have to be honest, didn't exactly epitomise the punk look in my opinion. He went on to say, 'If we become friends, I'd love to pamper your feet.' Malcolm concluded the first side of the page with 'I do hope you'll write to me soon and tell me your...' I hesitantly turned the page over, expecting the next phrase to be 'shoe size' but, sadly, Malcolm was playing hard to get and only wanted my phone number at this point. I responded to Mal-

CHAPTER 1

colm's admirably honest letter with a picture of a giant footprint and said, 'Pamper that if you can.' Since then, I've always assumed that all foot fetishists are called Malcolm and that all Malcolms are foot fetishists. Correct me if I'm wrong. I wasn't shocked or offended by Malc's toe fascination, but he was not the kind of weird I was looking for.

The second response I received was from Graham. Graham had included a photograph of himself in which he had very normal brown hair.

'Dear Box no 13561' started Graham. 'I reckon I'm weird and punk…' I took another look at the photo of Graham. I reckon you're not, Graham, I thought to myself. But wait, Graham continued…

'My best mate is into GBH, Crass, The Damned, Pistols, Varukers, Charge, Vice Squad, etc, etc,' he claimed. My best mate has a penis, I thought to myself, but that does not make me a man.

'I like peppermint tea, rosehip tea, and joss sticks,' continued Graham bewilderingly. Had Graham confused punk with hippy?

Graham concluded his letter by apologising for not having written sooner because he had been 'busy with the DHSS and drinking'. It's good to have hobbies, Graham. Malcolm was beginning to sound like the better proposition.

It was a few days later and I was beginning to think it was going to be just me, Malcolm and a shoehorn, when a third letter arrived. It was from a sexy boy with a Mohican haircut who lived in London and whose name was Joe. I'll have some of that I thought and, taking a chance, I wrote back to him and included my phone number.

Over the next couple of weeks, letters piled in from 'weirdos' of all shapes and sizes, and from all over the country. I thought *Sounds* was a music paper! I had definitely learned that my bold use of the word 'weird' had been a grave mistake, as was confirmed by the arrival of Derek's letter, which came with an accompanying photograph of said Derek in bed sexily reading a porno mag. Luckily, the portion of the photo below Derek's waist had been tastefully removed to preserve Derek's modesty and in order to create a little mystery.

Derek described himself as 'six-feet tall, of slim build and VERY

WELL ENDOWED.' He went on to say that he was 'not so much a punk, as SEX MAD'. Eurgh.

'I have no place to rest my aching loins and I have no girlfriend,' he whined. You will not be resting your loins anywhere near me, Derek, you fucking pervert, I thought. I sat down and sensitively composed a reply to Derek: 'You will not be resting your loins anywhere near me you fucking pervert!' I replied. And I'm not sad to say I never heard from Derek again. Some other lucky lady won that prize.

Happily, most of the correspondence I received in reply to the *Sounds* ad was from like-minded people with similar interests. I often wonder whether Malcolm ever managed to find a woman whose insteps he could adore. Or perhaps he was just an arse-sole and ended up alone, touching his own feet for pleasure.

A few weeks later, I got a phone call out of the blue from a guy called Perry. I didn't know anyone by that name, and it didn't match up with any of the letter writers I'd been corresponding with. Yet, during the course of the conversation, Perry told me a few accurate details about myself, such as what I looked like, my age, where I lived and other personal details and, if I'm honest, I was feeling a little uncomfortable. I thought it might be an old school friend fucking with me. Perry asked me to meet him that night at a remote Tube station in London at 6pm. I still thought it was a wind-up. However, Perry seemed offended when I said I was suspicious. So, purely out of curiosity, and with a modicum of naivety, I agreed to meet him.

I had crimped and backcombed my paper white peroxided hair to within an inch of its existence and ensured it would never again move with a generous application of the strongest hairspray known to punk-kind. I wore a white second-hand dentist's tunic with a black belt, a black skirt and black tights. My make-up was dark and heavy.

I stood outside the Tube station and, after a while, an obese skinhead boy showed up. He even had a swallow tattoo on his neck. How original. Perry wore a green bomber jacket, tight jeans and Dr Martens boots – full-on skinhead attire. We got talking and I immediately wanted to know how he had got my phone number and knew my name and so much more about me. Perry told me to stop asking questions and just enjoy being with him. I didn't find him phys-

CHAPTER 1

ically attractive but he seemed interesting and I was really curious about how he knew so much about me. Plus, I was 18 years old and extremely naive, especially when it came to the opposite sex.

Outside the station, Perry pointed at the pavement and said, 'This is where I work.'

'I work on a London souvenir stall,' he said in answer to the puzzled look on my face. An obese skinhead who sells cheap crap to tourists – that's original, I thought.

Perry treated me to a cup of tea in a cafe. I was still feeling wary and as if I couldn't relax until I knew how this obese, swallow-tattooed, fridge magnet-vending skinhead had managed to get my number, and why he'd phoned me in the first place. Conversation flowed though and, after the cafe, we went on to a pub. Perry generously offered to buy drinks for me and, being 18, I was impressed as I thought that must mean he liked me. I wasn't very experienced with men at this point in my life. Eighteen-year-olds then were like 13-year-olds now. It never once occurred to me that Perry might have an ulterior motive. That he wasn't just a generous young man wishing to be kind to a young girl with no money. We went to a small place in the backstreets of Soho called the Sound and Vision. It had a video jukebox – I had never even seen one of those before.

Perry bought me a pint of cider and black, a popular drink with young alternative types back then as it was alcoholic, very sweet, a funny colour and there was lots of it – what more could a young punk want from a beverage?

Perry told me all about himself and that, apparently, he had been the secretary for the Sex Pistols and had roadied for Toyah and the Boomtown Rats. I didn't know whether to believe him or not or whether he was just bragging. Anyway, a few pints of cider and black later, and with very little experience of alcohol, I have to admit I was feeling very merry. Two men on the next table joined us for a while and they both bought rounds too. Soon, I was reeeeally drunk. Perry took advantage of my state – which was way closer to pissed on the scale than it was to sober – and kissed me. I really didn't fancy him and I wanted him to stop but I was drunk and young and wasn't sure what to do or say.

11

I should mention at this point that, when you have low self-esteem, there is a tendency to let anyone treat you how they want to treat you. This might be difficult for someone with healthy self-esteem to comprehend. Someone confident with a good, strong level of self-assurance would have had no hesitation in telling Perry to fuck off and leave them alone. But I had no idea how to deal with this situation.

'I suppose you want to know how I know you,' Perry said eventually.

'I'd forgotten all about that,' I slurred.

It turned out that Perry lived in the same house as Joe with the Mohican who had responded to the *Sounds* ad. Joe had shown Perry the ad and mentioned he was going to write to me. However, by the time my reply arrived, Joe already had a new girlfriend (which explained why I hadn't heard anymore from him). Perry had liked the photo I'd included and had cheekily memorised my phone number without Joe's knowledge. I must admit I was amused by Perry's boldness, although that might have been the several litres of cider 'talking'.

The pub finally closed and I said it was time for me to go home. Perry invited me back to his for more drinks but I said I didn't want to miss the last Tube. I barely knew this guy and, had I been sober, I definitely wouldn't have done what I did next. However, I wasn't sober, I had drunk my weight in cider and black and Perry successfully managed to persuade me to go back to his place, even offering to pay for a cab home a bit later. I lived 15 stops away on the Tube, so it seemed like a very generous offer, and I assumed he actually liked me. The alcohol had robbed my mind of any common sense at this point so I stupidly agreed to go back to Perry's for a nightcap before getting a cab home. Innocent enough, I thought.

Perry lived on the top floor of a Victorian house in West London that had been converted into a type of hostel. I was full of booze and staggered up the four flights of stairs to get to Perry's room.

The room was smallish but strangely tidy for a boy. We sat on his bed, as it was the only place available to sit other than the floor. Perry put on a record, poured us some gin and pulled out a scrapbook. The scrapbook was full of press cuttings featuring many bands that I loved, including the Sex Pistols. And there amongst them was a pic-

Chapter 1

ture of Perry, and a reference to him being their secretary. As a drunk 18-year-old from Morden I was, of course, very impressed although this was a feeling that was, sadly, rather short-lived.

Perry encouraged me to finish my drink and drew closer to me. 'You don't think I bought you all those drinks for nothing, did you?' he said out of the blue.

It was at this point that I realised that I was probably in a very precarious situation. My mouth went dry and I suddenly felt scared and sober – or at least much less drunk. All of a sudden Perry lurched towards me. I was completely incapable of defending myself. Even if I'd been sober, he was a heavy guy and he caught me off guard. Perry was groping me and I knew that I really didn't want to have sex with him. I definitely didn't fancy him and now I had decided very recently that I really didn't like him either. What I thought had been a gesture of kindness I now realised had been a horrible ruse. Like I said, I was naive. Catholic schools in the 1970s didn't prepare young girls for situations such as this.

Perry yanked my skirt up and I tried to push him away. I wasn't going to give in or make things easy for him.

'I'm not just after your body. You can stay the night if you like,' Perry said, as if this would convince me. However, his actions belied his words as he continued to slide his hands roughly up and down my legs. Thankfully, due to the fact that I was wearing a combination of tights, underwear and a skirt, Perry suddenly seemed put off. That, or he realised that if he continued to have sex with someone against their will then it would make him a rapist, which is kind of illegal. He stopped and pulled my skirt back down.

'I think you'd better go,' he hissed.

'You said you'd get me a cab,' I said. The last Tube had long gone by now and I had no idea how to get home. Even if I'd tried to walk home, it would have taken hours and I had no idea of the route.

Perry reluctantly agreed, and actually appeared to be sulking. After his behaviour. Incredible! How wronged he must have felt. We walked back out into the night and I was exceptionally relieved not to be trapped in that tiny room any longer with a potential rapist. A black cab was eventually hailed and I gratefully climbed inside. As the cab pulled away I realised Perry hadn't given me any money to pay the driver and I had none either. I didn't care. I was just glad to be out of his reach and to be heading towards home. I rooted around at home and managed to get together enough cash to pay the cab. It was a narrow escape from a very undesirable scumbag and a lesson learned. Note to self, Gail: not all men are honourable.

Chapter 2

South Kensington

Not all the people who responded to my advert in *Sounds* were 'bad', weird or sex maniacs. Flick, for example, was a dramatic girl who I exchanged a few letters with before we finally met. I recall that she had the tiniest precise handwriting (so very different to my own chaotic scrawl) that belied her lively personality.

Flick and I had been penfriending for a while when she caught me completely off guard by telephoning me. And I'd never heard such a posh voice! She sounded like a voiceover from the 1940s. Flick had left her home county of Norfolk (where, like most, or at least many, teenagers, she didn't get on with her parents) and had gone to live with her aunt in London. At 17, Flick was a year younger than me, and what a typically fiery Leo she was.

Flick and I met for the first time outside the Hammersmith Odeon. She had striking short pink hair that was crimped and backcombed to perfection. She was wearing a black gay-biker cap, luckily without the handlebar moustache that often accompanies it, and bondage trousers covered in straps. Her make-up was as dramatic as she was. I loved her the moment I met her and we immediately got on like a large house on fire.

Flick and I started going to gigs and nightclubs in London and pretty soon we were inseparable. Although Flick seemed to be on a mission to get herself a boyfriend, I really wasn't too bothered about romance. Perhaps Malcolm, Graham and especially Perry had put me off boys for a while. And besides, I was having loads of fun as I was.

Pretty soon, Flick suggested that we should get a place together in London. I was simply dying to leave Morden and become more independent – the Tube journey from Central London to Morden was interminable and I'd been feeling increasingly asphyxiated by my parents, who failed to understand their teenager daughter's quirks – and

I couldn't think of anyone else I'd rather live with. So I absolutely ran and jumped at the chance. Fun and freedom on tap in an exciting city crammed full of venues, punk bands and nightclubs; living with my best friend; two pairs of crimpers to choose from – count me the fuck in.

So a week before we were due to move in together, I was giving a bloke I'd just met at a gig a goodnight kiss when Flick suddenly materialised. 'Isn't Gail lovely?' she said, and then promptly stuck her tongue halfway down my throat. A lot of people were sexually experimental on the alternative scene and being bisexual was definitely not uncommon. However, kissing girls really wasn't my thing. My sister's, yes, but not mine. I pushed her off. Seven days before we were due to move into a place together, and now I was beginning to have les-ervations. Was Flick after more than just friendship? The last thing I needed was someone hassling me for sex whilst I was drinking Cup-a-Soup in my PJs. Thankfully, I didn't have anything to worry about. I think I'd made it clear to Flick that I was definitely heterosexual, as she never tried it again.

So Flick and I moved into a bedsit in South Kensington. Ideally, we'd wanted separate rooms (with a spiral staircase, a sunken bath and a small but loyal staff) but a cramped bedsit with a shit sink was all we could afford. The exterior of the house was well posh with impressive white pillars and the works. It would have been a family home at some point, but now it had been divided up into studio flats or rooms and we were in the room closest to the front door, which meant that every time one of the other tenants slammed the door on the way out or in, our walls rattled. It was like living in a snare drum. We were happy, however. We had our independence. The room consisted of two single beds and a sofa so ancient it probably should have been on display in the Victoria and Albert Museum. It was hard to believe that it had ever been comfortable. In fact, it was hard to imagine that it had ever been new.

'Where's the kitchen?' I'd asked optimistically, as the landlord showed us 'around', which, incidentally, didn't take him very long. The landlord – complete with blonde wedge '80s haircut – strode over to a wardrobe in the corner of the room and proudly threw

CHAPTER 2

open the doors to reveal the tiniest handbasin I'd ever seen and a one-ring electric hob. No fridge, no oven, no anything. Instead of having kitchen cupboards, we had a cupboard kitchen. No wonder we didn't need loyal kitchen staff.

Still, we were young punks with our first home in London and the last thing we cared about was cooking. Fuck nutrition, we thought. And there was always the humble Pot Noodle. I would go back to Morden every Friday night as I had a cash-in-hand Saturday job there for which I earned the princely sum of six quid for the day. And so my mum would make sure I'd get to eat a proper meal once a week at least.

Despite the cramped conditions, Flick and I were having the time of our lives. We entertained each other, played cards, wrote letters and still managed to go out cheaply pretty much every night. We found all sorts of ways of making our money stretch. Many clubs handed out flyers that enabled us to get into other events and clubs for half price or free. We'd neck a bottle of cheap Merrydown cider before we went out to save money on drinks, usually as part of the getting-ready ritual of crimping our hair into oblivion and applying excessive quantities of black eye make-up. The cider was cheap, sweet and highly effective, so it pretty much ticked all the boxes. We'd be pissed before we even left the house. And once we were out, we would 'minesweep' drinks that unsuspecting nightclubbers had foolishly left unattended on tables. These days you don't leave your drink unattended to avoid getting Rohypnolled. Back then, it was because people would nick them. How times change!

The process of hair crimping was part and parcel of being a punk or goth in the '80s. It involved dividing the hair into sections, dousing it in cheap lacquer and then crimping each section of hair from root to tip. Usually the hair was so damp with holding product that it would emit a satisfying sizzle and steam would rise from the crimpers. After a while, the crimpers would be covered in a thick layer of gunge from hair dye and hair product. Often, and not surprisingly looking back, people's assaulted hair would snap off from repeated bleaching, colouring, crimping, backcombing, lacquering and general abuse. The '80s was not a great time to be hair. Luckily, my hair was miraculously robust and, thankfully, impervious to misuse. This was possibly down to the one nutritious meal a week I had at my mum's.

Our favourite drinks – and indeed the drinks popular with a large majority of punk and alternative types at that time – were cider and black (blackcurrant cordial) or Pernod (an aniseed-flavoured liqueur) and black, if you were feeling rich or if someone else was buying. Flick used to chat men up and try to get them to buy her drinks, but I was way too shy. Flick loved Pernod and black to the extent that most of the time she stank of aniseed and probably did purple poo.

We stayed in South Ken for about eight months. During the winter, we couldn't afford to use the fan heater as it used up too much electricity – we had to feed the meter 50-pence pieces like you wouldn't believe. It was like having a child. A noiseless one. That ate money. I'd often spend the day walking around the nearby Natural History Museum or the Victoria and Albert Museum (where the sofas were more modern than ours) as they were free to get in and had a thing called 'central heating'.

It was long before the advent of digital cameras but we were always taking photos on my cheap little plastic camera, which you had to load with a cartridge of film, then snap merrily away and hope for the best when you posted the film off or dropped it into a chemist's for processing. You'd have to wait a couple of days – unless you paid extra for next-day processing – before you could see how many pictures had actually come out all right, and then pay all the same, even if none of them came out OK. There was none of this instant imaging and deleting the ones you're not happy with that we have the luxury of these days. I'm happy now to have so many photo albums bursting with memories of friends and events and the various eras of my life. So many hairstyles and hair colours documented. Flick and I also kept diaries, in which we would scribble down all the scabrous details of our nightlife. Every morning, after I had written my entry for the previous night, Flick would make me read out what I had written. I soon realised this was in order to make sure that I hadn't written anything negative about her, so I always made sure that I worded my accounts carefully.

Chapter 2

It was through Flick that I met Sebastian. Sebastian had changed his name to Sebastian as he was a huge fan of the band Sex Gang Children who had a song called, you guessed it, 'Sebastian'. Sebastian thought the name Sebastian was exotic and gave him an air of gothic mystery. More so than a name like, for example, Eric. Which was Sebastian's real name. Actually it was Dave, but I'll refer to him here as Eric to avoid confusion with later Daves.

As I mentioned previously, Flick's goal in life was to find herself a man, and she made it her secondary mission to find one for me, regardless of whether I actually wanted to find myself a man or not. And to be honest, I wasn't really that bothered. Life was good already. As soon as we arrived in a venue, Flick would start scouring the place for suitable male victims – like an avid huntress sweeping the horizon for potential prey.

The now-legendary 100 Club is one of London's oldest venues. Punk and alternative acts such as Siouxsie and the Banshees, The Jam, the Sex Pistols, The Damned, the Angelic Upstarts and Buzzcocks all played gigs there in the '70s and '80s. Tuesday night at the 100 Club was punk night, at which Flick and I were regulars.

'See anyone you fancy?' Flick would say the moment we entered a club. This was Flick's mantra and she would deliver it whilst simultaneously scrutinising the clientele for suitors to her punk throne.

One night, she asked me the same question as usual and, as I looked around, I saw some random bloke with lovely crimson hair – which was about all I could see of him to be honest. More out of a desire to get Flick off my back than because I was interested in anyone, I said 'I quite like his…'

Before I could finish my sentence, Flick had already pounced and was already uttering the extremely embarrassing and well-worn chat-up-line-by-proxy 'my mate fancies you'. I stood there totally embarrassed waiting for the floor of the 100 Club to swallow me up. Which it failed to do. Nightclub floors were pretty basic back then. A bucket of dry ice and a mirrorball was as technical as it got. I remained unswallowed.

'Come and meet Eric' – as he was still calling himself then, before morphing a few weeks later into Sebastian – 'he's really nice,' said

Flick. But my eyes and Eric's had already met and neither of us seemed particularly interested in the other. Eric had had surgery to fix a harelip and he also had acne scars – but he did have gorgeous hair. Flick, as always, was as persistent as a hungry lion chasing down a wildebeest and kept insisting that I talk to him. 'He's really nice,' she told me. 'I'll introduce you.' Despite Eric and I doing our very best to ignore each other and resist Flick's stubborn attempts to matchmake, she eventually succeeded and, once she had introduced us, she immediately fucked off, kindly leaving us to it.

After several minutes (that felt more like centuries) of awkward silence, Eric told me that he liked animals. 'That's nice,' I said. And I could hear time drumming its fingers.

Eventually, going with the animal thing, Eric revealed that he had a mini zoo in his flat, which was aptly located in Elephant and Castle. Why do I always end up with the odd ones, I thought, fondly remembering Malcolm the foot fetishist and, rather less fondly, Perry the almost-rapist.

I love animals too and was intrigued when Eric went on to tell me that he had had a kestrel and tarantulas and that the kestrel had eaten the tarantulas or vice versa, I can't quite recall – who am I? David Attenborough? – something ate something, OK.

I was just deciding that I actually quite liked Eric and his small and murderous SE1 menagerie when Flick reappeared, clearly dissatisfied with the romantic progress Eric and I were making, and suggested that Eric and I kiss. I looked embarrassed. And so did Eric. And so Flick, being a good best friend, kissed Eric for me. 'He's such a good kisser!' she exclaimed. Eric leaned in to kiss me but, as soon as I opened my mouth to latch onto Eric's, I suddenly felt the compelling urge to vomit. This was due to the substantial quantity of powerful cider and lager combos (aka snakebites) that I'd been necking since I arrived, rather than because Eric was repellent and vom-inducing.

Luckily, I managed to pull away and sprint to the toilet, which was over the other side of the venue and through throngs of dancing people, just in time to projectile-vomit five or so pints of second-hand snakebite into the toilet pan. Afterwards, aware of the fact that I was

Chapter 2

coated in post-sick sweat and that I smelt mainly of vomit, I thought better of going back to Eric, and persuaded Flick to take me home.

We were to bump into Eric several times over the next few weeks and it was during the course of knowing him that he changed his name from a very-down-to-earth-and-normal Eric to an interesting-and-exotic Sebastian. At first, we avoided each other like we were both carrying a medieval plague but eventually we turned into good mates, yet nothing more. Apparently, almost vomiting in someone else's mouth when they are about to kiss you and then sprinting inelegantly in the opposite direction is not considered foreplay. Romance can be so confusing.

Luckily, Flick eventually found herself a man, which meant that she dedicated more time to him than she did to finding scarred zookeepers for me to vomit in. She started dating a goth bloke called Si. Si had hair dyed jet black (of course) and wore very pale foundation and a ton of black eye make-up. Because that's what goths did.

Flick and Si met during a gig at the Lyceum. A Flock of Seagulls were a new-wave synth band from Liverpool whose biggest hit was 'Wishing (If I Had a Photograph of You)' in 1982. The name A Flock of Seagulls came from a line in a Stranglers song. The band were more famous for singer Mike Score's dodgy '80s haircut, than for their music.

Anyway, as always, Flick and I had been drinking pretty heavily and, for some reason Flick stepped backwards and toppled over. Luckily a man caught her. This hero was Si. Si's black Mohican hair flopped sexily over his eyes. Immediately, Flick started chatting to him and within minutes they were laughing. Before I knew it, I had been introduced to Si's mate Gary, who was also gothic-looking with an even longer and floppier black Mohican. Gary was much taller than Si and didn't say much. In fact, he didn't say anything at all. He was 120 per cent goth.

Flick dragged me along to their first date at the Fulham Greyhound, a pub that often put on live bands in a dismal room at the back between the '70s and '90s. All kinds of bands played there but, during the '70s, it was very much a punk venue. Sadly, it's one of the many small venues in the UK that is no longer with us. It fell into disuse during the '90s and has recently been turned into another much-needed sports bar. Sad, but true.

Si was lovely and extremely likeable and we all got on really well, so I didn't feel like that much of a gooseberry. And, as it turned out, Si was a witch. Not a warlock, he insisted, but a male witch. I come from a psychic family, so the concept of the supernatural was not alien to me. I knew a little about witchcraft and was intrigued by Si's witchery. I didn't share the common misconception that modern witches were spooky virgin-sacrificing Satanists. And anyway, Si lived in Croydon – not a location notorious for the dark arts as far as I knew.

One day, Flick looked fearfully at me and told me she had been looking in Si's wardrobe and had found two knives.

'What did they look like?' I asked curiously.

'One had a white handle and one had a black handle,' she replied, eyes wide.

'Oh!' I said. 'Don't worry, they're just witches' knives.' Witches' knives (or ceremonial knives) were not allowed to come into contact with blood. 'It's unlikely that he'll stab you or anything,' I added, reassuringly.

'Unlikely?' said Flick.

Si later confessed that, the night he had met Flick, he had done a love spell in order to find a girlfriend. So when Flick had drunkenly fallen into his arms at the Lyceum, he knew it was no accident, and that fate had delivered her to him, as requested. I wonder if he should have specified that he wanted a girlfriend who wasn't a total nut job when he performed the love spell.

Though we'd agreed that boyfriends weren't allowed in our space-restricted bedsit, I made an exception for Si as I liked him a lot and was as interested in mysticism and white witchcraft as he was. We'd often go clubbing until 3am (which is the time clubs shut back then) and as Si worked during the day delivering bread (not the most occult profession I could think of) he had to be at work at ridiculous o'fucking clock and so he would get a bit of kip on our sofa and then go straight to work.

Si would often take us all out to clubs and gigs in his tiny delivery

CHAPTER 2

van – the preferred transport method of punks and goths – him and Flick sat up front like bread-van royalty whilst little old me and silent Gary were squeezed in amongst the bread crates at the back.

Initially, Si did sleep on the sofa, but it soon become apparent that as soon as they thought I was asleep, he would tiptoe into Flick's bed and magically return to the sofa before I woke up. And then after a few weeks of this, he didn't even bother returning to the sofa. They started to make excuses to get me out of the way so that they could spend time together in the room without me, which was understandable as they were a young couple in the throes of romance and Flick and I slept in the same room. They would often tell me to go on ahead to gigs we were supposed to be going to together, saying that they'd meet me there and then fail to materialise. I certainly didn't begrudge them this time together, although they could have just told me outright as I had no interest in watching goths canoodling. Luckily, anyway, I had other friends who I would hang out with.

Bizarrely, at around the same time, strange things started happening in the flat. We were convinced we had a resident ghost; either that, or someone had a key to our room and was helping themselves to what few belongings we had. Flick had also started to have major mood swings and could turn suddenly aggressive for no apparent reason. I sometimes saw her take her aggression out on Si, even hitting him a couple of times. Si seemed to take it all in his stride and, after each outbreak of craziness, Flick would smother him with kisses and apologies. I recognise this now as domestic violence.

The first thing we noticed going missing was, curiously, our cutlery. Not just one knife or fork – the whole bloody set and the container it was stored in disappeared, never to be seen again. Then my Snoopy-shaped moneybox, containing just a few quid, went missing from my wardrobe. Sometimes, things would inexplicably vanish and then turn up again in the exact same place a short time later. A skull earring I had 'went on holiday' for an entire week and then was found exactly where it should have been. At first I think we silently accused each other, but then things started happening when we were both out of the room. We'd go for a walk down the nearby King's Road, come back and something would have changed places in the room or gone missing completely. Once I left a map folded up on my bed whilst Flick and I went out. When we returned, the map was spookily open on the floor, as if someone had been reading it.

I started to doubt my own sanity. We tried to be logical and assumed that perhaps a previous tenant still had a key, and so we tried to catch the person out. We also wondered if it was the landlord letting himself in and trying to make me and Flick fall out as it was generally her belongings that went missing, and so it naturally looked like I was to blame. Her Public Image Ltd album (*Metal Box*) went missing, as did some new white tights, and I knew she was suspicious of me. I invited her to search my wardrobe to check that I didn't have them and pointed out that it was me who had given her the tights in the first place. Did we have a Johnny Lydon-loving poltergeist with a penchant for hosiery?

A few weeks later, with our relationship already destabilised by her burgeoning mood swings, and the continuing inexplicable disappearances, Flick pulled back her bedclothes to discover reddish-brown marks on her sheet that looked like dried blood.

'Maybe you cut yourself and didn't realise,' I suggested, helpfully I thought.

'Gail, I would know if I cut myself!' she snapped.

On closer inspection, the marks looked more like scribble than blood, as if someone had drawn on her bed-sheet. The colour looked very familiar to me. I went to my wardrobe and took out my artists' pastels, which I hadn't even opened since leaving art college a year or two previously (around the same time as dyeing my hair blue/green/blue) and discovered that each and every pastel had been deliberately broken in several places.

I confronted Flick: 'You think I did that to your bed, don't you?' I said. She glared back at me. 'Well, look. The colour of this pastel matches the marks in your bed, but do you really think I would break my own expensive pastels like this?' I showed her the broken pastels. She seemed to see my point but I'm not sure she was totally convinced that I hadn't broken them myself to make it look more convincing.

We never did get to the bottom of these strange events but I have often wondered since whether Flick wasn't at the root of everything

Chapter 2

that was going on. I'm not sure why she would do these things. On one occasion, before hooking up with Si, I recall she'd met a bloke at a gig and decided to visit him at his flat, taking me along with her, for backup, as usual. He wasn't expecting her and was busy cleaning the loo and told us to wait in the living room whilst he finished. Unhappy at being 'ignored', Flick grabbed a bunch of keys off his coffee table and we left. The poor guy must have known it was her who had taken them. He rang her later but she flatly denied it.

'That'll teach him a lesson for ignoring me,' she said bitterly as she tried to justify her crazy behaviour. Back at the bedsit she stuck the keys into her diary as a souvenir. The key fob included the poor guy's door keys and the key to his moped. I wondered how he'd manage without them but Flick didn't seem to feel any remorse. In fact, she felt justified.

I was still sharing the bedsit with Flick when I joined Adventures in Colour, the band my penfriend Dave Hughes played in. Flick and I were still hanging out together and drinking excessively but the odd occurrences in the flat and her violent mood swings had caused a definite tension between us and things were not as they used to be. Perhaps she resented me for being in the band. I had begun to realise that Flick was extremely possessive and very controlling, not to mention unpredictable.

One night, we were on a train going to a gig out of town. Flick had put her camera in my bag, or so she said, because when we arrived at the gig she looked in my bag and there was no camera. In fact, I hadn't even seen her put the camera in my bag and I certainly hadn't volunteered to be responsible for it, but her reaction was volcanic. She verbally attacked me, screaming and pulling at my clothing like a volatile crimped-haired demon. I was shocked and shaken by her behaviour.

'I didn't even want to look after it!' I said, incredulously. 'YOU put it in my bag!' I tried to reason with her, saying that it could still be at home, and that perhaps she was mistaken, but she was having absolutely none of it. I was frightened her verbal attack would escalate into a physical attack. She was out of control and it was starting to be unpleasant to be in her company. As soon as we got back home,

Flick started tearing the place apart looking for her fucking precious camera.

I urged her to leave it until the morning. 'It's late now. Go to bed,' I reasoned, but this raging little woman was having none of it. She pulled everything out of her wardrobe, and then proceeded to do the same to mine. Surprisingly, no camera was found.

'It's your fault!' she screeched. 'YOU were meant to be looking after my camera – you said you'd look after it and now you're going to have to buy me a new one!'

'Anything for a quiet life,' I acquiesced, feeling bullied into submission, not for the first time. I was beginning to feel unsafe around this crazy wench.

In the morning, Flick was up super-early, still searching through the two wardrobes she'd already destroyed the night before in search of her stupid sodding camera. Luckily it was a Friday, which meant it was band rehearsal and so I had a good reason to get out of Flick's way for a few hours.

My hair was short and neon pink around this time, with blonde streaks. I wore it crimped and backcombed. I applied large quantities of dramatic '80s make-up, which consisted of heavy black geometric eye shadow and blusher applied in wide strokes and not blended. Subtle was not a word I would have used to describe my look.

During my journey, I went to the post office to buy a stamp for a letter I needed to post. I was just throwing the letter in the letterbox when Flick suddenly appeared like a crazed banshee and bellowed:

'IF YOU'VE GOT MONEY TO BUY STAMPS, THEN YOU'VE MONEY TO PAY ME! I WANT MY MONEY FOR THE CAMERA!'

'GIVE ME MY FUCKING MONEY!' she screamed as she grabbed a handful of my hair and pulled me to the ground. She was like a crazy Staffordshire bull terrier and I was like a meaty bone. Flick had my hair in an unremitting grip and was refusing to let go. I tried to push her off but still she wouldn't let go. I had a perspex tambourine in a carrier bag in my hand that I tried to hit her with, but the bag split and the tambourine disappeared musically down the high street. She still didn't let go. I tried to kick her away but my shoe flew off. It

CHAPTER 2

would have been funny if I wasn't so scared. Surely the police would come along any minute now and pull this possessed woman off me, I thought. Surely someone would see I was in trouble and come to my rescue? No one got involved. And still Flick wouldn't release me until I stuffed money into her hand. She released her grip on me immediately, and then calmly walked off as if nothing had happened.

I was in complete shock after this attack. Nothing like this had ever happened to me before. I took the Tube to Ladbroke Grove, shaking and crying with my make-up running all down my face, making me look more dramatic than ever. People on the Tube were staring but, typical of Londoners, no one bothered to ask if I was OK.

When George, our keyboard player, opened the door, I burst into tears again, but I managed to pull myself together enough for when Dave and Lisa, the other band members, arrived. Dave was my boyfriend by then and he gave me a massive hug and I began to feel better. Halfway through the set, though, the communal phone rang in George's hallway. Somehow, Flick had found the phone number (must have gone through my phone book, the cheeky bitch). I refused to go to the phone, though. I was still in shock and she was the last person in the world I wanted to talk to.

'She wants to apologise,' George assured me. 'She sounds really remorseful,' he added. Reluctantly I went to the phone, and Flick told me she was sorry.

All the same, I was full of dread later when I made the journey back to the bedsit in South Ken, not knowing whether she would try to attack me again. I tentatively opened the front door, as quietly as I could manage, half expecting a crimped Tasmanian devil to hurl itself at me and wrestle me to the ground.

'Oh Gail!' she gushed. 'Oh, you've been crying! Oh, you are silly, aren't you?'

She really had no idea of the anguish she had caused. My scalp was tender where she'd yanked out a handful of my hair. In fact, I had a bald spot in that place for 10 years where my scalp was traumatised, before the hair eventually grew back.

My trust in Flick was gone. I knew that I didn't feel safe in that bedsit or even in her presence. I knew that I could never trust her again.

I headed back to Morden on the Tube. When my mum saw me, I broke down in tears and related the event to her.

'I know you say you don't smoke, but this is an emergency,' she said as she lit me a cigarette, which I declined, and listened with horror as I described Flick's behaviour.

'That's it! You're moving back here. Don't argue. You're not staying another second in that room. You're not safe,' she ordered and, the next day, my lovely mum helped collect my possessions.

'I'm moving out,' I told a shocked Flick, as we loaded my meagre belongings into my mum's car.

'But what about me?' Flick protested. 'What about the rent? I can't afford it on my own,' she whimpered.

'Well, you shouldn't have done what you did, should you?' I retorted, and my mum shot her a classic close-range, don't-fuck-with-my-daughter glare. The kind only mothers can do.

Chapter 2.5

Excerpts from the diary of an 18-year-old punkette

I went to a lot of nightclubs in my late teens and early twenties. Those that stood out were Skin Two and Cha Cha's, which was located next door to Heaven in the Charing Cross Road, not far from Trafalgar Square – handy for the London night buses, if you didn't mind sharing public transport with drunken people who were ready to vomit at any second (and often did, and maybe I was one of them?) or people screeching loudly from one end of the bus to their mate at the other end, all whilst suffocating in billows of smoke. (Yes, smoking was not only allowed on buses at the time, but also cigarettes were advertised both inside and outside the buses and on the Tube, although that changed within a few years.)

Punk gigs were taking place in abundance and my favourite haunts included the Clarendon in Hammersmith and the Fulham Greyhound, where the barman refused to serve me pints of snakebite but would serve me a half pint of cider and a half pint of lager. Go figure. Mind you, sometimes at other venues, when the lager and cider were mixed in the glass an alchemical process occurred and a strange lava lamp in a pint manifested before your very eyes…

A FLOCK OF SEAGULLS
THE LYCEUM
15 NOVEMBER 1982

Flick and I were two of the five people there tonight who weren't mainstream. It was so different to a punk gig, as everyone just stood there quietly watching the band like they were admiring a work of art in an art gallery, whereas at a punk gig people bounce around and break things – often themselves and each other. This gig seemed very conservative by comparison.

A Flock of Seagulls were brilliant. The lead singer actually LOOKS like a seagull! He has a strange hairstyle that really looks like a seagull coming in to land on his head. Brilliant.

Flick had planned to be there without Si, and was enjoying her freedom when he suddenly appeared behind her and gave her a red rose of all things. I felt a bit in the way.

Later, we saw Knox, lead singer from the Vibrators standing at the bar. He was wearing a white cap. Flick knocked it off as she went past. I thought she was going to keep it, but she threw it back.

I later saw Flick with the bloke she'd seen outside, the one with the blond spiky hair. She said he'd just grabbed her. As I stood talking to them, I felt an arm go around my waist. It was a friend of the bloke Flick was with. He introduced himself as Tomor. I asked him if his surname was Hawk. Corny I know. I liked him a lot. He was very handsome and punky too.

UK SUBS / VIBRATORS
KLUB FOOT
18 NOVEMBER 1982

I met Flick outside Hammersmith Odeon before going to Klub Foot. There was a bit of a queue. Flick had her eye on a man with blond spiky hair who was leaning over the railings. We got pissed inside and spent the evening just wandering around. Soaphead, whom I'd met at previous gigs, was also there so I spoke to him for a bit.

Outside, after the gig, one of their friends was wearing Knox's (the Vibrators' singer) hat. Me and Flick grabbed it but then someone else managed to grab it off us – it was a free for all as everyone was after his hat. We never got it in the end. Tomor asked for my address so he could write. We are moving into a bedsit on Saturday(!) so I gave him the address.

CHAPTER 2.5

24 NOVEMBER 1982

I met up with Rich, the bloke I met last night, at South Kensington station. I didn't think he'd turn up, so only wore jeans and a T-shirt, not much make-up and only slightly backcombed my bleached hair – but I was really pleased when he did show. We went to his mum's in Fulham because he wanted to go back there to live. He'd been sleeping in a water tank in Mortlake. He was homeless. His mum was out, so we went to Barnes to see his mate but he was also out. I asked Rich if he'd told Jeff he knew me.

He looked at me and said, 'Oh, you're not the same Gail as the one from the magazine (*Sounds*) are you?'

'I bet that's put you off me,' I said laughing, but he said it hadn't.

He said that Jeff and Colin had seen me and Flick standing outside Charing Cross Station a few weeks ago and had wanted to go up to us. In the end, Rich had got so pissed off with them for dithering that he'd said *he'd* go approach us, but Jeff had said: 'No! Don't go! They're really transvestites!'

Rich's hair was black then and I wouldn't have recognised him. Most punks change their hair colour every week. He didn't recognise me either. Later we went for a drink in a pub in Hammersmith, and he played pool with a mate. I was bored, so I went home and arranged to meet him later at The Batcave – a club that only opened a few months ago. I thought it odd that he didn't give me a proper kiss goodbye or put his arm around me all day. I put it down to shyness on his part.

Later on, whilst I was getting ready, Flick was in a hurry to get me out of the house, and kept saying that I would be late meeting Rich and that I should get a move on.

So I was stood waiting outside The Batcave for my date in the pouring rain, but thankfully under a big umbrella. I was wearing a lot of make-up and I was scared I'd be mistaken for a prostitute as I was in the middle of Soho [an area notorious in the early '80s for sex clubs and prostitution]. Shortly, two policemen came up to me and told me to get back in the club.

'I didn't come from any club – I'm waiting for someone,' I said.

They gave each other a knowing look and one of them said: 'Wink, wink!'

God, even the police think I'm a prozzie, I thought. I tried to protest my innocence but it was really humiliating. I took refuge in the nearby McDonald's where families kept gawping at my spiky bleached hair and dramatic make-up whilst they stuffed French fries in their mouths.

I had a cup of tea and then went back to meet Rich. A foreign man with a beard came up to me and asked me the name of the street we were on, which was really fucking obvious as the street sign was clearly visible.

'Fuck off,' I said and he did, but later he came skulking back over to me and quietly said, 'How much do you charge?' I felt so insulted that I marched off in my high heels and took the tube home, crying my eyes out. I never did find out if Rich turned up that night. I'm not sure he had my phone number.

THE BATCAVE
1 DECEMBER 1982

Finally made it into The Batcave! The Batcave doesn't open until 11pm. and closes at 3am. There was a queue of weird/alternative looking people outside and it was really weird and dead good inside. I was beginning to sober up, but Flick just got worse. We danced to a David Bowie song. A band called Alien Sex Fiend played live. They were ok. We saw Stevo there (the manager of Some Bizarre Records and Soft Cell). Si said he saw Marc Almond from Soft Cell in the men's toilets combing his hair and talking to himself in the mirror, which we found amusing. The DJ – Ollie from The Specimen – looked amazing in black blusher and was wearing fishnet tights on his arms like gloves.

*

CHAPTER 2.5

SPLODGENESSABOUNDS
100 CLUB
7 DECEMBER 1982

Si drove me and Flick and a load of his mates to The 100 club in his bread van. We reckoned we were probably the only weirdos arriving in a baguette delivery vehicle. The van was full and Flick had to sit on my lap in the front. Si's mate Gary kept knocking the window and poking his tongue out at us. We arrived pissed on cheap cider. Splodgenessabounds were great. We kept a look out for Angel, another of my mates from the *Sounds* advert but couldn't see her. Soaphead was there though, propping up the bar as usual with his sleeves rolled up on his leather jacket.

THE ALTERNATIVE FASHION SHOW, KINGS RD, CHELSEA TOWN HALL

THE ADDICTS
KLUB FOOT, THE CLARENDON, HAMMERSMITH
9 DECEMBER 1982

We were bored all day until Flick remembered that the Alternative Clothes Sale was on at the Chelsea Town Hall, so we went. It wasn't worth the 40p entrance so in the end we went window-shopping down the King's Road as it was cheaper! We went to look at the clothes on the Kahn and Bell stall in the Great Gear Market, forefront of new romantic and alternative fashions.

I was still bored later on and so I tried to get Flick and Si to come and see the Addicts at The Klub Foot, but Si was sulking, so I ended up going on my own. I had been drinking gin but it was still pretty boring on my own with no Flick to have a laugh with and to ask me if there was anyone I fancied.

When I got home, Flick was alone and already in bed. Si had walked out for no reason and she had been on her own all night. Si had left some confectionary snowmen he'd made at work, so we ate them.

THE DAMNED
THE MARQUEE CLUB, SOHO
15 DECEMBER 1982

Si was giving me and Flick a lift to The Marquee in Soho to see The Damned. I was in the back of the bread van as usual, rattling about with the breadbaskets. When the van stopped and I got out I stepped right into some wet cement.

I'd never been to The Marquee before. It was tiny and dark inside and the floors were sticky. I liked it. As soon as I got inside I bumped into the blond bloke who'd kissed me last night. He said hello, but I ignored him as I don't want any trouble from his angry girlfriend. He said hello to Flick but she ignored him too. Sebastian with the red hair was there too – he bloody gets around! Although I guess that means I do too.

Dave [Reeves], a bloke I'd previously met from a band called The Straps [a punk band from Battersea whose lead singer was called Jock Strap, possibly not his real name] came up and told me about their new album. He showed me a copy and told me to buy one and he'd sign it for me. Typically, I didn't have any cash to buy records so I suggested he bought one for me instead. He laughed at the suggestion and I never did get a copy.

Flick and I got really excited when we saw Captain Sensible and Dave Vanian from The Damned in the audience, whilst the support band – Johnny Moped – were playing.

Whilst I was watching Johnny Moped, I became aware of a young bloke with short black spiky hair staring at me. After a while he came over with his mate and stood next to me.

'What are you doing, stood here all on your own?' he asked.

'Waiting for people to come up to me and ask what I'm doing stood here all alone!' I replied cheekily.

CHAPTER 2.5

I smiled and said I liked his T-shirt. He told me his nickname was Sid, as he looks a bit like Sid Vicious, but his real name is Will. His mate was called Spike but his real name is Mark. I liked Sid, and so we went into the bar where it was quieter so we could talk and he practically told me his life story. He told me he thought I was beautiful and kept saying, 'Gail is *bella*,' explaining it was Italian for beautiful, which I thought was rather odd at the time, as he was Welsh. He said he'd been looking at me all night from the moment he saw me walk in. Sid wore a studded leather belt with pyramid-shaped studs. I said I liked it, so he gave it to me. He told me he'd had all his clothes stolen in a hostel, so I might as well have his belt. We arranged to meet at the dole office the next day, as we both sign on at the same time and place in Fulham.

I didn't get the bread mobile as usual but got the tube home with Sid and Spike. Spike was really funny and extremely likeable but for some reason, Flick couldn't stand him. He told us a really funny story about his pet spider which had no legs and had to bounce around on a thread of web looking for food. Everyone at the tube station could hear him and lots of people were laughing.

GBH
THE KLUB FOOT
16 DECEMBER 1982

We were on our way to see GBH play at Klub Foot when we were spotted by two black men who screamed, 'Back! Back!' like we were vampires and made cross signs with their fingers, which made us all laugh.

We were in the bar when a boy with a red Mohican stuck his tongue out at Flick. We went and sat on some empty beer barrels and saw a hippy bloke with long black hair head butt a punk girl and pull her hair out. Someone had to separate them and calm the punk down, as she was hysterical. We had no idea why he'd head butted her.

The boy with the red Mohican, who'd stuck his tongue out, kept going past us and smiling at Flick, so we asked him what had happened. He said he wasn't sure but that the girl deserved all she got. A few moments later, a skinhead boy came right up to me, screamed in my face and walked away, which shook me up.

Later, I was sitting on my own by the bar when a fight broke out amongst a table full of skinheads nearby. I thought if I didn't move sharpish, I'd be beaten up too.

Flick was by the stage talking to Soaphead later, he was messing about trying to pull her hat off. So, for a joke, I pulled it from behind, thinking she'd play along. Instead, she turned on me and started to hit me and pull at my hair, which actually really hurt. I hadn't meant to upset her, so I was slightly alarmed at her reaction.

'I've got a bone to pick with you,' she hissed when we were at home later. 'Would you mind NOT pulling my hat off? It really annoys me. You only do it when Soaphead is around.'

I was upset by what she said. It wasn't true. I'd never touched her hat before. I don't know why she was being horrible.

VICE SQUAD
100 CLUB
21 DECEMBER 1982

We had arranged to meet Angel (*another* from the *Sounds* ad) down the 100 Club tonight. Me and Flick were already pissed as newts. I'd never met Angel before. She has long orange hair spiked up like inverted ice cream cones, only sharper and her make-up is incredibly intricate and amazing. She had drawn a design like a red and black protractor around her eyes, tapering into a point down her nose.

Flick and Angel got on very well. I looked terrible that night, my hair wouldn't go right and kept falling down on one side but wasn't too bothered about it. We were all messing around by the bar, taking photos, and Flick caught Soaphead (whom I had a bit of a crush on) in a few when he wasn't looking.

A skinhead boy came up to us, asking to take a photo of Flick and

Chapter 2.5

Angel, but he ran out of film, so I took one with Angel's camera instead, and included him in the picture. The skinhead started kissing Angel, and ended up with her black lipstick all around his mouth. It looked really funny. Then for a laugh, Flick decided we should take some pics in the girl's toilets. As I stood next to the tampon machine, I realised it was broken, so I removed all the tampons and stuffed them in my jacket pockets. I cut my thumb in the process. Just as I was seeing to my thumb, a load of male skinheads burst into the ladies. I looked up as someone grabbed my arm. Looking up, I realised it was Perry! The bloke who tricked me into meeting him outside a London tube station. The one who'd tried to roughly 'seduce' me.

I was really pissed and he practically dragged me out the toilets and over to the opposite bar to buy me a drink. He was trying it on again. I was struggling to stay in control of myself. He kept trying to get me to come back to his place with him. I realised he was trying to use me, trying to get me to agree to have sex with him, I'm not sure if it was because I was drunk, that he thought maybe I'd be less resistant to his advances. I gave him an emphatic NO.

'Ok, so I was a bastard,' he admitted, 'but I want to show you I can be nice. How much did your taxi home cost you?' he asked, referring to that horrid night a few months ago.

'Eight quid,' I replied [the equivalent of about £80 these days]. He offered me a fiver, but I said I didn't want his fucking money. He kept hassling me to come back to his and wouldn't drop it.

'You like vodka don't you?' he said.

'No,' I said.

'Whisky? Gin? I *KNOW* you like that.' He then offered to take me for a meal to show he wasn't just using me and I could even stay the night this time! I almost gave in, and not because I wanted to, but his persistence and my drunkenness were not a good mix. Thankfully, looking away, I saw Flick and she came to my rescue, taking me home with her. Perry is a cheap and nasty scumbag.

CONFLICT / CHAOS

GEORGE ROBEY, FINSBURY PARK
3 JANUARY 1983

Angel rang earlier to invite me to a gig. Flick stayed home as she was skint. I just started to get ready and plugged the crimpers in, when Angel rang and told me to meet her in 45 minutes at Finsbury Park tube station. I panicked as it usually takes me an hour to get ready, but I managed to get there on time and rushed into the toilets in the George Robey to finish backcombing my hair.

On the way in our hands were stamped with the letter J. Daz, Angel's boyfriend, said it stood for 'jerk'. Daz is very nice, a good laugh and friendly. He is a lot younger than Angel and in a band.

The gig area was dead small like someone's living room! There was a studenty looking man standing in front of us when the bands were on. He wore a weird crochet waistcoat and had long black hair. Angel found his top hilarious and said she was going to knit one with matching trousers and wear it down the 100 Club tomorrow. The man then put his tweed jacket over his shoulder. 'Oh look, he's trying to cover it up!' Angel exclaimed. We cracked up laughing. I think he must have heard us, because he walked away. After the first band had played, we went in the ladies so I could smuggle some glasses into my bag. We didn't have any at home.

I helped Angel repair one of her hair spikes as she'd got her hair caught in the closing doors of the tube – luckily she was on the inside of the tube, not the other way round, that could have been deadly!

POISON GIRLS
100 CLUB
4 JANUARY 1983

Before heading off to the gig, Flick and I downed a bottle of cider and half a bottle of Martini Rosso, so we were drunk before we got there. I was dressed entirely in black and wore severe blue make-up to go with my blue (not green) hair.

We chatted to a few people we knew and the bar man gave us some free drinks as he has a crush on Flick.

CHAPTER 2.5

A repulsive boy who looked about 15 tried to chat me up. To discourage him me and Flick put our arms around each other and pretended we were gay. He asked me how I got the scar under my chin [a five-inch scar I've had since I was four years old]. Flick said she'd slashed me one night. I told him that Flick was a sadist and beats me up every night and that I'm a masochist and enjoy it and he actually believed us! It was fun winding him up. I ponced half his lager and he said: 'You can have something else as well... I may be small and young, but I've plenty of tricks up my sleeve...'

He then scrounged all the slops off the barman from the beer drip trays. It turned my stomach as the barman tipped them into his glass. I guess I shouldn't have nicked his beer, then.

COMBAT 84
100 CLUB
6 JANUARY 1983

Flick and I intended to see The Exploited tonight but when we got to Klub Foot the gig had been cancelled so we went to the 100 Club to see if there were any bands on. Despite it usually being punk night, the band playing was a skinhead band called Combat 84. Neither of us had heard of them but decided to give it a go anyway, rather than go home. The door lady only charged us two quid as we said we wouldn't have enough to get home if we paid the extra 50p.

Once inside, the place was packed with skinheads and I was scared we'd get beaten up, so didn't dare talk to anyone. Normally, I'd chat someone up for a sip of their beer, but this time I didn't dare – there wasn't a punk in sight. However, I noticed the skinheads were linking arms and dancing together, very happy and friendly. Very different to the aggressive dancing and pogoing of punk gigs.

A decent looking skinhead stood right in front of me with two full pints but I was too shy to ask for a sip at first, but then thirst got the better of me and I plucked up the courage to ask. To my total surprise, he gave me the whole pint! It was cider and blackcurrant, my old favourite tipple. He told me his mates called him Barney Rubble

– like the character in the Flintstones cartoon. I forget his real name. He invited me out on a date the following night. I agreed. He wanted my phone number, but we couldn't find a pen.

When Combat 84 finished, a smoke bomb was let off. I was choking, and ran to the ladies toilet where I chatted to some friendly skinhead girls who'd also taken refuge there. We were choking from the smoke and our make-up was ruined as tears streamed down our faces.

A few moments later, Barney Rubble came in looking for me. He was asking everyone for a pen, so he could get my phone number. I suggested we went outside as I wanted to find Flick. At the tube station, going home, Flick and I sat on an empty bench. A skinhead lad came over asking if we had change for 50p. He sat himself next to me and we started chatting. Some other skinheads came over and a girl sat on the lad's lap. A good-looking tattooed skinhead bloke sat himself on Flick's lap. 'I hope you don't mind, but my trousers are wet,' he told her. We all boarded the tube. When me and Flick got off at South Kensington, they assumed we were dead posh. The skin who'd sat next to me gave Flick his phone number. She never rang him.

THE STRAPS / BRIGANDAGE / CHAOS
100 CLUB
11 JANUARY 1983

I wasn't planning to go to tonight's gig, but during the day I went for a job interview for a window display person. I didn't get it. In fact the boss ridiculed me asking, 'What makes you think you could dress my windows?' I wanted to say I could do a darn better job than they'd already been done, but I bit my tongue. Maybe I should have said it – what did I have to lose? I was feeling so depressed I decided to go to the gig and cheer myself up. Well, I needn't have bothered as it was shit, but maybe that was a reflection on my mood rather than what the bands were like.

Si gave me and Flick a lift. We tried getting pissed on a bottle of cider each. I had to sit in the back of the van with Gary, who was being his usual quiet self. I tried talking to him, but gave up in

Chapter 2.5

the end. I could have got more conversation out of one of the bread crates.

We saw Cindy, another of my penfriends, outside the 100 Club. She'd been waiting for her boyfriend for over half an hour, so I said if he didn't show she could hang out with us. Her hair was also in big spiky cones. A bit like Angel's but with shaved bits at the sides. She'd dyed it red but it didn't look so good as when it was black.

Flick took loads of photos. I had my camera too, but wasn't in the mood for taking pics. I wished Barney had come down. (He was planning to, but rang me on Monday to say he couldn't afford it and he'd probably see me on Sat.)

I walked away and went to the toilets to do my hair. There was a punk and punkette kissing by the mirror, so I asked them to shift over so I could see myself in the mirror. The punkette stared at me. 'Are you from Wimbledon?' she asked. It was Renata! She had been there when I first dyed my hair blue aged just 16. It was great to see her. She said she hoped to see me on Friday down the Marquee as Chelsea were playing. Not sure I can afford it though.

THE ADDICTS
100 CLUB, OXFORD STREET
25 JANUARY 1983

I was itching to see The Addicts tonight, as they are one of my favourite bands. As I entered the 100 Club, the first person I saw was Eric/Sebastian with the red hair. He bought me a drink and we sat on a table talking. A bleary eyed punkette came up to him wanting to scrounge some of his drink, so he let her have some but then she wouldn't go away, so he got annoyed and told her to go away and annoy someone else. A handsome punk bloke appeared and put his hands on the girls' shoulders and stared at me. He was so lovely, I smiled back at him. He brushed past me later and knocked the drink out of my hand. I exaggerated my annoyance and he produced a bottle of whiskey from inside his raincoat and offered me some. I took a few swigs and then he kissed me and I enjoyed it. I was still sitting next to Sebastian and he got up and moved away. I felt bad about that. [I had already split up with Barney after just one or two dates. My love life moved fast in those days!]

The boy I was kissing turned out to be Tomor (hawk). The same lad I'd met a while ago at The Vibrators gig. We swapped addresses. He lives in Leeds. He asked if he could crash at mine, but knowing Flick would disapprove, I said no, even though I would have loved him to stay!

SKIN TWO – OPENING NIGHT
31 JANUARY 1983

I didn't really want to go to this new nightclub at first, but I'm glad I did. I loved it. Inside it was dark and cosy and everyone was dressed in rubber and leather as it's a fetish club. Flick and I wore black lace dresses as we couldn't afford rubber or leather. There was a strict dress code. The place wasn't too packed and the clientele select.

Flick spotted Si and Gary at the other bar across the room. She was annoyed because he'd rung her during the week to say he wasn't going out all week as he was skint. So she went and chatted to the DJ who liked to be called Arthur, although it wasn't his real name. We asked him to play some David Bowie, Soft Cell and John Foxx and went on the dance floor. No one else was dancing, so we had it to ourselves. Arthur told us they'd been planning the club for over a year. He said Rusty Egan was there and Col, the other DJ had deliberately ignored him.

Tik and Tok [alternative robotic dancers from the dance group Shock] arrived dressed head to toe in Jane Khan clothing. Jane Khan was there too as Tok is her boyfriend.

We got chatting to Tok, who was sat on the same group of seats as us. He was very nice and not at all like a big star – down to earth. He told me they had a new single out and they weren't dancing because they'd been recording for *The Kenny Everett Show* all day and were worn out.

CHAPTER 2.5

Tok asked if we knew who they were, so as a wind up and to see his reaction, I pretended I didn't, although I actually did know who they were, so he started to explain about Shock, which made me laugh.

Tok had small cameos of the Mona Lisa stuck to the shaved parts of his head. We took some photos, one of which was of me sitting on his lap. He squeezed me so very tight, I could hardly breathe!

SKIN TWO
7 FEBRUARY 1983

Me and Flick got really pissed on cider and vodka before going to Skin Two. Flick was wearing her ripped Kahn and Bell dress with chains around her wrist and ankle. She looked really good. I could never get away with wearing such a short dress, I'm too self-conscious.

Mulligan from the new-wave band Fashion was there. He's really good looking, so we asked him if we could take his photo. He bought us both a drink and we chatted for a while when Stevo, the manager of Soft Cell and the owner of Some Bizarre record label, came up and we took photos of him as well. Somehow or another, Flick ended up being handcuffed to Stevo, when he was messing about and then he told her he didn't have the keys to unlock them with. Flick went off with Stevo, well, she didn't have much choice.

I was woken up at 8am.(!) the next morning, by Flick, who'd had to stay the night at Stevo's house in Hammersmith. Eventually he'd unlocked the handcuffs and they'd had an all-night party.

RECORDING STUDIO, LEYTON
ADVENTURES IN COLOUR
10 to 11 FEBRUARY 1983

I was telling Flick how I was really pissed off with meeting one bloke one night and someone different the next and that I wanted someone permanent. Later, when Flick was almost asleep, and I was dozing, the doorbell rang. I opened the door wearing no make-up, with flat hair and wearing a grotty black T-shirt dress, red socks and leg warmers. The stranger at the door was Sid, the bloke I'd met at the Marquee a while ago but hadn't seen or heard from him since.

Sid told me he'd come back from Wales yesterday and had just been thrown out of the hostel, so he'd got pissed and was just wandering around. He said three of the guys behind the desk at the hostel had tried to beat him up and his mate Spike had also been thrown out and he didn't know where he was. I invited him into the hall as it was snowing outside and Sid looked frozen.

'I haven't seen you in ages,' he said with his soft Welsh accent. 'I've been around about five other times, and that *cow* (meaning Flick), said you were out. Didn't she tell you I'd called round?' No, she bloody hadn't! I had been rehearsing a lot lately with my new band – Adventures in Colour – and hadn't been around much.

I knew then, that he still cared about me and I felt bad about being cold towards him, so I said, 'Do I get a hug?' We hugged each other really tightly. I didn't want to let go. It was really emotional.

Flick begrudgingly let Sid come into our room where it was warmer. She clearly didn't like Sid, but I did and I certainly wasn't going to let him sleep in the snow.

Flick went to sleep and Sid and I sat on the sofa talking. He had his arm around me and was obviously glad to see me. I kept shivering so he pulled my duvet over the both of us. I asked him to come to bed with me.

'What's Flick going to say when she sees me in the morning?' he asked.

'I'll tell her that you're my hot water bottle,' I replied. Later he said something about me being the prettiest hot water bottle he'd ever seen.

He asked me if I wanted to get a flat or house with him, but I didn't feel ready. I'd only met him twice, so I said no.

The next day, I went to band rehearsal. At a proper rehearsal studio for the first time. The studio was in Leytonstone and the same one used by our idols Rubella Ballet. It went well. I had a new song to

CHAPTER 2.5

learn, which sounds a bit like *Cars* by Gary Numan. I like it and I loved singing through a mic. I'm looking forward to our first gig, even though I'm terrified I'll make a mess of it. The band gave me a red perspex tambourine that used to belong to Motörhead.

After rehearsals, Sid came back to Morden with me. My mum and dad have gone on holiday and the house is empty. We bought some bread and gin and orange to take back with us. We sat in the front room with the fire full on, drinking and listening to The Stranglers and Stiff Little Fingers, but before long we made our way upstairs. We made love and I was really happy. The next morning, I had my Saturday job in the chemist. Sid came in and said he was going down the Kings Road to find Spike and he'd left his stuff at my house. [However, I never saw him again after that. It took me years to forget him.]

LOOK MUMMY CLOWNS
STREETS, ISLINGTON
4 APRIL 1983

Dave, Lisa and I went to this gig after band rehearsal. Lisa met her boyfriend Steev from the Lost Cherrees outside. He told us Youth in Asia weren't playing, as intended. All the bands were really shit.

Dave was hoping someone would recognise us. Later, a skinhead came up to us and asked if we were Adventures in Colour. He said he really liked us and could he have a tape of us sent to him. We were all flattered and chuffed to bits. When Look Mummy Clowns came on, the rest of us left.

SEX GANG CHILDREN
FLICKS, DARTFORD
5 APRIL 1983

We took lots of cider with us to drink on the train journey to Bexley.

Si was waiting for us at Bexley station and drove us to Dartford. Flicks (the club, not the person!) turned out to be a disco venue and was very posh inside. The punks that packed it out looked out of place. Later, I couldn't find Flick's camera. I said she might have left it at home by mistake. She gave me her can of beer to put in my bag but it didn't fit so I told her to hold it instead.

When we came out of the toilets, she wasn't holding the can, so I asked her what had happened to it. We started to argue over who was meant to have it, but neither of us had it. She was angry about the camera too, and blamed me for losing it, but I couldn't remember having it in the first place.

Sex Gang Children were excellent. Andi, the lead singer, has dyed his hair black and put it in a tiny ponytail on top of his head.

Chapter 3

Cherree red and other colours

Since placing the advert in *Sounds* I had been writing to a bloke called Dave Hughes, who lived in Silvertown in East London. Silvertown was famous for being the home of the Tate and Lyle sugar factory. The Sarson's malt vinegar factory was also close by, meaning the entire area often smelt of sweet vinegar.

Dave was over six foot and slender with short black hair and Irish ears. In his letters, he had told me all about a band he was in called Adventures in Colour. He played the synthesiser and co-wrote the songs with their bass player. He said they needed a new lead singer and asked if I could sing. I said yes right away, without really considering whether I actually could. I'd sung in the choir at school: surely that counted for something?

The audition was held in a Ladbroke Grove bedsit rented by George, the other keyboard player. George was an olive-skinned Greek Cypriot with curly black hair and a wide, cheeky smile. He fancied himself as a ladies' man. During one rehearsal, he boasted about the armchair being broken because he'd 'entertained' two ladies on it simultaneously the previous night. I think the only person who believed this was George.

I also met Lisa, the bass player and other founder member of the band – a petite and boyish girl with a quirky dress sense and hairstyle, which was not at all unusual in the '80s. Her hair was cropped and dyed a two-tone mix of amber and shocking pillar box red. She wore blue plastic clip-on earrings that she'd bought in a flea market and had revamped with big red feathers. I was taller than average at five foot nine and took a size-14 dress (voluptuous I like to think), whilst Lisa was a diminutive five foot four and took a size eight. But despite her weeness making me feel like I was on the wrong side of hefty, I liked her immediately.

In fact, we all got on well together and before I knew it I was the lead singer in a band. I WAS THE LEAD SINGER IN A BAND! I am not sure why I passed the audition. Whether it was for my voice, or because my short spiky peroxide-blonde hair with pink sides and dramatic '80s make-up fitted the image of the band. But what the fuck… I was the lead singer in a band.

I was quickly instructed that I was not allowed to dance or move around much on stage or wave my arms around like other bands, and that chatting to the audience between songs was definitely out, as we weren't *THAT* kind of band. I wasn't much of a dancer, arm-waggler or chatterer between songs anyway, so none of that bothered me much. *I was the lead singer in a band!*

Six-foot Dave with the sticky-out ears grew closer and closer as the weeks passed. We used to down tins of Special Brew (an exceptionally strong lager, and the preferred tipple of many an alcoholic due to its high strength-to-price ratio) during rehearsals as we were convinced we sounded better after a few cans. Looking back, I'm not entirely sure this was the case, but it certainly helped us to relax and provided necessary lubrication for my throat, as I had never had singing lessons and was prone to explosive bouts of violent coughing between songs. Well, that was my excuse.

Our sound was contemporary and electronic. The electronic sound had become extremely popular since the '70s as music technology had advanced exponentially. The band consisted of two cheap buzzing synthesisers that were played in a simple style by two self-taught keyboard players. George played a JEN – the cheapest keyboard available in his mum's catalogue. And it really doesn't get any more anarchic than that! The JEN made some interesting sounds but the other keyboard, the Wasp, created unique noises. Its most distinguishing feature was a two-octave keyboard with touch-sensitive non-moving keys, which we considered to be incredibly modern at the time, although I knew nothing about such technical things: I just liked the quirky sounds it made. Apparently the Wasp was so-called due to its yellow-and-black keys – although at times it literally did sound like a sizeable and unremitting wasp.

My vocal style wasn't exactly singing (this was the '80s!) but I was

CHAPTER 3

tuneful enough. As I was still incredibly shy and it took me quite a while, and copious quantities of Special Brew, to gain confidence as a frontperson, I guess it was just as well that I wasn't supposed to move about and chat to the audience between songs.

Lisa's boyfriend, Steev, who was the bass player in a punk band called the Lost Cherrees, managed to secure us some gigs. And so it came to pass that my terrifying debut gig with Adventures in Colour took place in a 'venue' called Streets on 5 March 1983. Streets was located at the back of the Angel Tube and has since been demolished. Which is sad in a way but also a blessing as the toilets were an underground experience in themselves. So many of the old London grassroots venues (also aptly known as the toilet circuit) have disappeared over the years. The only saving grace being that their toilets went with them.

As you can imagine, as a shy kid with little self-esteem who had never performed publicly before I was incredibly nervous. The saying 'butterflies in the stomach' just doesn't cut it. My intestines were playing host to a pair of lively squid. I had to keep nipping to the really rather appalling toilets to, well, y'know, but at least I hadn't thrown up. Not yet, at least. The last thing I wanted to do was to have to kneel down in those dodgy bogs. The venue really was an utter dive but it *was* a venue and that was really all that mattered to us.

The stage was conveniently located in a corner of the venue (which was actually just a normal-sized room) opposite the stinky toilets. Plonked in the middle of the room just in front of the stage was a pool table that no one had bothered to move. Obviously expecting a full house then.

At least, as a new and unknown band, we were first on the bill, which meant that I could get the performance over and done with and avoid any further visits to the offensive toilet facilities. Flick and Si had come along to provide much-needed moral support (this gig was before Flick and I had our huge row) and Dave had brought his brother with him to take photos, so we had three 'fans'. It was one band playing to another band really, but everybody has to start somewhere. Secretly, I was really glad that there were so few people to watch me flummox around (not moving though, remember) with a microphone in my hand during my very first gig in front of actual, real, living, breathing human people.

I gingerly clambered up onto the stage and fidgeted with the mic to check that it worked. My mouth was suddenly dry like I'd been gargling with pencil sharpenings and parts of my body that had never sweated before suddenly discovered that they had the ability to do so. Prolifically.

After what seemed to me like a torturous fortnight, the synths and drum machine started, and were followed a few bars later by Lisa's throbbing bass. I sensed the moment I had feared getting closer and closer. There were bones in my toes so tiny they'd never been medically named that were shaking with nerves. But then, amidst a ripe bouquet of fresh shit, old piss, mildewed walls and stale cigarette smoke, with a base note of spilt lager, I actually began to sing.

A life without the worry
'cept the problem pages
doing what's right for who?
You're simply in existence
to fill the population
how does that really make you feel?
Greed, envy, formality…

Sexes clearly parted
there's nothing in between
a smile is not worth nothing
you're simply in existence
to fill the population
how does that really make you feel?

We got to the end of the set and were rewarded with cursory applause.

'It was really good!' enthused Flick, who now loved the idea of her flatmate being in a band. And despite having suffered an aerial attack of nerves, I had absolutely loved being on that stage. I was riding a wave of beautiful and swooping adrenaline and I felt a tremen-

CHAPTER 3

dous sense of achievement. Me, shy, unconfident Gail. From South Morden. On stage. In a band. I was already hooked. Jesus Christ, the venue smelt of piss.

When I went to the loos later, a girl with massively backcombed bleached hair came up to me and said how well we'd done. She told me her name was Janice and she was in a band called Evil I. I was being acknowledged and admired by fellow musicians on the alternative circuit. I loved it and I wanted more.

I have a live tape of that gig somewhere and in the background you can hear the sound of billiard balls clacking together as a group of skinheads were playing pool in front of the stage during our set. Bet that doesn't happen at Madonna gigs.

Also on the bill that night, although I barely noticed them as I was so high after my prodigious performance, were the Lost Cherrees and Four Minute Warning. Sean was the lead singer of Four Minute Warning. He had long brown hair that had been shaped into footlong spikes with soap. A bit of a messy job, but hey, that was punk! He was immediately given the nickname Gummidge (as in *Worzel Gummidge*, the popular kids TV show starring Jon Pertwee as the Scarecrow Worzel Gummidge who'd come to life) as he came from the countryside.

Later, the skinheads who had been playing pool asked us if we had a cassette of ourselves. (In those days, bands often gave away cassette tapes for free as a way of marketing themselves.) I was flattered until someone pointed out that they were probably going to tape over it with other stuff.

We played with the Lost Cherrees again on 20 May 1983, along with the Screaming Bongos, and with Rubella Ballet headlining. Rubella Ballet were a band I'd heard a lot about who had their own following, so this was a particularly exciting gig for me. They wore fluorescent clothes that were handmade and performed under UV lights. Back then, most bands didn't pay much attention to their visual aesthetics, so they had quite a stage presence.

After I had a few gigs under my belt I began feeling like a puppet in the band and felt stupid standing there singing and unable to move. My confidence had improved and it felt natural to move about a bit

51

– a primitive response to music if ever there was one. Lisa was also saying she wanted to try singing again, and why didn't I learn guitar? Listening back to the tapes several years on, I think this was a passive-aggressive way of saying she thought she could do a better job.

Dave and I split up at the Feltham gig. I can't remember why I was dumped, but I had noticed he seemed very close to Lisa, although they always insisted they were just friends. I'd had the fight with Flick and moved back to Morden by then. I had dyed my hair with red henna to condition my brittle over-bleached hair and help treat the bald patch I now had from having my hair relocated by Flick for the sake of £1. I'd kept the sides pink though. I was wearing a homemade skirt and top in a '50s rose-print orange fabric, with borders of hand-painted snakes I'd designed and made myself. I'd set up my own tiny clothing label called Rubella Rat.

Outside the venue, I told Steev I'd just been dumped and he was sympathetic as he'd recently split with Lisa. On the journey home, Steev asked me out and a few days later we went to see Dario Fo's *Accidental Death of an Anarchist*, which was a popular stage play at that time. Steev revealed that Lisa had told him they were planning to drop me from the band as Lisa wanted to be the singer and was jealous of the attention I'd been getting. It's no wonder so many bands break up due to 'musical differences'. I guess it was understandable, as I was singing the songs she'd written and was getting more attention than her. Steev suggested I should leave the band and not give them the satisfaction of dumping me. He also suggested I join the Lost Cherrees.

In-between leaving Adventures in Colour and joining the Lost Cherrees, I had gone into the recording studio with Steev, Nuts (the drummer) and Andy (the guitarist) from the Cherrees and recorded two tracks: 'Oohh la la la' and 'Lavender'. With Steev's encouragement, I wrote the lyrics to the chorus of 'Lavender' and felt emboldened to sing it in my own style. OK, so I only wrote two lines – '*Collect old photos by the fire*' and '*Lavender hangs out to dry...*' – but it was nice to have some musical freedom, even just two lines of it.

The two songs were recorded as a muck-around in the studio. I never thought they would ever see the light of day, but they now feature on the Lost Cherrees' album *In the Very Beginning*, which was released in 2007. Had I known they were going to be committed to CD someday, I'd have taken the recording session more seriously but I barely put any effort into my vocal part at all. Ho hum. All the same, it was great fun recording the songs and I liked the other band members.

After we had recorded the two tracks, I was asked to join the Lost Cherrees. I pointed out that they already had a singer, so Steev suggested I play keyboards instead. I highlighted the fact that I couldn't actually play keyboards, or any other instrument for that matter. But in the spirit of punk I was told by Steev that they didn't know how to play their instruments either. The great thing about punk bands was that you didn't need talent or musical ability. Desire, enthusiasm and attitude were enough. So, that's how I joined the Lost Cherrees.

Chapter 3.5

Letters from Dave

20 December 1982

Dear Gail,

So you say you can't play any instruments... well, neither can I, but I'm a good actor. A synthesizer or drum machine doesn't require musical ability to play, as they are more mathematical than tuneful. Keep an eye out for our adverts starting this week in *Sounds* looking for guitarists and other synth players, hopefully by January we should be starting rehearsals again. Because Lisa wants to stop singing, we got in an old friend to do vocals, but every day, it becomes plainer and clearer that she's only along for the ride. I get the distinct impression she'd rather be with her mates boasting about being in a band than actually doing anything for it! For this reason, we'd both like to find someone more genuine, so a singer is on the shopping list too. Whether you still fancy the idea, I don't know, but anyway, think about it.

We've no more gigs lined up until we've a stable line-up, but we will be doing studio work in January – probably at Xnrtrix, because the Poison Girls and Rubella Ballet are two bands I really admire and it would be beneficial for us to use their facilities. We sat in one day when Youth in Asia were having their soon to come tape EP mixed and we were very impressed with the whole set-up. Lance D'Boyle makes very nice tea.

Blah blah blah...

Love Dave X

*

10 January 1983

Dear Gail,

The only thing I find frightening about guitars is that there are six strings and people only have four fingers and a thumb – illogical! I like basses though. I like making next-door's ornaments walk on the shelf with the low frequencies. The synthesizer that I have at the moment was an innovation when it first came out in 1979, cheap and very varied in the sounds it could achieve. Now most synths are made to do certain things. Moogs are usually used at the bass end because of the fat notes they can produce. I'd quite like a Moog Source, it's digital instead of millions of knobs, which means that instead of turning the decay switch halfway, all you do is program [sic] the numbers DE50 and it's perfect every time. Better start saving the £865 I suppose. Next week, Lisa and I will be touring the music shops of London to try out a few synths and drum machines as it's obvious I need to replace the 'Wasp' soon. It's got no keyboard and sometimes the touch sensitive keyboard does a dance of its own. I really want you to come along, so please keep an afternoon free for me.

You seem to go to a lot of gigs. Did you ever like Joy Division? Do you ever pig whole boxes of chocolates? Do you steal in order to visit the Chinese? Do you realise I do all these things?

All regards, fondest wishes and other goo,

Dave

PS Will you take me to see E.T.?

*

CHAPTER 3.5

Somewhere in London E16
10.40pm
15 February 1983

AND THE IMAGE SPOKE:
'DO YOU WANT TO BE IN LOVE OR JUST TO BE LOVED?'
THE IMAGE DIED.

Dear Gail,

Here I sit in my kitchen with the oven on. I'm not cooking, you understand, but with the central heating turned off, it's quite the simplest way of keeping my veins from freezing up.

The rehearsal on Friday I felt went very well, at last we sound like a group! I thought your vocals were excellent, it's exactly what we wanted – every word could be heard. Please don't leave for Christ's sake! I can feel it in my bones, the line-up is complete!!

I want to be respected more than anything else; I want people to think 'he's got it sussed.' Being in a group is the easiest way to communicate – if there was a better way, then I'd do that. I'm doing what I'm doing to hopefully make people more aware of the problems and injustices of the world – I can't just sit back and say nothing, there's far too many doing that already.

One thing annoys me more than any other, the 'I'm alright jack' syndrome. 'I've got my car, my house, and my bank account. Fuck the underpaid Africans, the rape of women, the rape of the countryside…' But what can Adventures in Colour do? Nothing more than a token. I would get very depressed if I thought it was ALL pointless.

I'd love you to come to my house soon. I've loads of type head lettering and paper, so maybe you can work out your fashion design advert in the world famous AIC office? You can also help out on the fanzine – I could meet you at the tube station. How about Sunday?

Thinking of you with affection…

Dave xxxxx

*

57

25 February 1983
Silvertown, London

Dear Gail,

I think I'd like the band to be as small as possible. Musicians can be replaced with tape recorders but vocalists are another matter. It's always hard to find someone who's prepared to sing another's lyrics especially when those words contain strong personal views. If you find any of our lyrics contradictory for you to sing, then please mention it and we can go through it together, reaching a compromise. Those gigs are not very far away you know!! I'm getting nervous already.

I really enjoy being with you, I feel really good when I travel back to the east on the clanky tube trains with you. Please keep being there... I'm trying.

All my love...

Dave x

9 March 1983

Dear Gail,

The gig on Saturday was great. I really enjoyed myself. Someone taped the whole thing and will be sending it on soon, hopefully tomorrow so we can find out just how we sounded – AND prove to my family that we got claps and cheers!

This Friday, we should be making tapes at the Leyton rehearsal studio to send out to places in London where I'd like to play: The Mitre, Greenwich – Ad Lib, Kensington, The Thames Poly, Woolwich, The Batcave!!, The Moonlight Club (those that instantly spring to mind).

Thinking of you...

Love Dave xxxxxxxx

Chapter 4

Lost Cherrees – in the beginning

By the time I joined, the Lost Cherrees were an established musical presence on the alternative scene, with the 7-inch single 'No fighting. No war. No trouble. No more' already under their musical belt. They were signed to Riot Clone Records, a very small label run by the band Riot Clone, who were friends with the Lost Cherrees. The two bands often gigged together.

My closest relationship within the band was with Steev, although I got on well with all the other members. However, since being attacked by Flick, I was now wary of other women and so gelled better with the males in the band.

'Gail's joining the band,' Steev had announced, and I watched the expression fall off Sian's face, as she knew I was a singer. But before anyone could say anything, Steev added, '…as keyboard player.' Sian immediately looked relieved.

So I joined my second band. I was a keyboard player who couldn't read music, didn't know what the notes were called and had never played keyboard before in my life. Kind of a steep learning curve, if ever there was one.

Steev took up the role of music teacher and was very patient, teaching me the basics of the keyboard. I never did learn what the notes were called, but instead relied on coloured stickers with numbers on for each song. Most punk bands used a less-than-diverse selection of three chords, as punk 'musicians' generally displayed an anarchic lack of musical ability – and we were no different.

Steev and Sian were the main songwriters but sometimes Andy would write too. I 'played' keyboard and sang backing vocals to Sian's lead. The subject matter of our songs was always along the lines of enthusiastic anarchy. We were young, angry and political. We were anti-politicians, anti-war, anti-religion, anti-meat, anti-vivisection, anti-establishment... anti- most things it would seem. Working-class youth had found its voice and the sound it made was more vociferous than that of any generation before us.

Sian's vocals were amazing. She sang loud and fast as she angrily delivered the lyrics like she was spitting out razor blades. There was no way I could sing like her although, over the next year or so, we started to slow the tempo down. This diminished tempo can be heard in 'You Didn't Care' – a song about the despicable practice of vivisection, something we all felt very strongly about. And like most people with a heart, I still do.

Gummidge came to almost every one of our gigs and would delight in standing directly in front of me, where he'd try to put me off my virtuoso keyboard-playing by gurning, which invariably worked and resulted in me missing notes. Although, in all honesty, I would often miss notes anyway as I found it hard to concentrate after imbibing several pints of snakebite, and because I hadn't learned the art of counting beats.

It was unusual for a punk band to have keyboards, and so many live-sound engineers would amp me via the vocal PA or through the guitar amp. Either way, I usually couldn't hear myself and just had to trust I was pressing the right keys which, due to unerring inebriation, I couldn't guarantee was the case. No one seemed to mind though. It all added to the chaotic energy.

One of our biggest gigs was with a well-known punk band called Conflict at a venue called the Ace in Brixton, which later became known as the Fridge. We had an audience of 2,000 people and unbelievably my keyboards didn't work. Looking back, I've often wondered if this was coincidental. I wasn't convinced that a professional sound engineer at a decent venue would be unable to deal with keyboards. My mic was also gaffer-taped to the stand. I'd heard rumours that main acts often sabotaged the support bands' sound, in order to make themselves appear better. Tsk tsk. That's not cricket.

On a few occasions, admittedly, I simply forgot to switch my keyboards on. Which can happen when you've marinated yourself in a cocktail of cider and lager and not eaten. I remember getting very drunk before a gig at the Metropolitan Club in Farringdon. I'd got

CHAPTER 4

on stage, which was a feat in itself to be honest having made several litres of alcoholic fluid disappear, and found that no sound came out when I pressed the keys. In my defence, I was used to not being able to hear myself through the monitors, as monitors in those days were crap but, halfway through the set, I had noticed that I actually hadn't switched it on. I drunkenly switched it on, forgetting that I'd been fucking about with the volume, which resulted in a long and painful screech of feedback. All heads turned to stare angrily at me. Ooops!

The Lost Cherrees were prolific giggers and in the two-year period I played with the band, we clocked up over 60 gigs – more than some bands achieve in a lifetime. We rehearsed every Sunday in the dank old cellar of a Victorian semi in Surbiton, Surrey. It was so damp in there that we used to find slugs navigating the walls. The steps to the basement were deep, which meant we had to negotiate them with heavy, awkward-shaped amps and music gear. Despite not being able to play the keyboard, I had still upgraded to a Korg electronic piano. I figured that if I was going to be a keyboardist who couldn't play the keyboard, I might as well be unable to play a good-quality keyboard. I had my reputation to think of. The Korg was three times the size of the original JEN and I had inexplicably had a heavy wooden case custom-made for it, just to add to the extra weight of transporting it. The number of hours I spent lugging a heavy instrument across London, in and out of vans and up and down stairs – just so I could stand behind it and not actually 'play' it. I should have joined Spinal Tap.

Sian eventually left the band as she wanted to go to university and it was decided that I would remain on keyboards and we would get another singer in. Another one of Steev's friends, Bev, a girl with a huge, dyed-black Mohican, joined us. For a while, both Sian and Bev sang together while Bev learned the songs. Bev had an extremely powerful voice. She had made a recording of herself singing 'You Didn't Care'. Her treatment of the track was haunting, and there was no way she wasn't getting into the band. We all liked the sound of two girls singing together and they worked well in harmony, so when Sian left we started to scour London for another female singer.

I found Deb at a party. I had been chatting to a man called Keith (Goldhanger) and casually told him that we were in the market for

61

another singer. He immediately introduced me to his friend, a petite girl with black crimped hair and a Siouxsie Sioux mode of dress. Needless to say, I felt like an inelegant and self-conscious giant next to petite girls. I'd been bullied at school for my size and for being different. Yet Deb and I remained lifelong friends after the band split.

We recorded a second single – 'A Man's Duty; A Woman's Place' – that was put out on Bluurg Records, a label run by Dick Lucas from the anarcho-punk band Subhumans. The studio belonged to Jon Hiseman – a well-known music producer whose studio was conveniently located next door to Sian's parents' house, so we got to use all his expensive studio gear. (His daughter Anna's voice can be heard during the opening sequence of the track 'Blasphemy'.)

It was taking such a long time for the single to be released that Conflict's new label, Mortarhate, offered to release it quicker than Bluurg were able to. So the single 'A Man's Duty; A Woman's Place' was finally released. I had thought up the title of the single, created the artwork for it and designed the fold-out poster inside. I enjoyed having some creative input and it made up for me not contributing to any of the songwriting.

At one of our early gigs in Stockwell, a young punk came up to me and asked if I used to be in a band called Adventures in Colour. I was chuffed to bits to be recognised. Having grown up being told by my father that I would be a nobody and amount to nothing (thanks, Dad), it was good to have a bit of recognition.

An album was later released called *All Part of Growing Up* along with a 12-inch single – 'Unwanted Children' – for which I did the cover photography. The image was of a child we'd seen on a council estate where one of my friends lived. We sometimes wondered how that kid would feel if, later in life, it discovered it had been a poster child for unwanted children. But hey ho, it was art and we didn't worry too much about that kind of shit.

We were often interviewed for fanzines, who would always ask us the same questions, such as whether we supported CND (The Campaign for Nuclear Disarmament, which was very topical at the time, with the Greenham Common protestors out in full force). Or 'Why do you wear all black?' Which was bordering on the ridiculous as I

CHAPTER 4

more often than not dressed like I'd been involved in some sort of an explosion in a factory that manufactured rainbows. The fanzines didn't even bother to tailor the questions to each band.

We got so bored of being asked the same formulaic questions that once Andy replied flippantly that we should 'bomb the bastards' when he was asked the inevitable CND question. To which the journalist failed to respond.

Most of us still lived with our parents during the day whilst singing angrily about our hatred of the establishment at night! No irony there then. Nuts and Andy were still at school, but I was working in a factory packing nursery furniture, Steev was a picture framer, Bev worked for British Telecom and Deb was a cook.

We used to receive a lot of fan mail, some of which I still have. The letters we received would be split between the band members and we would often strike up penfriendships with various fans. This was, of course, in the days before emails, websites and mobile phones.

Our fans were usually young and as poor as we were, so they would apply soap to the postage stamps that they attached to their fan mail, which meant they could be easily reused, without having to steam them. 'I've soaped the stamps,' they would write. They would also send blank cassette tapes and we would record our music for them free of charge. We knew what it was like to be young and broke – *we* were young and broke – so we didn't mind.

Plus we were ferociously anti-capitalist and so the last thing we wanted was to profit from our music. We would insist that the words 'pay no more than 86 1/2p' were printed on the covers of our singles, as several bands were doing at the time as a political statement against capitalism and the corporatisation of the music industry. It also meant that the shops couldn't sell the record for more if the price was already printed on the product.

Much of the fan mail we received was covered in anarchy symbols and made references to the ALF, The Animal Liberation Front, a pro-animal rights activist organisation which engages in illegal action to save animals from laboratories, etc. The ALF now has active cells in over 40 countries dedicated to animal welfare, although critics have classed them as a terrorist organisation, despite the organisation remaining adamant that they are non-violent. Many punks were getting more and more involved in vegetarianism and veganism. Some would participate in animal rights demos and were fox hunt saboteurs.

As soon as the album was released, full of anti-establishment and pro-animal rights lyrics, our fan mail suddenly ceased. We believed that this was because it was being intercepted by the police, as we had heard that the same thing had been happening to other outspoken punk bands whose political messages were considered inflammatory.

There were wider-reaching implications of being involved in a band with such antagonistic and political views. I was called a communist and a 'red' at work for refusing to join the union. Anyone speaking up for themselves or seen to be 'rocking the boat' was frowned upon and victimised. One of my cousins joined the Royal Navy and we later discovered that the Ministry of Defence investigated the entire family and somehow knew all about me and my anarchistic points of view.

Whilst I identified strongly with the animal rights beliefs, I felt like some punk musicians were trying to score 'punk points' off each other. There was a hierarchy of snobbery in which vegans looked down on vegetarians, who in turn looked down on meat-eaters. People would check the labels on each other's groceries and food products in order to catch each other out, instead of encouraging each other. It was becoming suffocating and the very people who claimed to be into freedom of speech and equality became judgmental and overbearing. I couldn't understand how this helped the cause that we all believed in.

But besides this churlish anarchic one-upmanship, I have many fond memories of other bands. Having to arrive early at venues to set up the gear and soundcheck left us with plenty of time to get to know the other bands and have a laugh before the punters arrived. I once swapped trousers with Mitch, the bass player from Hagar the Womb – a band we sometimes gigged and giggled with. I gained a pair of baggy metallic-blue trousers, pleated at the waist and with tapered legs that fitted like a dream. I don't think a pair of more '80s trousers could possibly exist. In return, Mitch got to wear a pair of

CHAPTER 4

stylish Noddy-print trousers, handmade by yours truly. A fair swap, if I do say so myself.

There was one pre-gig confabulation in which a bunch of us were confessing to venial sins such as thefts. To shatter any preconceptions people often had about punks, usually based solely on our appearance and bad publicity garnered by the likes of the Sex Pistols, most of us were either totally innocent of any such heinous crimes or had nicked nothing more impressive than a few penny chews from the local sweet shop when we were kids.

Then one bloke piped up that he had once stolen a *KERRANG!* We all fell silent. A *KERRANG!* What the fuck was that? No one knew. And no one wanted to own up to not knowing either, but we guessed it was something major. I (for some reason known only to myself) imagined it was a piece of heavy machinery, like a JCB or a tractor or something. We all eyed this bloke with new-found respect, elevating him to celebrity status whenever we discussed his bravery and gall in the years to come. 'Wow! That's major!' someone actually said. Years later, of course, I discovered that *KERRANG!* was a heavy-metal music magazine that probably cost about 70p at the time.

Another memorable gig was on our home turf in an assembly hall not far from where we regularly rehearsed. Conflict were headlining and the venue was packed. After we finished our set, the police raided the venue and a riot broke out. Luckily, Steev and I had sloped off early as we'd seen the other bands play countless times. We had noticed police cars parked down every side street as we walked towards the station, which was unusual for a quiet suburb, but we'd just assumed it was a stakeout. I'm not sure why we thought this, it's not like we lived in The Bronx. So anyway, there we were, safely back at Steev's enjoying a nice cup of tea, whilst just a few streets away the infamous Surbiton Riot was taking place, or at least that's what the media called it the next day.

My favourite-ever gig was also on home turf in New Malden. We'd hired a hall and booked our mates the Screaming Bongos to play along with an up-and-coming band called New Model Army (NMA) who headlined. NMA had just released *Vengeance*, which had been confidently climbing up the Independent Album Charts. I had already bought the album and it had become an instant favourite so I was feverishly excited to be playing on the same bill as such a great band. Our own single and album were also doing well and had made it high in the Indie charts too. At one point, we were number nine alongside The Smiths, who you might have heard of. John Peel was regularly playing our single and we were invited to go into the Radio 1 studios to play a live session on air. Sadly, this never actually happened as the powers that be decided not to put on live sessions for a while.

Anyway, we were used to playing with other bands who were around the same level as us, and who had no egos. Like I said earlier, most punk bands were in it for the music and the anarchy and as a vehicle to spread social and political messages. We'd had the luxury of dressing rooms once or twice, but we all shared them and stored our gear there until it was our turn to play. NMA were different. They insisted on using their own drum kit, which took up most of the stage, and wouldn't allow any other band on the line-up to use it, so Nuts had to squash his own drum kit in front of theirs, leaving even less room for the rest of the band.

In the dressing room, NMA kept themselves to themselves, barely acknowledging anyone else and not making conversation with any of the other bands. They also had a platter of sandwiches as part of their rider (the free drinks and food given to bands when they play as part, or even sometimes instead of, payment) and ate them all without sharing, which was against the very spirit of punk. We were used to sharing our drinks not only with the other bands but with the audience too. It was a shame as I really liked NMA's music and they did play a blinding set, but it was difficult to forget their snobbery and lack of dressing-room etiquette.

Being a local gig, however, most of the fans were Cherrees's fans. We played really well and someone videoed the gig, which I believe is available on DVD somewhere or somehow. Funnily enough, there were no night buses at that time in New Malden and the bands were all running late so most of the audience pissed off home after we played, leaving NMA to play to a half empty hall. That's karma right there for you.

There is a saying that goes something along the lines of 'to over-

CHAPTER 4

come your bullies you must become successful.' During a gig in Bristol, before we went on stage, I heard someone call my name and turned around to see a girl I went to school with. She told me that she was there with another girl that we had both been at school with, one that used to bully me. Great, I thought, they've come all this way just to harass me. But I was wrong. Both girls paid the entrance fee without trying to blag their way in and even bought band merch. The girl who had bullied me was now full of admiration. That was a huge and much-needed confidence boost. No mention was made of her previous treatment of me and I was too shy to broach the subject, but I didn't care about that. Let bygones be bygones and all that.

After years of suffering with extreme low self-esteem I was beginning to develop some serious self-respect – it had been a long time coming – and I felt like I could finally hold my head up high around other people.

It's another popular misconception that punks are punks because they are aggressive, when in actual fact most punks or alternative people who I have met have arrived at a punk/alt lifestyle directly from a difficult childhood or because of a dark past. The punk/alt contingent also often attracts disabled people, people with deformities, people who are extremely shy or fat or ugly, or shy, fat *and* ugly – anybody really who has not been allowed to fit in with their peers for whatever reason. Prime examples include Poly Styrene from X-Ray Spex, who was mixed race and wore braces on stage, and Vi Subversa from the Poison Girls, who was a large middle-aged woman. There was also Ian Dury from Ian Dury and the Blockheads, who was crippled from having polio as a child. Punk/alt culture provided lonely kids and outsiders with a family or urban tribe they could belong to. Punk was not just about the music, it was about finding like-minded individuals and about finding some form of acceptance. In a way, primary-coloured hair, tattoos, piercings and outrageous clothing are ways of distracting attention away from other issues or problems that people have. They are also a method of expressing and celebrating individuality – an individuality that had been seen as negative at school, for example. In some ways outrageous dress was a smokescreen and in others it acted as a beacon of pride. If you don't fit in, you might as well capitalise on that fact and make sure you REALLY don't fit in.

A gig we played in Norwich was memorable, although it was nothing to do with our performance or the headlining band refusing to share their crisps with us because they had an album in the charts and were therefore better than us. Some local punks had arranged for us to play in their local Scout hut. The best thing about punk was that it was so DIY, everyone was doing it for themselves, from designing and making their own clothes and jewellery to forming bands, putting on gigs, marketing themselves and writing fanzines. No creativity or imagination was wasted. This, for me, was the very essence of punk. And so very, very different to the contemporary music business, which sadly seems to care only about profit and how marketable a band is.

So after the gig we piled into the back of the van, and it soon became apparent that, whilst we'd been busy on stage performing, Gummidge et al. had removed all the toilet seats from the men's bogs and raided the Scouts' tuck shop. Sweetie war broke out instantly. Foam shrimps flew through the air like pink flack above a battlefield and sherbet flying saucers were taking flight and spinning through the air.

It was no surprise then that we were never invited back to play the Scout hut in Norwich. And, in fact, all punk bands were banned from ever playing the Scout hut in Norwich again, for the rest of time. I felt kind of bad about that, as the people who had asked us to play there were only trying to bring a bit of life and youth culture to their boring hometown. Well, they certainly accomplished that. By this point, the friends of the band were referred to as our 'wrecking crew'.

There was one other momentous gig, again not memorable because of our performance, which took place at the Clarendon in Hammersmith. The gig was being held downstairs but the PA had failed to materialise so the rest of the band got bored and fucked off home. I bumped into a bloke who knew our new singer Deb and he offered me a swig of brandy from a large bottle he was carrying, which was very odd. Most people who attended our gigs were young and broke and brandy is expensive liquor. What was doubly strange

CHAPTER 4

was that he was more than happy to share some of it with someone he'd never met.

Anyway, it was getting late and the PA still hadn't shown up, so I was in the pub upstairs drinking with friends. The landlord of the pub came over and asked if there was anyone here from the bands. Thinking the PA had finally turned up, I volunteered myself. He asked me to follow him downstairs to the venue (a room in a basement). It was empty. There was absolutely no sign of the PA. But as soon as we got downstairs he began shouting at me, 'You bands are to blame for this!' and pointed towards the empty optics at the back of the bar, his face crimson with anger. I didn't understand what he was talking about. All I could see was an empty bar behind the shutters. Then the penny dropped. *That* was the point he was trying to make. Someone had stolen every bottle of spirit from behind the bar. I recalled the generous lad with the large bottle of brandy, but I decided to keep quiet about it.

I protested my innocence but the landlord wanted someone to blame, and that someone was going to be me. He grabbed my arm and gripped it tightly whilst continuing to shout at me. I tried to pull away but he refused to let me go. Friends I'd been drinking with upstairs came down and confirmed that I'd been upstairs the whole time, but the landlord was having none of it and retained a vice-like grip on my arm until the police arrived 20 minutes later.

Sebastian (who still came to all my gigs, bless him) confirmed that I had indeed been upstairs all night. But just to make matters worse, it then emerged that whoever had buggered off with a couple of hundred quid's worth of booze had also broken into a cupboard and made off with several microphones. The landlord was still intent on blaming me, because I was the only one from the band still there I guess, but thankfully the police could see I was innocent and persuaded him to unlatch himself from my arm and let me go. I had a bruise on my arm for a week afterwards. Generally, in my experience at least, punks weren't thieves. People assumed we were criminals based on our appearance but there were few amongst our number who were criminally minded. (Not counting the heinous crime of stealing a few quid's worth of foam shrimps from a Scouts' tuck shop, of course.)

Later that week, all the bands that had been billed to play, despite not actually playing, had to report to Hammersmith Police Station to provide statements. I'm not sure if the perpetrators of the crime were ever discovered, but we were banned from ever playing at the Clarendon again. Ironic really considering we never got to play there in the first place.

Our 12-inch single was being released on vinyl at the time so we put the scratch 'Banned from The Clarendon – Ra Ra Ra' on the run-out groove, with 'Where's the Mics?' on the flipside.

By then, I had split up with Steev and had started dating Dylan, a friend of a friend I'd met at another party. I'd dated Steev for a year. I had seen it as a proper relationship, but he didn't seem to want to see it in the same light, so we blew hot and cold for several months before I eventually admitted to myself that it was never going to be what I'd hoped for.

When I finally split up with Steev, I hoped things would improve if we were just friends/band mates, but if anything the situation worsened. I was still in the band and I still loved the process of making music and playing gigs. My keyboard-playing had improved, although I needed a lot of help to work out the riffs. Now, though, my keyboard-playing became the focus of criticism, which was strange as I had never pretended to be a proper keyboard player in the first place. I would come away from gigs and rehearsals confused and hurt.

One day, during a band meeting, we were discussing the release of the *Unwanted Children* album at Alaska Studios in Waterloo – this would have been about 1985 – and I asked if anyone had any ideas for the album's cover. 'If it's one of yours, then no!' a certain band member retorted suddenly and bitterly. The rest of the band fell silent with embarrassment, not quite knowing where to look, nor attempting to stick up for me. I was feeling pretty much like an unwanted child myself.

And then, a couple of weeks later, I was phoned and asked what my ideas were as it turned out that no one else actually had any. I could have told him to fuck off, but I'd studied photography as part of my art diploma and I liked the idea of my artwork on the sleeve. And I was probably way too forgiving.

Chapter 4

After I'd been asked for my ideas, at our next gig Bev's boyfriend was shown the photos I'd done. Steev had sneered at my idea of applying a green or pink wash to them, which I thought would make us stand out from the monochrome anarcho-punk stereotype. And Steev was clearly expecting Bev's boyfriend to concur with him. However, realising that Steev was trying to malign me, he said he thought the coloured wash was a great idea. Oh how I could have hugged Bev's boyfriend. (In a non-sexual way of course!) *Na na na na na*, I thought. However, I was sick of negative attitudes towards me and I was disappointed that no one else in the band had the balls to defend me, so I decided there and then that this would be my last-ever Lost Cherrees gig. I was beginning to feel animosity towards Steev because of his apparent hostility towards me.

I rang the rest of the band one at a time and they all wished me luck for the future. I left Steev until last, dreading what his reaction would be. I told him I was doing them a favour as they were now free to find a proper keyboard player. 'If we'd wanted a professional keyboard player, we would have got one a long time ago,' he said. 'It was YOU we wanted.' I was stunned. Talk about running hot and cold. It was the first time I'd been given any indication that I was actually still wanted in the band. But I'd already made up my mind and I left the Lost Cherrees.

Around 2004, I was handed a flyer that a friend had randomly picked up from a gig she had attended. Apparently the Lost Cherrees were reforming. I went to the website that was included on the flyer and discovered that Bev, Steev (now Steve again), Nuts (still Nuts) and Andy had reformed the band but were trying to locate me, Deb and Sian, and were asking if anyone knew where we were. I admit to having been dubious and curious in equal measure but eventually bit the bullet and sent an email, not knowing whether this was a can of cherry-flavoured worms that I really wanted to reopen.

I quickly received a reply from Steve saying how nice it was to hear from me again. We ended up chatting on instant messenger and he apologised sincerely for how he had treated me in the past, and admitted that he had been nasty and that I didn't deserve it. I felt instantly transported back to the 1980s and started to cry, cos I'm soppy and because I'd still been carrying the hurt feelings around with me for many years. Of course I forgave him.

Chapter 4.5

Lost Cherrees fan mail

10 May 1985
Brixton, London

Dear Lost Cherrees,

I came across your band through a friend some months ago and have since been watching out for new releases and gigs. Out of all the political punk-type bands I've heard, I think the Lost Cherrees have got something different and I really enjoy listening to your records. I agree with everything the band has to say and it makes a change to see females in a band.

I got the LP when it came out and I think it's really good, especially *And the Rape Goes On* [sic]. I feel really sick every time I hear about a rape or child molester – the bastards should suffer for it, but half of them do it again and all those '*macho moronic men*' that walk about and think they are great, make me sick.

Blah blah blah…

Dom

Dear all of you, being the Lost Cherrees,

I first heard of you on the Mortarhate *Who What, When, Why, If, But, Where, This, That* etc compilation LP and was very impressed by your song 'The Wait' and this inspired me to buy your second EP *A Man's Duty, A Woman's Place*. This EP is absolutely great! (This is my opinion, as well as everyone else's who've heard it!) Especially the

Lost Cherrees flyer

songs 'Blasphemy', 'No Trouble', 'Living in a Coffin' and 'Sexism's Sick'… oh, that's the whole EP! Well, I said I liked it! Seriously, 'Sexism's Sick' is one of my favourite tracks. The way part one ends and part two begins is brilliant!

Blah blah blah…

CHAPTER 4.5

Sincerely, Costos

p.s. could you please return my stamps!

13 October 1984
Birmingham

Dear Gail,

It's been ages since I last wrote but there hasn't seemed anything to write to you about, until now... At the mo, there is a really great LP track about that has gotta be the best song of the moment (ie best song I've heard lately!) and that particular song is called 'F Plan, G Plan' taken from you and your fellow fruits' latest release. It's such a good song (at least I think!) that it inspired me to put pen to paper to find out what's happening.

Blah blah blah...

Love, Tom

p.s. Are you RUBELLA RAT? I remember you mentioning before that you designed clothes. Is that you with the fleas and stag beetles?

11 November 84
Nottingham

Dear LC's

I've just finished listening to the album for about the tenth time this week, it's brilliant, one of the best things musically to come out of 84. It's great to see a band side step from the moronic thrash that seems so prevalent in a lot of todays 'punk' music (apologies for the label). Most people have just dismissed a lot of what's gone on before simply because of the noise. A lot of people I knew just aren't interested in listening to an unintelligible squawk, regardless of the message held in the music, but, with All Part of Growing Up, people have listened and read the lyrics saying they enjoyed it. So I've told them to have another read of the lyrics and think about them. I don't suppose it'll get much airplay but that's only to be expected.

The Omega's 'Hard Life' was pure brilliance as well and rivalled the best crap in the charts, but did it get played on daytime radio one or another music station I've heard... not a chance of it.

Keep up the pressure in '85, '86, '87...
LOVE AND PEACE,

Pete

Chapter 5

Not all men are created equal

At some point during my Lost Cherrees era, I went to a Roman toga party that was being held in a flat somewhere in North London. When we got there, as was to be expected, everyone was wearing togas – well actually they were wearing bed-sheets wrapped around them toga-style – but the will was there. Angel, who I went with, was given the last toga sheet to put on and, typical of my luck, I ended up with a toga blanket. Sexy. I wrapped the blanket around me, over my jeans and jumper, in order to get into the spirit of things and, besides, it was a cold evening and so I might have looked like the world's worst Roman but at least I was warm. Flattering, no; practical, yes.

Of course, everyone was drinking heavily – it was England in the '80s after all. Angel knew the guy having the party – Pongo (not his real name) – because he was in a punk band and because they lived quite close to one another. I knew the band he was in but it wasn't the kind of punk music that I liked. (I wasn't a fan of shouty male vocals and preferred more tuneful or female vocals.) A couple of hours into the party and Angel had found herself a Roman and was doing some quite serious heavy petting on the sofa. He had his hand up her toga and she was reciprocating, if you get my drift. It was getting to the point where some people were staring voyeuristically whilst others, myself included, were finding the display of drunken romance a little bit embarrassing, and weren't exactly sure where to look. I went into the next room as I was bored, slightly uncomfortable with the erotic display and didn't feel like drinking anymore.

Suddenly Pongo materialised and casually asked me if I wanted to dance. I was naturally surprised as he had barely acknowledged me since I'd arrived, but I nodded and we walked into the living room, where a few people were already dancing to very loud punk music. Then all of a sudden Pongo grabbed my hand and yanked me through a door off the living room, which led to a small bedroom. As soon as we were through the door he turned around and bolted the door behind us. It all happened so fast that I barely knew what was going on. Panic shot through me, turning the contents of my veins to ice.

'You didn't really think I wanted to dance with you, did you?' Pongo sneered.

Fear sobered me up in a matter of seconds. If ever there was a quick cure for drunkenness, fear is it. I immediately went from pissed to petrified. I was pretty sure Pongo's intentions were not altruistic. I thought that, if I could just get past him, I could undo the bolt and make my escape. The one large problem with this plan being the presence of a large odious man clearly with no morals, who was currently standing between my terrified and recently drunk self and the bolted door. Screaming would have been useless as the music in the room next door was way too loud for a mere human scream to penetrate.

With a big angry hand he suddenly pushed me towards the bed and forced me down, groping me fiercely through my clothes – thank God for my blanket toga. With the other hand he grabbed a wooden chair that must have been next to the bed, and used it to pin my arms and shoulders down so that I couldn't struggle. He kept his weight against it whilst he located the fastening of my jeans and ripped it open. I was terrified. I kept quiet and didn't struggle as I was aware that by doing so I could put myself in further danger. There was no way I could fight this man. If he wanted to rape me, violently assault me, murder me or all three, I stood no chance.

Pongo was ramming his big dirty rapist's fingers deep inside me by now. He was rough and angry. My body was most definitely unprepared for sexual intercourse, so it was dry and extremely painful. Not to mention embarrassing. I disassociated mentally; it was like I was no longer inhabiting my body at all but hovering slightly above myself, and looking down at what was happening to me. I felt numb and frozen. I just prayed that he would stop, and then when I realised he wasn't going to stop, I willed it to be over.

He started yanking my jeans off and I braced myself for what was

CHAPTER 5

about to happen, soundless and compliant with fear and so terrified that he would hurt or kill me.

Suddenly, there was a loud hammering knock on the bedroom door and a female voice demanded to know who was in there. It must have been Pongo's girlfriend as he released me immediately, pulling the chair off me and throwing it on the floor. I yanked my jeans back up and wrapped myself up in the blanket and as soon as Pongo unlocked the door I seized the opportunity and bolted through it. Pongo and his really lucky girlfriend stood in the doorway and started to argue. She must have known what was going on inside a locked room but must have assumed it was consensual. I'm going to assume that she didn't actually know her boyfriend was a rapist. And if Pongo was raping someone despite having a girlfriend, that makes him even more of a sick fuck.

I was numb and in shock. My thigh muscles were gelatinous and I could barely walk properly. I sat on the floor against the wall with my head in my hands, huddled up with my arms wrapped as tightly round my knees as I could get them. I thanked God (or someone) that I'd been wearing jeans and a thick blanket. I tried not to think about what had just taken place. My very insides were trembling and I felt like I would vomit.

Eventually, I managed to calm my blood down and went to find Angel so we could get the fuck out of there, as I was meant to be staying at her house that night. The man she had been entwined with was long gone and she had passed out on the sofa. I tried to wake her but she was pretty much unconscious.

I realised that I didn't know where I was, other than that I was in some suburb of North London. It was 2am. I was 19 years old. Even if I found my way to a Tube station, the Tube had long since stopped running. I had no money for a cab. No map. And I didn't know where Angel lived. I was completely stranded, stuck at a dreadful party hosted by Mr Fucking Rapist and, instead of being able to run from the most dreadful experience of my life, I had no choice but to stay where I was. I would have to wait until Angel sobered up or the Tube started running, whichever came first. The Tube, I imagined, looking at the state of Angel. At least Pongo's girlfriend might

79

keep an eye on him, I hoped. I mean, perhaps he could have sex with her? There's a thought.

I curled up into the smallest bundle I could on the other end of the sofa to Angel. There were other people in the room besides – so safety in numbers at least, I reasoned.

Eventually I managed to fall asleep. Sometime later, I don't know how long I'd slept for, I awoke to find a man – a complete stranger – trying to kiss me, while I was asleep! I opened my eyes and pushed him off me with all my might. Then, looking over, I saw that Pongo was on top of Angel and was fucking her. Angel's eyes were closed and she didn't seem very responsive considering she was in the throes of sexual intercourse. Then it occurred to me: was she even conscious? Her head was lolling from side to side but I'm not sure she was aware of what Pongo was doing to her. I was both disgusted and horrified. I tried to speak but I couldn't form the words. I guessed his girlfriend must have been asleep in their room. I hadn't known Angel that long and I didn't know how well she knew Pongo. Had she had sex with him before? Was this normal behaviour for them or was he now rap-ing her? I was terrified. I didn't know what to do. Would I be next?

I could see Pongo thrusting away at Angel's possibly unconscious body and I couldn't move to do anything. My limbs felt foreign to me. My brain was sending signals to them, but they weren't picking up the messages. I closed my eyes to block out the repugnant image of this pathetic specimen of a man thrusting in and out of someone who was oblivious. What kind of a sick creep does this?

I don't know how but I eventually fell asleep – I was mentally, emotionally and physically exhausted, not helped by the large quan-tities of alcohol I'd imbibed earlier in the night. I woke up, I don't know how much later, and the strange man was trying to kiss me in my sleep again. What was wrong with the men at this fucking party? I pushed him away, angrily.

There was a man nearby who I'd noticed earlier in the evening. He looked kind and gentle and my gut feeling was that he was a good person so – and I know this might sound bizarre – I went over and asked him if he would like to sleep with me. I was terrified of Pongo and the weirdo who kept trying to kiss me in my sleep – clearly a

CHAPTER 5

friend of Pongo's – and I wanted to feel safe and protected. I felt that the only way of doing so was to be around other people. I instinctively knew that this man would fill the role of protector. I had always enjoyed sex in the past, when I had been given a choice in the matter, and I felt that I wanted to have sex in an environment where I was in control. I wanted to choose who I had sex with, as I'd recently had that decision taken out of my hands. Mainly, I wanted to feel protected and safe until I could get myself away from the 'party' as soon as I possibly could, which was still several hours away.

We found a quiet corner in another bedroom and settled ourselves on the floor in each other's arms. I asked him his name and he asked me mine. And then I allowed this man to make love to me. He was extremely gentle. I needed something pleasant to replace the horrible experience with Pongo. After we'd had lovely tender sex, we fell asleep, me wrapped securely in the warm arms of my new acquaintance. He had no idea what had happened to me earlier on that night and absolutely no idea how much his gentleness had helped me. (Years later, when I received counselling, I was told that it isn't unusual for a victim to have sex with someone else after being raped: apparently it's part of a survival instinct. It's a way of owning your own body again; taking your power back; and being able to make your own choices. Getting right back in the saddle so to speak.)

In the morning, Angel woke me as if nothing had happened and we wordlessly went back to her house. I just couldn't find the words to address the subject. Neither of us ever mentioned what had happened. I felt terribly ashamed. I guess I felt stupid for allowing it to happen. I was very shy, only 19 years old and didn't know how to approach such a subject. I was not a virgin, but I was extremely inexperienced.

I was at a friend's a few weeks later when she mentioned that her period was late. I had found blood in my knickers the morning after Mr Fucking Rapist had jabbed his dirty fucking rapist's fingers into me and, at the very thought of bloody knickers, I burst into tears and eventually confided in her about what had happened. She hugged me and tried to convince me to report Pongo to the police, but I was scared. I was scared no one would believe me. I was scared it was his word against mine. I was scared because he was well known. I was scared I would have to relive the trauma. I was scared I would be blamed for being drunk. I was scared he would get away with it. And I was scared of ever seeing Pongo again.

The physical reminders of such a harrowing event lasted a week. The mental scars have lasted a lifetime. The pain rape victims experience does not end just because the act of rape has ended. Not even close. Rape can – and often does – lead to drug addiction, alcoholism, eating disorders, self-harming, difficulty in maintaining close relationships, depression, anxiety, sexual dysfunction, sometimes promiscuity, self-loathing, an inability to enjoy sexual intimacy, flashbacks and post-traumatic stress disorder. So nothing serious then.

Ironically, the Lost Cherrees had a song called 'But the Rape Goes On'. Other than my friend, I never told anyone, not Angel, not even anyone in the band what had happened to me. I was way too ashamed. Rape is weird in that it is the victim who feels shame. In other crimes, it is the perpetrator who is ashamed. People whose homes have been burgled don't feel embarrassed. So why do rape victims?

We blame ourselves because we must have given them some kind of unknown signal as a come-on, that we allowed it to happen, that we attracted it by being in the wrong place at the wrong time – and why me? Why not anyone else?

Despite not letting on to my band mates, whenever we played 'But the Rape Goes On' live I would scream the lyrics vociferously into the microphone:

Young girl lying, crying in the street
The old woman dying, lying in the street
The squandered innocence, the shameful abuse
But the rape goes on (and there's no excuse)

It could happen to me, happen to me
Happen to you, happen to you
Happen to me, happen to me
Happen to you

Thousands of women, battered, beaten, bruised or killed

CHAPTER 5

But the rape goes on
All those complaint forms that can or can't or won't be filled
But the rape goes on
All those women suffering the indignation
But the rape goes on
The sexual offenders, minds that reek with depravation
But the rape goes on

The problems there to realise not analyse
The problems there to realise not analyse
The problems there to realise not analyse
So realise now before the coward strikes again

Social workers signed to give the best advice
But the rape goes on
Case dismissed, the victim cannot testify
But the rape goes on
Because rapes becoming such a common accusation
But the rape goes on
The judge puts it down to flirting provocation
But the rape goes on

The problems there to realise not analyse
The problems there to realise not analyse
The problems there to realise not analyse
So realise now before the coward strikes again

Law will never do enough to justify my fate
Sometimes I wonder if there's anywhere that's safe
It's in and out the countryside, it's in and out the city
But the rape goes on and on and on

It could happen to you, happen to you
Happen to me, happen to me
Happen to you, happen to you
Happen to me

It's happening now
It's here and there and everywhere
But the rape goes on
The average person, do they really think to care
But the rape goes on
Sexual violence is happening, it's here today
But the rape goes on
It's sick and its callous and it must be stopped in any way
But the rape goes on

The problems there to realise not analyse
The problems there to realise not analyse
The problems there to realise not analyse
So realise now before the coward strikes again

The problems there to realise not analyse
The problems there to realise not analyse
The problems there to realise not analyse
So realise now before the coward strikes again

(words written by Lost Cherrees)

It did happen to me.

Years later, I was watching the daytime chat show *Kilroy* in which they were appealing for rape survivors to take part in a future show entitled '*If a woman dresses provocatively, is it an open invitation to rape?*' Now here was a subject close to my heart and one that I am still vociferous about to this very day. And what's more, I am living proof that a woman can wear jeans and a blanket and still get raped. Clothes don't make a rapist rape. The urge to rape makes a rapist rape.

Many years had passed since the attack and I felt strong enough now to speak about it. I seized the opportunity to give voice to all the emotions that I had been keeping bottled up inside me for so many years. *Fucking fuck it*, I thought, and picked up the phone.

Chapter 5

When I arrived at the BBC studios, I was amongst many other women who were there to relate their own harrowing stories of attacks at the hands of cowardly men. Realising that, sadly, I was really not alone in my experiences was eye-opening. For the first time in my life, I felt a sense of solidarity with other women. Whilst the scenarios in which we'd been attacked were invariably different, we definitely shared the terror, shame and years of trauma that had ensued. All of us had struggled with self-esteem issues, anxiety and depression following our ordeals. All of us felt worthless. We'd all been profoundly affected by the experiences that we'd undergone.

Kilroy asked if wearing skimpy clothes encouraged rape, and then pointed the microphone in my direction. I was still a punk and had dyed my hair bright purple for the occasion. I explained that I didn't think rape has anything to do with what you wear and had my say for all of two minutes before the microphone was whisked away while I was in mid-sentence.

Although I had publicly admitted that I had been raped – on TV! – and had a new-found sense of solidarity, having been surrounded by others who shared my experience, I was left feeling disappointed. I'd hoped that appearing on the *Kilroy* show would give me some closure, but it didn't. However, the following day in my usual pub, some women told me they had seen the programme and recounted their awful rape experiences to me. I no longer felt like I was the only one it had happened to.

Many years later, close to a nervous breakdown, I went through a series of therapy sessions and, as part of a commitment to healing, I recounted the details of the rape and other sexual abuse I'd been the victim of to a counsellor. I was also in contact with WAR (Women Against Rape) – an excellent organisation with a great staff of extremely helpful people – and they helped me greatly. In return, I helped out with a bit of administration to assist their campaign.

There was another edition of *Kilroy* due to be recorded and aired, this time on the subject of male rape. WAR asked me to represent them on the programme. They said it was great that male rape was gaining recognition, and that men were getting help, but they didn't want the fact that women have been raped for centuries to go unmentioned. I agreed. WAR insisted that the BBC pay me a fee for my appearance because programmes like *Kilroy* capitalise on controversial topics such as rape and trauma because they are topics that guarantee good viewing figures. They reasoned that, if the programme was making money from the topic, then the brave people who agreed to appear on the show should also be remunerated, not exploited further.

I struggled – like all victims of sexual abuse or trauma – with the knock-on emotional and psychological effects for over 30 years. I have invisible scars that have never gone away. Luckily, with the passing of time and thanks to many positive experiences with other individuals, they are gradually fading. But I don't think they will ever really disappear completely.

For a very long time I avoided any form of sexual contact. There were times when I didn't have or want a boyfriend. I wanted my body to remain covered up and the last thing I wanted to do was undress in front of a man. I felt vulnerable and dressed accordingly. I carried a sense of shame with me like an invisible suitcase, wherever I went.

In 2014, approximately 30 years after brave old Pongo had held me down with a chair and forced himself upon me, a friend posted some photos on a social networking site of a friend's wedding he'd recently attended. To my horror, the friend getting married was the wonderful Pongo. I felt instantly livid. How dare this vile 'man' negatively impact every single sexual relationship I've had for the last three decades, yet be standing smugly smiling and happily married. What kind of a monster was this poor bride agreeing to spend her life with?

I had never been married. I was too damaged and felt too unlovable. Seeing the wedding photos of Pongo not only opened up the old wounds, they began to bleed with a vengeance. I spent the ensuing days crying uncontrollably.

After a few days of feeling like utter shit, I suddenly picked myself up and brushed myself down. I decided that I no longer wished to be a victim in my own life. The disgusting and evil actions of one human being had scarred me irrevocably but it was time to put an end to that. I had never known Pongo's real name, so when I saw that the photographs of his happy day on the Internet included his real name – I immediately picked up the phone and dialled Women's Aid.

Chapter 5

The publicity surrounding the 1970s children's TV presenter Jimmy Savile had recently been monopolising the news in the UK. Savile had been posthumously exposed as a child abuser and rapist, and new victims of his repugnant behaviour were coming forward every day, more than 30 years later. The laws and attitudes had changed over the years. It was 30 years since I'd been raped but I was still affected by it at a profound level. My 13-year-old son saw me crying and I had to lie to him about what was wrong. I couldn't tell him what had happened to me. But the fact that victims of Savile's fucked-up sexual shenanigans were suddenly coming forward gave me strength.

Women's Aid were fantastic and put me in touch with a specialist rape and sexual assault unit. I was asked if I wanted to report the rape to the police, and I decided that, yes, it was the right thing to do. I was scared but I felt that it needed to be done. I was interviewed at home by two lovely female police officers and, a week later, I was driven to a centre where I was interviewed in front of a camera. One of my reservations over all those years had been that no one would believe me. That the law would favour him. So I was incredibly relieved when it became obvious that they believed me. I was amazed at how strong I was and how I was able to talk and recall so many details of what had happened. (The beauty of having something replayed over and over in your mind ad infinitum helps commit it to memory, I guess!)

Reporting Pongo was both a relief and terrifying in equal measure. I was petrified of the backlash. Would he turn up on my doorstep or send someone to beat me up or worse? I, more than most, knew what he was capable of but I was given the assurance of police protection.

Pongo was never prosecuted as the crime had taken place so long ago and it was difficult to prove because there had been no witnesses. None who would come forward, anyway. But I do have a sense of satisfaction that his name is now on file, and that if he ever touches another woman again in the way that he attacked and abused me and Angel, he will at least be punished for it. Plus I have the knowledge that his wife (who I seriously pity) might find out one day. I just hope he treats her with more respect than he does other girls.

I was finally offered counselling and I met a wonderful woman called Katia, who was exceptionally helpful. I was able to tell her everything, safe in the knowledge that she wasn't judging me. (Katia also told me that many victims of post-traumatic stress disorder become psychics and healers because they are so tuned in all the time. There's a thought.)

Men like Pongo are ultimately cowards. I don't know what our society does to compel so many men to act in such abusive ways. I've never been much impressed by people who enjoy using power over the weaker. Rapists, child molesters, animal abusers – fucking cowards and bullies, the lot of them. How much better and more beautiful our world would be without them sullying it.

I wonder if Pongo ever explained to his wife why he was being interviewed by the police? I wonder if he fobbed her off with a diluted (aka bullshit) version of the events of that night? I wonder if he claimed that I was willing and then changed my mind? I wonder if, in recounting that evening, he ever mentions the words 'consent' or 'chair' to his lovely bride?

I'm glad that Pongo remembers me now. Because I have never been able to forget about him.

Chapter 6

Home is where the hurt is

I'd been living back in Boreden with my folks after leaving my job as a cot finisher in the hope of doing something slightly more creative with my precious time. As I'd been to art school I considered myself a bit of an arty wench and I needed a creative outlet. Having played in bands and designed and made clothes, applying the finish to cots in a factory just wasn't cutting it.

The unbelievable monotony of working on the production line of a factory really didn't suit me and as I'd also had a few issues with the union rep, due to my outspokenness, I had been moved from the slightly skilled job of cot-finishing to packing high chairs (every day was a thrilling adventure, I assure you). If you are imagining that it was an incredibly boring and pedestrian job unsuitable for a creative personality or anyone with a desire to enjoy their life then you are correct. I felt I was destined for far more interesting things.

I'd stopped working at the chemist's on Saturdays but had remained friends with a girl called Laura who was what we used to call 'straight', which back then was nothing to do with her sexuality but indicated that she wasn't a punk/alternative/goth or part of any of the other youth cults. Laura was a natural blonde and very pretty. She was a few years younger than me and lived round the corner in Lower Morden. When she started working at the chemist's, I was already there with my green hair. Which is odd in itself, looking back. The manager must have been incredibly broad-minded to unleash me on the unsuspecting old ladies who queued up to get their prescriptions filled at 9am on a Saturday. Laura was clearly so gobsmacked by my vividly green bonce (not such a common sight back then) that she went home and told her mum about me. Mummy Laura was horrified that such a degenerate could be allowed to work in a chemist's amongst nice and normal folk and forbade Laura from ever returning, lest my evil influence subvert her innocent daughter and she spend the rest of her life burning in hell. Which would at least have been more interesting than living in Morden all her life.

Luckily, Laura managed to persuade her dismayed mother that I was not in fact a ne'er-do-well intent on ruining her daughter but that I was just a girl who happened to have colourful hair – and much more likely to offer Laura a nice cup of tea than gob on her or shower her with expletives. Punks had a bad reputation, and there were some who were into screaming obscenities and randomly expelling phlegm, but I was not one of those. Most of us were enthused by the image, the music and the politics rather than mindless violence. I liked bright colours and I enjoyed expressing myself using colour.

Laura's mum came to meet me the next day, in order to check that my intentions were honourable I guess, and, to my absolute surprise, she took an instant shine to me, giving me the affectionate nickname of 'Polly Punk' which, of course, I loved.

Laura and I stayed good friends and, despite our contrasting tastes in music, we would often go round each other's houses and put the world to rights over a bottle of Rosé D'Anjou wine and a diverse selection of music that spanned Lionel Richie and X-Ray Spex. I cannot put my hand on my heart and say that I liked Lionel Richie, whose music was as far from punk as it was possible to be, but I tolerated it for Laura's sake. And she, in turn, endured my punk collection. And I did eventually manage to convert her into an X-Ray Spex fan. (The same cannot be said for me becoming a Lionel Richie fan, I'm afraid.) Laura and I would put on X-Ray Spex and belt out the lyrics at the very tops of our voices. Laura even bought a copy of the record and learned all the words. Her favourite lyrics were: *Freddie tried to strangle me, with my plastic popper beads, but I hit him back, with my pet rat.* (Which certainly beats the shit out of *Hello? Is it me you're looking for?* – Sorry, Laura.)

Romance-wise, I was dating Dylan by this point. I mentioned him earlier, right? Keep up now. Both of us wore crowns of magnificent bleached-blonde hair crimped to the very edge of oblivion, and of similar length. I found him instantly attractive and felt drawn to him, possibly because we looked similar. When I'd first met him at that party, we'd chatted, probably awkwardly, for a while, until someone had serendipitously pushed past me forcing my body against Dylan's warm body, who took full advantage of the situation, wrapped his arms around me, pulled me gently towards me and kissed me. (Note to Pongo: no chair necessary.) We remained in each other's arms the entire night snuggled warmly together like a pair of happy blonde punk puppies.

Dylan was a postman and lived in a bedsit in Guildford, Surrey, where I would stay with him at the weekend. One Valentine's Day, he placed a classified advert in the paper, with a cryptic message for me using our pet names:

'BIG NOSE LOVES PUFFBALL'

An incurable romantic! He also treated me to a weekend in Amsterdam and came to see me at most of the Lost Cherrees gigs. He knew I had a hard time being in the band towards the end and was always nearby to provide me with support and man-cuddles when I needed them. Dylan was kind and fun and generous. A noble gentleman if ever there was one. Why did I ever split up with Dylan?!

Like a typical doley, I was staying up until 3am and not rising from my boudoir until 3pm. My mum soon got fed up with me sitting around the house looking miserable, and so demanded that I pay rent from my dole money. I had to cough up a massive 50 quid a week out of each giro – which didn't leave much for purchasing the finer things in life, like hair dye. Looking back, I'm glad my parents pushed me. I wasn't achieving much on the dole and needed a bit of a stern nudge in the direction of employment.

I had set my hopes (ambitious beyond my actual ability, as always) on establishing my own silkscreen-printing business. I wanted to design and print my own T-shirts. I figured I was already a keyboard player who couldn't play the keyboard. I'd been a singer without any musical ability. And I'd designed and made my own clothes despite not knowing the first (second, third, fourth or fifth) thing about cutting patterns or sewing. How difficult could being a silkscreen-printing entrepreneur be?

I went to a career mentor and fervently relayed to her my fabulous dreams of being the figurehead in my very own printed T-shirt empire. She was less enthusiastic about my entrepreneurial ability than I'd anticipated and suggested that, before I started my own silkscreen-printing company, I should learn how to silkscreen-print. No imagination, some people. In actual fact, I'd already had a bash at silkscreen printing during my art diploma, so I felt like I had the essential skills required to establish my small empire. She told me that there was a street nearby where she was sure there were some silkscreen printers and suggested I go and strike up a conversation with them, which I did. Life was dramatically easier then. Before the Internet, if you were looking for employment it was thoroughly acceptable to go in person and ask someone to give you a job. Now, you probably need a degree in silkscreen printing before you can get an entry-level position in which they will train you to silkscreen-print. So I left the careers advisor, and trotted happily off to find the street she had recommended, which was located between Waterloo and London Bridge train stations.

My hair was peroxide blonde again, wild and backcombed and lacquered stiff. Not even a force-10 gale would have been able to penetrate that do, I can tell you. I had on my usual dramatic make-up and a dress that I'd made from some very bold fish-print fabric. The frock was set off nicely by complementary blue fishnet tights and stilettos. I was also modelling a pair of brightly coloured plastic-toy fish earrings, designed and made by yours truly, thank you very much. Now, this is probably not the typical interview attire that you might find recommended in a book on interview etiquette. But I looked and felt good, both slim and confident, as I strode into Golder and Richardson silkscreen printers. I had smelt the printing inks as I walked past, like a bloodhound driven by colour, and had decided to try my luck.

The manager eyed me suspiciously, as most businessmen would when being approached by a woman dressed head to toe in fish print, with hair like a terrified peacock and make-up like an angry drag queen. Bizarrely, and completely unbeknownst to me, they had been advertising for a screen printer, so my timing was spot on.

The manager said he had never taken on a female printer before.

CHAPTER 6

Sexism was still pretty rife back then, although this was the 1980s and things were definitely improving. Equality was a prominent theme and women were finding their voices. He tried to discourage me, as it was clear he wasn't really keen on employing a 'printeress'. He said he was worried I might break a nail or complain if I got ink under my nails (which was bloody sexist in itself) but he knew the law was in my favour and, according to the Sex Discrimination Act, he had to give women a fair shot at any jobs they wished to apply for.

I assured him that I was a tomboy and that I didn't give the slightest fuck whether I bust a nail or went home marinated in a thousand shades of ink and – what do you know? – he gave the fish girl a week's trial.

On my first day in the job, the boss's 16-year-old son was given the job of demonstrating how to print wallpaper. The company was the only one left in London that still hand-printed wallpapers, the others having succumbed to advances in technology.

Hand-printing wallpaper involved using a huge machine that fed the blank paper from a massive roll under the screen, where the machine sucked the paper to the table and held it in place whilst the design – in this case, an intricate bird pattern – was printed onto the paper. I stood and watched for a while and then got stuck in. The boss came to see how I was doing at 10am, took one look at me, enrobed in a cocktail of vivid colours, and said, 'Well, I needn't have worried about you, then.' He smiled and walked away. He needn't have worried about me as I was as happy as a pig in shit. Or as happy as a punk in ink. I was working with fabulous designs and amazing colours. I don't know whether you've realised yet, but I love colour. They thought I was one of the designers when I'd first showed up looking for a job because of my colourful attire.

The boss later admitted that he'd taken me on as he'd been struck by my cheekiness and impressed by my willingness to work. He had really taken quite a shine to me. This didn't stop me from being completely stunned one day when he asked me into his office. *Oh my god!* I thought, *I must have done something wrong.* Internally, I was adopting the brace position whilst I waited for him to reprimand me, or perhaps even fire me. So imagine my surprise when he asked if I would like to have an affair with him. Well, that was unexpected. I politely declined, as messing about with married men wasn't my bag. Also, his son worked there and I would never have been able to look him in the eye again. The boss reacted nobly and the subject was never mentioned again, which was a relief as many men would have become angry and resentful at having been rejected in that way.

I was lucky that, despite being the only girl in the print room, all the guys accepted my presence completely. There was no issue with my gender. The camaraderie in that job was great and we laughed and mocked each other good-heartedly whenever we were given half the chance, which was most of the time. We had a tape player on the factory floor and would take it in turns to play our own music. One guy would play Elvis (who I had grown up listening to as my dad was a fan of The King), another Motown and I of course, in turn, subjected them to my favourite bands of the time: Siouxsie and the Banshees, The Damned and Stiff Little Fingers.

Sebastian had become a close and valued friend by then and we would often share bottles of Merrydown cider together before heading out to gigs. My boss asked me one day if I knew anyone who would do the cleaning for the company, so I suggested Sebastian. He still had his bright red hair and I think the boss liked having two punks brightening the place up like a pair of macaws.

I loved the job and I loved the people there. But sadly, a year later, I was laid off, as the company was beginning to struggle due to other firms' lower prices. So it was back on the dole for me.

Of course, with all the printing inks and screen wash that we employed during the screen-printing process, I was exposed to an endless supply of potent fumes. We were never provided with any form of breathing protection (health and safety was not what it is today) and simply opened a window to air the place, during the summer at least (all four days of it, in England). I would get the train home after work, as high (and as colourful) as a kite and stinking of screen-wash chemicals. The upside of this was that no one wanted to sit next to a toxic, ink-covered punk, and so I often had part of the train carriage to myself – like a multicoloured leper. The downside was that a few years later it suddenly occurred to me that I no longer had a sense

CHAPTER 6

of smell. Having worked at the screen printers and handled powerful solvents in the previous factory job, and without adequate protection, my poor sinuses were, if you'll forgive the sophisticated medical terminology, fucked.

When I managed to escape Morden again around 1985 or 1986, I had no idea that I'd soon be sprinting right back again at an even greater velocity than the one I had used to leave it. I was totally unprepared for the total chaos that unfolded after I moved into a squat – a sturdy Victorian three-storey house in Stamford Hill, North London. I think perhaps I had underestimated how difficult it would be to live in a house with seven male inhabitants and no other women. Especially bearing in mind the recent experiences that I now had under my belt, if you'll pardon the tasteless pun.

Then I met Max, who had fluffy peroxided white hair like cotton wool and a girlfriend with long purple hair, called Nina. Max once admitted to having a crush on me but, due to various reasons, one of which was that Nina had threatened to kill herself if he ever dared to split up with her (not really the best way of keeping a partner interested in you Nina, but whatever), I had politely declined.

Max lived in a room in a squat in Kyverdale Road and told me that there was a spare room available if I wanted to get out of my parents' house, which I really, really did. No offence, M & D, but I was 20 years old and Morden ain't all that.

The room was the smallest in the building, and so long as I was prepared to overlook the fungus growing on the wall (or convince myself that it was ornamental), Max told me it was all mine. I moved house using a porter's trolley, the same one I used for carting my keyboards around, and a combination of Tube train and bus, more or less in one go.

I had just enough living space to accommodate a small wardrobe, a single mattress on the floor and my treasured keyboards and sewing machine, so long as I didn't mind turning sideways and sidling crab-like between the mattress and wardrobe should I want to actually move anywhere. The room was cold and damp, but rent-free, so long as I didn't mind sharing it with the large fungal growth the size of a man's hand on the ceiling. It sat there intimidating me, like something from another planet come to observe life on earth. None of the men in the house had wanted the room because of it. Taking a deep breath, I scraped it off with a knife.

Unlike many other squats, ours was pretty much five star, in that it had running water and electricity as there were people who knew how to rig the utilities, bypassing the meters so that we got them for free. There used to be a squatters' handbook, full of such useful tips, which is now banned.

Along with Max, there were Robin, Tom, Simon, Gavin, Dev, who had a beautiful black cat, and Ken. Ken was positively rich by comparison with the rest of the household as he had both a motorbike *and* a job. We all slept on second-hand mattresses that we'd rehomed from skips or found in the streets. I don't think bedbugs and fleas had been invented then. Either that, or we were young and carefree. Or is that careless?

Like I said, being the only girl living with a bunch of guys was a bit unnerving at times. Especially as I knew only too well what effect a blanket could have on a man. One day, whilst Ken was out, Max took me into Ken's room and pulled back his mattress to reveal a rather scary-looking hatchet. Was Ken as untrusting as me or was he a hatchet-wielding psychopath? I had no way of telling.

Despite my reservations, the rest of the household seemed cool enough. Simon was quiet and pleasant. Tom produced a high-quality fanzine called *Vague* which genuinely looked like posh women's rag *Vogue* as it used the same typeface, glossy cover and weight of paper. Except *Vague* featured articles relating to creative writing, politics, opinion and punk culture. The magazine was well known in punk circles and had a strong readership. Boxes upon boxes of the magazine fresh from the printers would line the hallways. We used to call him Tom Vague, because we were a) hilarious and b) imaginative.

Tom was over six foot tall with short black messy hair. He spent his days invariably slaving over his manual typewriter, producing features for the magazine. I heard years later that he had retired from punk fanzines and had turned his talents to writing and producing football fanzines. Being the studious and intellectual type, Tom was,

CHAPTER 6

of course, like Simon, pleasant enough and extremely quiet. Especially when compared to some of the others… sigh.

Gavin was one of my favourites – a natural extrovert who was super-friendly and dead easy to get along with. He had short brown hair and dressed in army surplus clothing.

The kitchen was small and badly equipped. When I first moved in there had been a cooker and a fridge but gradually, and somewhat inexplicably, these things disappeared. I'm not sure whether they'd been jettisoned or sold. Luckily, I'd brought a Breville sandwich toaster along with me, which meant that the majority of my meals consisted of some interpretation of that classic '80s gourmet dish – the toasted sandwich – generally constructed using cheese, baked beans, baked beans and cheese, cheese and onion or some other such combination (food of the gods!). That, or the epicurean delight that is the Pot Noodle. How I didn't get scurvy and die at least once, I'll never know.

Dev I vaguely knew from gigs and because he'd played in both Tom's Midnight Garden and Flowers in the Dustbin. Dev and Gavin were good mates and shared an interest in post-industrial gothic music. Or was it industrial post-goth music? Or post-goth industrial music? I forget.

Gavin played bass guitar and for a while played in No Remorse, although that was long after we squat-shared. No Remorse were considered a right-wing skinhead band. Gavin and Dev had both been developing an unsettling interest in World War Two and Nazi Germany, which I felt was a genuine reason for concern. But despite their burgeoning interest in Nazi paraphernalia, I still got on better with Gavin and Dev than with the other squatters. Gavin endeared himself to me when he made me a cup of tea after my kitten died, which had only recently been given to me by my friend Fiona. Gavin and I would often sit in the living room together and chat.

For whatever reason, the other guys had taken a dislike to Max long before I'd moved in and would often gang up on him like a pack of dogs trying to oust a feeble pack member. I moved in at the height of it. I think, looking back, Max had wanted me to move in so that he would have an ally in the house.

One day, the others moved all of Tom Vague's boxes of magazines and piled them up outside Max's door whilst he and Nina were inside the room, meaning that they were unable to get out. The others found this hilarious. Max and Nina did not. The final straw came when someone let off a CS gas canister in Max's room whilst he was actually in it. Which was both dangerous and fucking stupid. Sick of being bullied, Max wisely moved out – wouldn't anyone? Perhaps Max should have slept with a hatchet under *his* mattress?

I stayed friends with Max but, at about the same time, Dylan and I split up. It was around the time that the full after-effects of being raped were starting to hit me and I just needed some alone-time and, sadly, we gradually lost touch. Years later, however, I bumped into Nina, who confided to me that I was lucky to be alive as she had seriously planned to burn the house down, because of what the others had done to her and Max, and that it was only because of me being there that she didn't. A chill tickled my spine as she described how she had intended to start the blaze. My biggest phobia as a child was of being burned alive. My blood ran cold and I made a mental note to keep my distance from Nina and certainly never to piss her off. I understood her anger at being victimised and humiliated, but I had no desire to become toast as I slept.

With Max gone, the remaining occupants had to find other cruel ways to keep their childish boy minds amused. Looking back, I really got off lightly. Tom Vague's typewriter (the tool of his trade, remember) found itself defenestrated from the second floor whilst he was out. The others thought it was the funniest thing that had ever happened in the history of comedy. Tom, however, was inexplicably livid. He managed to retrieve the machine from the overgrown jungle of a garden, but it was broken and he could no longer use it. Hilarious, right? Ken moved out too. I think he went back to his mum's. A wise move.

The remaining housemates were nocturnal, whereas I wasn't, so luckily the house was often very quiet during the day, which meant I could monopolise the living room and sew in relative peace. I took a stall at Camden Lock Market on Saturdays to sell my wares. I'd taught myself to sew aged just 15 and I experimented with making my own clothes, although if I said I knew how to properly use a sewing pat-

CHAPTER 6

tern, I'd be a big fat liar. I liked to use conventional sewing patterns but then add my own touch. Yet I literally had no idea if I was doing it right and it was a long time before I realised what the direction-of-grain arrows were for. That was a lightbulb moment. The pattern layout suggestions were completely ignored by me, because I could find a better way to fit the paper pattern onto the fabric by placing and cutting it at odd angles. Of course, the consequence of this meant that the pieces would stretch after I cut them and sit oddly together, but what the hell did I know or care, it was punk.

I was still making clothes for myself too and then, because I was feeling broody but wasn't ready to have my own children, I started making clothes for anarchic babies. There were no pink-and-blue towelling Babygros in my infant collection. I used cartoon-print fabrics in the brightest colours known to man, which I picked up cheap from the local textile markets in London.

I'd also made jewellery from unusual beads and toys and sold them at the legendary market. Steev from the Lost Cherrees had previously made me a lovely display board from three hinged-together framed boards, using his skills as a picture framer, so that I could exhibit my creations.

Well, when I say I took a stall, I was deemed a casual trader, which translated into getting there early on a Saturday morning and putting your name on a list. Your name would then be pulled from a hat by the market superintendent (or 'Toby') and he would allocate you a vacant stall. It was meant to be a fair system but I somehow always wound up with the shittiest stalls that no one else would accept. Often the stalls smelt of beery piss, which my ruined sense of smell was still able to perceive, from the homeless tramps and drunken pub-goers from the night before. They were also more often than not covered in a beautiful veneer of bird droppings and were located at the very back of the market, where only the hardiest of shoppers, or those who were impervious to the smell of old wee, would dare to venture or bother to look.

On my little slightly pissy stall I sold kids' and women's clothes in funky cartoon fabrics such as My Little Pony, Star Wars, Rainbow Brite and the Mr Men, and vibrant jewellery made from plastic toys, plastic fish, fishing lures that glowed in the dark and bright pink cocktail monkeys and elephants. I soon added solid-silver chains and rings and earrings to my remit.

I had first started making earrings whilst I was still at school, using beads and miniature liquorice allsorts that I varnished with clear nail polish. It was this primitive jewellery-making that led to my first encounter with punks. I'd been told about a bead shop down the legendary King's Road in Chelsea and had gone to check it out. I must have been about 15 at the time. I'd found the atmosphere on the King's Road intoxicating and had admired, but been slightly intimated by, the infamous King's Road punks I'd observed for the first time in my life. They were a few years older than me and I looked on in awe at these exotic creatures with their multicoloured clothes and incredible coloured hair that had been wonderfully crafted into fabulous shapes.

I soon started to dye my hair (remember blue/greengate?) and I would get my supply of Crazy Color hair dye from a chemist's on the King's Road, which made me feel like an extremely grown-up punk, when in fact I was still just a baby punk.

As well as the stall that smelt of wee, I also began to take my creations to gigs and made a small killing selling them to band members and punters alike. I would often come away from gigs with more money than I took with me in the first place, and inebriated to boot. I had learned to pierce ears whilst I was still at the printers (the boss's 16-year-old son had been my guinea pig) and so I would also take my piercing gun to pubs, clubs and venues, where I often had a queue of people willing to pay me to perforate them for a much cheaper rate than the salons. Many a person emerged from the ladies' loos in the Bull and Gate pub in Kentish Town with a freshly pierced nose or ear, courtesy of yours truly and my weapon of choice. It was common for punks to have multiple piercings in each ear, so my cheap rates and accessibility (in the bogs) meant I was in demand, especially as punters would often magically summon up the courage to visit me in my mobile piercing toilet booth after they'd downed a couple of beers or three.

Speaking of toilets, I was really enjoying running the stall on the

CHAPTER 6

market in Camden, despite my insalubrious location. I was (geographically) close to another trader called Bob who sold punk fanzines. Neither of us did very well as far as profits went, but we were motivated more by happy enthusiasm than the desire to appear on the cover of *Forbes* magazine. Still, we managed to cover the rent on our stalls. Most weeks, at least. I noticed that Bob was selling copies of *Vague* and we got chatting about it. Bob was very impressed that I lived in the same house as the editor, as he idolised him slightly. I eventually introduced them.

The living room in the squat was sparsely furnished with an old sofa. In an attempt to be 'arty', my other housemates had built a sculpture using junk that stretched along the entirety of one wall. The 'sculpture' contained all manner of things, from old furniture to shopping baskets and TVs. If you were ever bored you could pass the time trying to identify the items of junk in the wall sculpture. (These days we have the Internet instead.)

They would also play a few (hilarious) tricks on me, although these were nothing in comparison to what they'd done to Max and Nina. One day, I arrived home to find that my beloved sewing machine had disappeared. Eventually, it was found 'hiding' in the wall of junk. I'd often find vinyl records nailed to the walls or melted to make ashtrays. Hahahahahahahaha! Thank God for Tena Lady. It was like living with not one, but several, Jeremy Beadles. A laugh a fucking minute, as you can imagine.

Often my squat-mates would bugger off to one of the local pubs. I never joined them: I was shy, felt I didn't fit in and was very nervous around men now. Plus they were an unpredictable bunch.

They drank ESB – which stood for extra-strong beer – which is all you need to know really. It was along the same lines as Tennents or Special Brew: beverages that are favoured by alcoholics due to their high strength-to-cost ratio. A couple of those and you'd be off your noggin.

In fairness, most of their antics were just childish and relatively harmless, such as stealing a huge outdoor pub table complete with benches from the beer garden of some local boozer. I discovered these new additions to the household when I tried to squeeze past them in the hall to go to work the morning after their arrival.

Another night, they got pissed and broke into the local off-licence. The owner was in prison so the shop had closed down. Other people had raided it first, which meant that, by the time my squat-mates arrived, all that was left to steal were a few bottles of Sanatogen fortified wine. Don't knock it until you've tried it. It's surprisingly strong.

Meanwhile, my mum had received a phone call at five o'clock one morning from a girl who informed her, 'Your daughter's going to die.'

'Why's that then?' my stoic old mum had said. Calmly, with just a hint of sarcasm. My mum was a tough old bird and she wasn't so easily frightened.

'I'm going to kill her,' the voice had replied.

'Oh yes. And why is that?' Mum had responded, still maintaining her cool.

The caller went on to say that her name was Sian and that I had stolen her boyfriend – Dave Hughes. Dave Hughes had been the keyboard player in Adventures in Colour and he and I had split up maybe two years earlier. Mum told the girl to stop talking crap, that I'd had the same boyfriend for over a year and that I hadn't stolen anyone's boyfriend.

Sian, of course, was the old lead singer in the Lost Cherrees, but she'd never even dated Dave. I wondered who it could have been and I had my suspicions it was someone pretending to be Sian and trying to stir up shit, but I really have no idea who or why or what I'd done to piss them off.

My mum remained indifferent throughout the entire conversation and eventually the crank caller hung up. Then the phone rang again and this time the girl on the other end started disparaging my mum for living in a nice big house in Surrey. Which means it definitely couldn't have been Sian as her parents lived in an even nicer and bigger house in Surrey. The tiresome calls continued for the next few hours and, in the end, my mum had to leave the phone off the hook for a while.

It was 1986 and, despite still being only 21 years old, a lot had hap-

CHAPTER 6

pened to me already and, without realising it, I had been suffering with stress and depression. When I'd dumped Dylan, a few months back, I'd been unable to explain why. I just knew that I needed to be on my own. I couldn't have a boyfriend. I didn't want to be touched. I didn't want to have sex. Dylan was a kind, lovely and noble bloke, but being in a relationship was more than I could handle at that moment, so we very sadly went our separate ways but remained friends.

The last straw at the squat came a few months later. Sebastian kept ferrets and they had got it on and produced a litter of gorgeous little kits. I agreed to give a home to two of them. Partly because I wanted to do him a favour and partly because, oh my god, they were so damn cute. I became the mother of two pretty little white albino females with pink eyes. I named them Verity Ferrety and Jarvis. They stank, as most ferrets do, but I'd already got used to the smell of seven immature men, so I figured I could handle two less than fragrant little animals that were adorable. And anyway I bathed them once a week to keep the pong down to a modicum.

We had a second kitchen that nobody ever used, which was where I kept the ferret babies so that they could run around like hairy lunatics instead of being constricted in a tiny cage. The guys seemed to take a shine to them too and would often go down and play with them. Until one night I discovered a couple of them had got drunk, removed the ferrets from the kitchen and took them to the basement without asking me, where they'd let them run up the chimney. The guys had been drinking ESB again and, when I came across them, Gavin was showing off in front of one of the others by gripping Dev's cat tightly by the scruff of her neck. The poor creature looked absolutely terrified. Gavin kept pretending to throw the cat against the wall, just stopping short of hitting it by a centimetre or so. He was tormenting a small, helpless animal. I was sickened and horrified. I can't remember what I said or did but the memory of the poor cat being tormented by that bully still sickens me to this day.

Some of my squat-mates had become increasingly destructive and nasty. The kitchen upstairs was disappearing in increments. After the fridge disappeared, the units and cupboards had been ripped out one by one and vamoosed. A young girl had come to stay for a few weeks

103

and someone had broken into the bathroom while she was running a bath and tried to push her head under the water. I'm not sure what the purpose of this was. I mean, was it supposed to be funny? The girl was OK but very shaken up, as you can imagine. Spurred on by one another they had become a pack of thugs happy to terrorise girls, cats or anyone else smaller or weaker than them. I was really not comfortable being around such people.

Concerned for my personal safety, I called Sebastian and he helped me put all my belongings into a trolley (Verity Ferrety and Jarvis included, of course) and transport them back to Morden (again), using a combination of bus and train (again).

Chapter 7

Oddities

If you've ever moved back to your parents' house (with two ferrets and all your belongings in a trolley) then you'll know what a tremendous backward step it feels like. I am of course eternally grateful that I had a safe place to return to but, once you've dipped your tootsies in the ocean of independence, you really don't want to be confined to a small paddling pool, and other analogies. Especially not in Morden.

Amongst the strong viewpoints I had that antagonised my parents was my commitment to vegetarianism. Vegetarianism was not the giant mainstream market that it is today. Back then, it was still considered, well, kind of weird and a bit hippy – which was a bad thing apparently. The fact that I chose not to eat meat inexplicably bothered my carnivorous folks, who really couldn't understand why I didn't want to eat my furry and feathered brethren. Especially on a Sunday: *if you put gravy on it, you won't even taste it.* This was just one of my idiosyncrasies that drove them mental. I seemed to be swinging Tarzan-like from one disaster to another, but without the leopard-skin loincloth. I had no little punk palace to call my very own, I was jobless and I had broken up with my boyfriend. Pffff. But at least I had Verity Ferrety and Jarvis.

Fortuitously, I was still sewing and making jewellery for Rubella Rat, which just about kept my spirits afloat. I advertised for free in various fanzines. Most punks only wanted odd earrings, as symmetry was a no-no, but most had multiple piercings, which was a boon for my business.

The squid earrings I made were sourced from a fishing-tackle shop in Wimbledon. The staff thought I was joking when I told them what I needed them for and when I showed them the one that I was currently modelling, which dangled down to my shoulder. Some of the lures were neon pink and covered in glitter and it was hard to imagine heterosexual fishermen handling such kitsch items. Perhaps they all sat in their fishing boats wearing lipstick and feather boas, and singing show tunes. Well, it must get lonely out there. I actually had no idea that squid were attracted to pink glitter. The sum total of my knowledge surrounding the behaviour of this tentacled mollusc failed to ascend beyond the fact that they were called squid. It was somewhat worrying that I was attracted to the pink glittery squid lures. Perhaps I was a squid in a previous life?

I was also still enjoying creating kiddies' clothes and began renting an indoor market stall, which at least didn't smell of drunk men's wee-wee, in the fabulously named Oddities Market in Chalk Farm, near Camden Town.

I moved in there with my sewing machine and sat making unique pieces, such as dungarees from unusual fabrics. Kids' clothes in the '80s were a little uninspired, to say the least, and mums would often squeal with delight when they came across my gaudy creations. It wasn't a big business as making the items was time-consuming and I didn't charge much for them, but I managed to make a little profit on each item. I also sold my crazy jewellery and still offered ear and nose piercing (body piercing hadn't taken off yet), so it was a bit of a strange combination – at my stall, you'd be able to find a punk with a foot-long green Mohican getting his nose pierced alongside a young mother trying kaleidoscopic dungarees on her toddler: a collision of disparate worlds if ever there was one.

Looking back, I don't know how I had the nerve to do what I did. But, much like playing in the bands, I just got on with it and waited to see what would happen. I was doing what I loved and nothing else mattered.

Oddities Market was located opposite the famous Roundhouse music venue in Chalk Farm Road, which was disused at the time. Now it's an upmarket venue with posh bars and restaurants and attracts bands and shows from all over the world, but at the time it had fallen into disrepair and only attracted graffiti and man wee. To get to the market, you had to weave through labyrinthine passageways between stalls. Other stalls were selling second-hand clothing, printed T-shirts, vintage albums and so on, but the most interesting

Chapter 7

stall for me was the one located directly opposite me – which offered tarot-card readings.

The stall was run by a slightly strange-looking duo: Alex was extremely tall with dark brown hair, wore glasses and had a full beard. Beards are all the hipster rage now, but in the '80s they were very much the antithesis of fashion. You wouldn't ever see Marc Almond trotting around Soho with a beard (unless it was a cunning disguise). Bill Grey was as short as Alex was tall and had dyed-black tightly curled hair almost like an afro and wore extremely thick cartoon-like bottle-top glasses.

Alex and Bill had introduced themselves to me and we were gradually becoming good friends. They explained that they were pagans. Witches. I had never met proper witches before, unless you count Si, Flick's boyfriend, and, based on the fairy tales I'd read as a child, they were nothing like the standard witches I'd come to expect. Not a pointy hat or broomstick in sight. Imagine my disappointment. Admittedly they did both favour dark attire, but then so did goths, nuns and police officers.

Alex and Bill went to great lengths to convince me that they didn't do evil spells and were only interested in the practice of white magic. Looking at them, I happily concluded that they probably wouldn't be capable of performing evil spells and turning me into an amphibian, even if they'd really wanted to.

I had come across the tarot before though and had been so intrigued by it that I'd invested in a deck of my own. I had attempted to learn how to read the cards and I had a rough idea of the significance of each card but I was very much a laywoman and lacked the confidence and proficiency to perform readings for other people. I'd never even had a tarot-card reading done for me so I excitedly booked myself in for a reading with Bill.

One of the first things Bill told me when he read my cards was that I was psychic too. I told him I thought he was right and that I also owned a deck of Aquarian tarot cards – a gorgeous design with obvious art deco and art nouveau influences. The last card in my layout was The Tower, which indicates an approaching time of disruption and chaos. Jesus, I thought, if the future is gonna be chaotic and disruptive, what the fuck have the last few years been? Horror must have been etched across my face, clearly visible despite my dense layer of rather dramatic make-up, as Bill quickly began to reassure me that the card could be read in numerous ways and probably wasn't as scary as I'd already decided it was judging by my expression. I breathed a thank-fuck sigh as I took a closer look at the card's image – a tower engulfed in ferocious flames – not the image you really want to see!

Oddities was a long trek from Morden, and the interminable journey encompassed almost the entire length of the Northern line. So, as luck would have it, I had been offered a place to live in another squat just a half-hour's bus ride away from Camden Town. Convenient. Nice.

About a week after Bill read my cards, the tower block I was living in actually did catch fire. Someone had set fire to the rubbish chute and the fire brigade had to be called, so it wasn't *Towering Inferno*-bad with pensioners dressed in highly flammable polyester dresses from the '70s being airlifted from the roof by a helicopter. It was a markedly less dramatic small fire, which was extinguished in a matter of minutes. No airlift was necessary. No animals died. But I was now totally convinced that there was validity in tarot reading, even if the cards often exaggerated, and felt instantly compelled to study them in more detail. How useful it would be to be pre-warned about events before they had even happened, I thought. How handy it would be to be pre-warned about some of the dodgy situations I'd later find myself in.

Bill took me under his magical wing and although he never actually taught me to read the cards, he was incredibly supportive and found 'clients' for me to give practice readings to. I was still a bit apprehensive about having occultist neighbours, even if they did wear thick glasses, or sport a full beard, so Bill loaned me books on the subject, and I could read all about it to appease my naturally suspicious mind. This alleviated any fears I still harboured about being dragged kicking and screaming by my squid-and-fish earrings into some fucked-up, beard-worshipping satanic cult.

Bill explained paganism to me and highlighted the links between Christianity and paganism. I had been brought up a good little Roman

CHAPTER 7

Catholic girl, remember, and was still under the impression that paganism was evil, wrong and very naughty. Now I was really confused. It seemed like everything I'd been taught as I was growing up had been, well, utter bullshit.

The Christian religion certainly had pagan roots. Bill explained that the cup or chalice in Christian mass originally represented the womb and that the red wine represented menstrual blood, the blood of life, which the Christians had adopted too, except they called it the blood of Christ. Menstrual blood was revered in paganism, because wombs were the source of creation from which we all came.

I was enthralled as Bill told me about the holy trinity of the goddess-mother, maiden and crone in the pagan faith, compared with the holy trinity adopted by the Christian faith, in which the father, son and Holy Spirit predominated. Paganism was a matriarchal belief, whereas Christianity was clearly patriarchal.

I definitely found that I could sympathise more with pagan beliefs, and so Bill invited me along to celebrate the festivals or Sabbats with him and his pagan friends. I was dubious at first, thinking it might all go a bit *Wicker Man*, but the events were extremely informal and friendly, unlike the rigorousness and pomp of Christian festivals. I always felt completely welcome and involved and there wasn't a sacrifice in sight.

Bill was a kind and loving person and just the kind of man I needed to be in close proximity to at this point in my life, having all but lost confidence in men. He would always greet me with a great big bespectacled hug. After suffering enough abuse and maltreatment to turn the warmest heart cold, it was a year before I felt safe enough to return his hugs. My fear being that a simple hug might be misinterpreted and turn into something sexual or into a situation that would scare the bejesus out of me.

Bill taught me that it was safe to be hugged and that it was safe to be loved. He always told me I was beautiful, even though I didn't believe it myself and he would often tell me that he loved me. And in return he expected nothing but my friendship. It took me a while to trust him and understand that, believe me, but from those foundations of trust, we built a brick-solid friendship that has spanned over 30 years.

Chapter 7.5

Alluring squids and creepy-crawly clothing – Courtesy of Rubella Rat

Before the invention of computers we did things freehand and on typewriters. Our cars also had square wheels

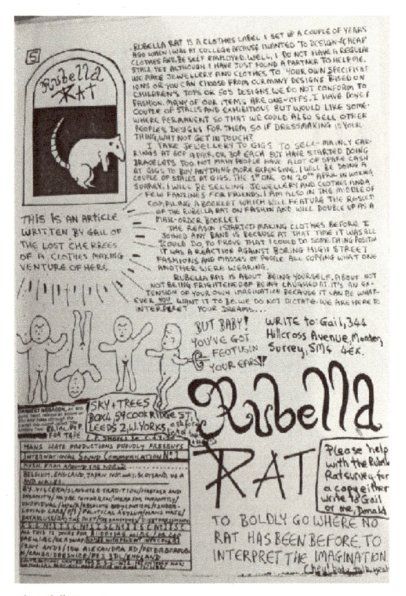

The Rubella Rat mission statement

Chapter 7.5

Rubella Rat clothing creations. People thought I was strange, designing skull fabric. 'It'll never catch on!' they said. And then goth happened

Soap the Stamps, Jump the Tube

Raw ingredients for the infamous squid earrings – and yours truly modelling some fishy creations

Chapter 8

Nightmare Estate

Cindy is another person who'd responded to my advert in *Sounds* years earlier, and we became friends. Hearing that I was depressed living all the way out in Morden, Cindy invited me to live with her and her boyfriend in a squat in the twenty-first-floor flat of a run-down tower block; the one that caught fire, as already mentioned, on the notorious Nightingale Estate in Hackney, East London.

Not only did I want to remove myself from the family home, but my dad had already suggested that I should begin looking for my own place after Verity Ferrety had escaped and found her way into my parents' bedroom, only to reappear some time later at my bedroom door with some strange object in her mouth. I examined what she was carrying and, to my horror/amusement, found that it was a sex toy.

The problem was that I then had to return the sex toy without my parents knowing, which would have been easy if I'd known where exactly it had come from. I had no idea so, in my infinite wisdom, I left it on their bed.

'I think you may have found something of ours...' my mother said awkwardly that evening. She stared at me like she was trying to continue the conversation telepathically, hoping that she wouldn't be forced to continue the conversation/confession out loud.

'Yes. I'm sorry about that. Verity found it and I didn't know where she'd got it from,' I replied, equally embarrassed, if not more so.

'Well,' she said finally. 'It belongs to your father.' Nice buck-passing, Mum. 'You know what men are like – never think they are big enough...' she muttered, providing her young daughter with far more information than she actually needed or wanted to hear, ever.

My father declared that if the ferrets didn't go, then I had to, which was quite dramatic considering it was his sex aid that had been discovered. But I was way too attached to my little bendy hyperactive squirrel-like pets to consider rehousing them, so I decided it was time for me to move out once again. Consequently, I eagerly accepted the spare room in Hackney and moved in right away. I can't remember whether a trolley was involved on this occasion, but I wouldn't put it past me.

To give you some idea of the calibre of the insalubrious Nightingale Estate, employing the word 'dismal' would in no way be a gross exaggeration. It was such an awful and fetid dump that it was referred to unaffectionately as 'The Nightmare Estate'. And that was the name given to it by people who actually lived there.

There were a number of other flats on the upper floors of the tower block that were occupied by squatters. There was no way that anyone would seriously pay to live there. Despite the bleak surroundings, a small community grew up amongst the squatters, who included a group of Italians who had fled Italy to avoid conscription. Everyone felt a sense of solidarity and we looked out for each other.

So I moved my paltry possessions into the new room. There were so many fly carcasses in my new palace that it looked like they'd filmed *The Amityville Horror* there. Once I'd swept the room, it instantly felt bigger.

Once again, my wing of the mansion was simply furnished with a second-hand single mattress on the floor, whose source was unknown, and my few meagre possessions. My precious keyboards came everywhere with me. By then, I had bought a Roland Juno 6 from a friend of Gavin in Stamford Hill. His friend had used it in a band called Death in June. It was polyphonic and produced some incredible sounds.

To heat our five-star palace we had a two-bar electric heater in the living room and... oh, actually that was it. Despite living in a squat we were paying for the electricity and had to be vigilant as we were all super-skint and out of work. Cindy and her boyfriend Mal were incredibly sociable squat-mates and a vast improvement on most of the guys at the Stamford Hill place.

Cindy came from Dorset and Mal from Cornwall. Cindy's hair was outrageous, with foot-long spikes dyed baize green on one side and flame orange on the other. The sides were shaved and dyed black. It

CHAPTER 8

often took her three hours to form the spikes and she wouldn't leave the flat until it was perfect. She would start by crimping and back-combing, and then form it into the spikes with half a can of hairspray. I swear us punks were responsible for the holes in the ozone layer, although we weren't even aware that such a thing existed in the early '80s.

A lot of people would pop in to visit Mal at the squat. We were all taking speed in those days and Mal had taken to dealing small amounts to his friends. One man called Karl used to visit us. Compared with us punks, Karl looked quite normal with tight black jeans, trainers and long curly hair, but despite this veneer of normality he was an intriguing character. He used to scale the outside of apartment blocks and tower blocks in order to break into empty properties and open a new squat for someone. We called him Rambo, although we should have called him Spiderman. How he managed to cling to those walls at great heights without falling to his death, I'll never know, but he said it didn't bother him.

Another regular visitor chez Squat was a punk who went by the charming moniker of Pus. Pus was part of the Hackney Hell Crew with whom Cindy had stayed when she first arrived in London. A lot of the punks became what we called 'wasters' or 'crusties'. A waster was someone who felt compelled to waste their life getting wasted on drugs and booze. Whereas a crusty was someone who not only neglected their appearance but bizarrely took pride in the fact. A crusty would often wear the same ripped and be-holed clothes without washing them, and would let their hair grow into matted dread-locks. Crusties would compete over who could achieve the accolade of most crusty. Which was quite an ambition. I think Pus fell conveniently into both the categories waster and crusty, although he didn't have the smelly dreads. Some of the Hell Crew took their quest for dismal hygiene a step further, and refused to remove their Doc Martens, even to go to sleep, for days or weeks at a time. We heard disturbing tales of people's feet becoming gangrenous due to consistent neglect. They were always trying to outdo each other in the ultimate goal of filthiness. I have no idea why this was considered a reasonable thing to do. Strange times.

SOAP THE STAMPS, JUMP THE TUBE

Pus turned up on our doorstep one night and ended up sleeping over mainly because, like a bad smell, we couldn't get rid of him. Neither could we remove his pervasive stench from the apartment for days after his departure. He'd bought a little puppy with him, which widdled on the floor, like puppies do. Pus's stench penetrated every corner of the apartment. We'd had to throw the windows open despite it being the middle of winter because it was a choice between breathing and freezing to death. When I awoke the next morning, Pus was still there, asleep on the floor of the living room in front of the electric fire, with both bars on full. Both bars on full! We never permitted ourselves such decadence. If we were cold we would put on additional layers of clothing. We would often sit around in our thickest jumpers and winter coats with our duvets wrapped round us huddled in front of the little fire, just one frugal bar alight to warm the entire apartment. Pus eventually left, leaving nothing but a stubborn black mark on the pillow he'd used that never, ever washed out and a miasma that refused to budge for weeks despite open windows and weapons-grade air fresheners.

Years later, we heard that Pus had been stabbed to death in an incident over drugs. Someone told me he also had AIDS. I can't attest to the authenticity of either of those stories.

Like myself, Cindy had gone to art school and had aspirations of being a clothes designer. Unlike me, she had completed a course in textiles and knew how to pattern-cut. She had started making punk clothes, mainly using black cotton drill, and had her own Damage labels printed that she would sew into the garments. Cindy knew another girl, Debbie, who was making jewellery out of old electrical components and circuit boards from radios. Recycling at its finest.

We decided to pool our collective experience and stock, and rent a new stall in Camden, splitting the rent three ways, which meant we could rent a better stall that was indoors and not exposed to the elements and passing drunks needing the toilet. Our stall was in the Electric Ballroom just by Camden Town Tube station. I had given up my Saturday stall in the Camden Lock Market, just further up the road, a few months prior to this new venture, which was now on the more busy Sunday.

118

Chapter 8

We were casual traders at first, which meant the dreaded 4am sign-up. The stalls were so popular that if you put your name down any later than that, they would already have been claimed. Luckily, Cindy was often on her way home from a club around this time, so she'd put our names down before heading home and I'd materialise after a few hours' sleep at 9am to claim the pitch. We were eventually offered our own permanent pitch, which had previously belonged to the experimental performance art/music band Psychic TV.

Debbie gave up after a few months as she wasn't selling much but Cindy and I persevered. I'd also started selling big chunky silver rings with skulls on which were popular with goths, bikers and punks. We were hardly raking it in but we made enough to cover the rent and materials, with a few extra quid left over to get us into clubs and keep us in beer at the weekend.

On Friday and Saturday evenings, the Electric Ballroom was a nightclub and by Sunday morning it had transformed into a market. On Friday nights the club was called Full Tilt and was dedicated to gothic and alternative music – I was a frequent visitor, needless to say. I often wondered how many worse-for-wear goths had to be extricated from the toilets to make way for the market.

Trading in the Electric Ballroom was loads of fun. Every stall sold something unique, colourful or different, from spiky rubber bags to stripy tights to vintage vinyl. It was always packed with tourists but sadly there was so much competition that we struggled to make a decent living from it and eventually decided to call it a day.

While living in Hackney, I went to a squat party with Sebastian. It had been quite some time since I'd split up with Dylan and, as I said, relations with the opposite sex were very low on my agenda. I couldn't help but notice, however, that a handsome man with a floppy black Mohican was staring at me. I looked up, smiled shyly at him and then proceeded to ignore him. He seemed to be with a girl and although I thought he was cute I gave him absolutely no attention. He could have star-jumped naked past me and I'd have feigned disinterest. I just wanted to sit and talk to my friend Sebastian.

Sebastian and I were still very close and we went to a lot of places together, the upshot being that people frequently mistook us for a couple. I often called round to his on my way to gigs or sometimes turned up unannounced with a bottle of cider for us to share. Sebastian's ferrets (mother and father and a sibling or two to Verity and Jarvis) would scoot erratically about the place. They'd made tunnels in the dilapidated sofa which meant they could disappear down one end and reappear at the other. It was like a theme park for ferret-kind. Sebastian also had a pet rabbit, ironically called Stew, as Sebastian was an animal lover and a strict vegan. If I stayed over on the theme-park sofa I'd often wake up with ferrets running all over me, like I was one of the attractions.

Anyway, back to the party and that hot young man…

Sebastian and I were chatting away when the handsome man approached and introduced himself to us, completely ruining my cool obliviousness. His name was Nigel. Not the sexiest name for a black-Mohicaned Adonis, but I decided I'd be prepared to look beyond that. His girlfriend was in another room, passed out. There is always at least one person completely passed out at a house party. Nigel kept looking lingeringly in my direction and eventually made some vague reference to me being Sebastian's girlfriend, obviously trying to find out whether we were a couple or not.

'Urrrgh! No way! I wouldn't go out with HER!' Sebastian said, letting Nigel know that I was completely available – just in case the tactic I had employed earlier whereby I had completely disregarded Nigel had gone unnoticed.

My veneer of nonchalance in tatters, Nigel and I got chatting and went outside to get some fresh air, and shared a cheeky and rather pleasant kiss. A month later, I was at a gig at the Clarendon in Hammersmith when Nigel approached me. He'd split with his girlfriend and did I want to go out with him? You can guess my response to that question.

Nigel always dressed in black and wore pointed black-suede Chelsea boots. We would go to gigs together and I would often stay over at his flat in Sunbury, which he insisted was haunted. Apparently there was the ghost of a man who would come looking for his girlfriend or

CHAPTER 8

wife. Nigel had seen him a couple of times, but it didn't bother him. Goths love that kind of shit.

One night, Nigel had stayed over with me in Hackney. He had to be up super-early to go to work. I heard him leave and the door shut behind him. I snuggled down into the warmth of the duvet, thankful I didn't have to get up early and leave my bed. Then suddenly I became aware of my bedroom door opening and I could feel a presence in the room, just to the side of me. I was working in Oddities Market and was friends with the witches. I had always believed in the supernatural, but I was still terrified of ghosts.

The blood in my veins turned to frost as I became aware of this presence next to me. I could feel it hovering close to the bed, and then suddenly scooting over by the window. I hope it doesn't think I'm its wife or girlfriend, I thought to myself. Perhaps I was dreaming, I thought, and I actually pinched myself in order to check. That's what you are meant to do, isn't it? I was definitely conscious of the pinch on my skin and my eyes were open beneath the duvet.

Everything felt strangely still and I had just about convinced myself that I'd been half asleep and imagining crazy things when I felt this 'entity' suddenly rush through me, entering me by the soles of my feet. I could feel it wrestling with me whilst inside of me. It was a terrifying and extraordinary sensation. It was like being in a fucking horror film. I felt like it was trying to suffocate me and I honestly thought that I was going to die any moment. I don't know how or why. I'd never heard of anyone being asphyxiated internally. Not by a ghoul. It's not something you read about in the papers.

To say that I was petrified is the understatement of all time. I was growing weak and losing the struggle with whatever it was and I succumbed to the idea that I actually might be about to die, here in a squat, in Hackney. With that realisation, for some reason, my entire body relaxed, and I suddenly felt like I was psychically tuned into the entity or energy or whatever it was. Just as I did so, the spirit loosened its hold on me and disappeared.

I sat up in bed. What in the world of strange fuck had just happened to me? My heart was banging so loudly in my chest that I thought it was trying to get out. Had the ghost from Nigel's place attached itself to him and travelled all the way across London on the Tube? I had heard of spirit attachments, and figured it must have left him when he went to work and jumped into me. Clearly not a phantom in favour of an early start of a morning. Perhaps not surprisingly, due to the fact that I'd just been supernaturally attacked from the inside by a disgruntled spirit who wasn't fond of mornings, I found it difficult to get back to sleep. In fact, I didn't get back to sleep for three whole nights. I was terrified in case it was still in the flat. I told Cindy and Mal what had happened, fearing they wouldn't believe me, but my description of the experience was so detailed and dramatic that they couldn't sleep that night either.

The morning after it happened, I was working at Oddities Market. As soon as I got the opportunity to get Bill alone, I recounted the experience to him. He clearly thought that I'd been gargling with bong water and that I was mistaking the event for a vivid dream.

However, later that afternoon, Bill approached my stall. He had a very anxious-looking woman with him.

'Repeat what you told me this morning,' Bill instructed. I described the event again, in as much detail as I could recall.

'Yes! That was it!' said the woman.

She had been standing by my unit earlier when she had felt the same thing enter her body, stifling her breathing, and then leaving as fast as it had come. It had then jumped briefly onto Bill, who'd experienced it for himself. Now he believed me. Bill talked me through some psychic protection exercises to stop it from happening again.

Nigel was flabbergasted when I told him what had happened. He'd assumed that the spirit was attached to the house. He then told me about a dream a friend of his had had about him in which she attended his funeral. She vividly recalled how a girl with bright orange hair wearing a green army jacket had walked behind the coffin. My hair was bright orange at that time and I always wore a green camouflage jacket that I had designed and made myself. The friend of his had never met me, yet she was able to describe me so accurately. We wondered what the dream could possibly mean – but thankfully, Nigel was still alive and well several years later when I bumped into him. It could have been that her dream foretold the breakdown of our rela-

Chapter 8

tionship, as Nigel and I parted company not long after that. And yes, I was sad.

Chapter 9

Bermondsey

I'd mentioned to Bill that I was feeling like a proper gooseberry living with Cindy and Mal, and he said that a friend of his knew of a squat in Rotherhithe New Road, Bermondsey in South London. It was one of a row of ex-railway houses that were due to be demolished. Demolition had been postponed as several people who lived there were still within their tenancies.

It was a beautiful old maisonette that oozed character. And when I say old, I mean it had an outdoor khazi, which meant wandering around outside in the dark on cold winter nights if one wished to relieve oneself. But considering it was a squat, it was in a very decent condition, with no interior damage such as graffiti or vandalism, and it even had the luxury of carpets. Moving here, however, heralded the moment in a mother's life that every mother dreads – the kids leaving home. My ferret kids were old enough now to move into a new place of their own. They had an entire downstairs room to themselves, which I filled with straw, sawdust and cardboard boxes for them to play in. Well, kids can't go on living with their folks forever.

Upstairs was my living area, or flat, which included not just a sleeping area but a living room. I'd scrounged furniture from my parents and I now had not just a living room but a living room complete with an armchair and a TV. The kitchen had a bath in it with a board that covered the bath to use as a kitchen worktop. It was surreal! I imagined a mum cooking dinner whilst dad sat naked in the bath in the same room at the same time.

Bill had lent me an electric Baby Belling cooker, which sat on top of a table and had two rings and an oven. It was basic compared with what most people had, but I felt like the fucking Queen. As it was a squat, the access to electricity and water was acquired (cough) illegally. A scruffy man named Sam, one of Bill's friends, came over one day to connect my electricity, bypassing the meter.

It was strange moving into a house on my own. I'd never lived alone before, and I didn't know anyone else in the street or in the neighbourhood. But I needn't have worried. I was soon introduced to Jim (who turned the water on for me), who introduced me to my new neighbours, a couple called Yasmin and Rupert, and Len. Yasmin was short with dyed-black hair and hair extensions. She was pretty with dark eyes and olive skin, making her appear like she was Mediterranean when in reality she was Scottish. Rupert was pale in comparison, and was tall and skinny. He had dark brown dreadlocks and wore a black leather jacket with one of the iconic Sisters of Mercy illustrations on the back, which he'd painted by hand. Len had floppy auburn hair that hung loose over one eye. He was pale-skinned, skinny and openly gay. Len was also an amazing artist and sculptor.

Most of the street was squatted, which meant that a tight and benevolent community had developed there. Squatters are, with a few exceptions, an interesting bunch of folk, made up for the most part of bohemians, anarchists, artists and musicians. Jim was not only a good water turner-oner, he was also a welder, which meant that there was often an old car or van parked outside his gaff while he worked on it. Jim was tall with short tousled naturally brown hair. He was lean with strong muscles and a flat stomach – not that I ever notice such details on men, of course.

Although I lived on my own in the squat, I never felt afraid. In fact, I always felt a sense of peace and contentment within my humble little palace. Although some nights I could have sworn I sensed the presence of a ghost on the landing outside my room, on those occasions it never bothered me. We had an understanding: I'd happily share my 'living' space with a spirit and, for its part, it promised not to enter my sleeping body via the soles of my feet and try to strangle me from the inside.

The house was extremely old and must have housed several generations of families in its time. The walls must have witnessed so many events: family arguments, births, deaths, changes of tenant, new years, new decades, the birth of a new century, etc. So much change. The

CHAPTER 9

lady who lived next door to me was an actual proper official tenant, who paid rent to live there and everything. I didn't think that would ever catch on. She had no intention of moving to a modern flat, as she loved her old house – it was her home. She was surprisingly happy that I was unofficially living next door to her, as an empty house is as much a lure for thieves and vandals as pink glitter is for squids. Many of us less-official neighbours would pop round to see her for a cup of tea – the community vibe was wonderful and it was really quite cheering to see people getting on so well together and looking out for each other. There was never any hostility.

Sometimes we would pool our food and prepare a huge communal meal for everyone. This came about when I casually mentioned once that I was hungry but only had some plain pasta at home. 'I've got some tomatoes and an onion,' Jim volunteered. And before you knew it, everyone had contributed a little something and we had a huge tasty pasta-and-vegetable feast between us. This sense of community and public spirit is something that I feel has been lost in the UK. It's a shame because, with just a little effort and compassion, everything becomes that much easier and more pleasant for everyone.

Jim and I soon became a couple. He owned a vivid purple Reliant Robin (an iconic three-wheeled car from the '70s that was considered a source of much amusement and was the butt of many jokes). Joe liked it because it was indeed reliant, and he didn't give a shit what anyone else thought. I liked it because it was bright purple – and because I didn't give a shit what anyone else thought.

Jim was the first ecologist I'd ever met. He was also interested in massage and shiatsu and, like myself and most squatters at that time, was strictly vegetarian and took a keen interest in a healthy diet and nutrition. He even made me a cake for my birthday that was full of nuts and healthy stuff, with my name spelt out in seeds on the top, in place of icing and candles. A man making a cake for a woman was about as likely as seeing a dolphin flying a helicopter in high heels. It was such a wonderful and thoughtful gesture, even if I did secretly wish it had been made of chocolate with my name spelt out in icing.

Anyway, it was because of healthy Jim that I cleaned up my diet. I had suffered from a knee problem since I was a teenager, a type of rheumatism that often meant I couldn't put pressure on my knee. The crunch came when I couldn't get out of bed one morning. I had to roll on my side and lever myself up ever so slowly, like a pensioner.

Jim immediately disappeared to the health-food shop and returned a while later with some herbal tablets to help relieve the symptoms, as well as a book by Clifford Quick that recommended deep breathing techniques and a complete dietary overhaul. The diet Quick suggested was extreme compared with what I had been eating and prescribed no caffeine, alcohol, sugar and salt – all the staples of my current intake!

For the first couple of days, I consumed only grapes and melons and spent most of the time pissing like a racehorse. After two days I was allowed to add in raw fruit and vegetables, which suited my very basic kitchen set-up. Within a few days, I looked like one of Jackson Pollock's paintings made human, as the clean food helped my body expel toxins or demons or something; but the spots soon disappeared and I lost half a stone and was feeling not only healthier than ever before but really happy to be alive. Just from eating healthy food! Who needs antidepressants?

Jim had many friends who were following alternative lifestyles and we would often jump in the Reliant Robin and go hurtling off (well, kind of) to visit them.

One day we were visiting some friends of Jim's who lived in an old single-decker bus. As we sat in the back chatting and drinking tea, the engine suddenly started up, and we ended up at a festival called The Elephant Fayre with just the clothes we were wearing, which in my case was a flimsy hippy skirt and T-shirt and black woolly jumper. In keeping with the community spirit, we were smuggled into the festival by hiding under blankets at the back of the bus. A makeshift tent was erected for us and we were quickly loaned bedding.

The festival was huge and I don't remember seeing many or even any of the bands. In fact, I don't think I made it as far as the field the bands were playing in. As we didn't have much money, we bought a loaf of bread and some muesli, which kept us going for most of the weekend. Jim found some wild watercress (which we were afraid to eat as cattle had been drinking from the water it was growing in and

CHAPTER 9

we were worried it might be contaminated and we would start mooing), but we also found wild garlic, which we did eat and was delicious. The nearby woods were lined with it and once you experience the pungent smell of wild garlic you never forget it.

One night I got chatting to a man who told me he was a Romany gypsy. He looked me in the eyes and said he could see I had a touch of Romany about me too. I nodded and told him it was rumoured that, on my dad's side of the family, there was indeed a Romany connection. The man told me that, like all Romanys, I could never lose anything. Anything that I 'lost' would always come back to me. I wasn't sure exactly what he meant and assumed he was talking some gypsy nonsense to beguile me.

Meanwhile, he could see me eyeing up his bracelet, a length of leather thong on which two small silver ladies' rings were hanging. He quickly removed the bracelet and offered me the rings. They were too small for me to wear properly, but one sat perfectly at the top joint of my little finger. I smiled and asked the gypsy if I could give him something of mine in return. His eyes rested on an earring I was wearing, a tiny pewter spanner.

'My friends call me "Spanner",' he told me, as I removed the earring and handed it to him.

The next day, Jim and I went for a walk to procure some cheap supplies, crossing several fields in which sheep were idly grazing. On the way back, we stopped and made a simple picnic from the bread and cheese we'd bought. Later, as it was getting cold, I reached for my black woolly jumper that I'd had tied around my waist earlier and realised it was gone. I must have lost it in one of the fields. It was the only warm item of clothing I had with me so I insisted we go back through the fields to look for it.

We retraced our footsteps through every field and were about to give up the hunt when I spotted a man sitting alone wearing an identical black jumper. A bit too much of a coincidence, I thought, but I didn't want to get all confrontational with this country dude. I'd seen *The Wicker Man* after all. I approached him nervously, cleared my throat and then tentatively asked him if he'd happened to see a black jumper lying about anywhere, please sir don't kill me.

'Like this one?' he asked, nodding in the direction of the black jumper – my black jumper – that he was now modelling for me.

'Erm, yes,' I stuttered.

He looked me up and down, fixing me with one of those we-don't-like-city-folk-around-here stares. Then suddenly he said, 'Well, thanks for the loan. I'm glad it's found its owner,' and with that he removed the jumper and handed it back to me with a smile.

So perhaps the gypsy man wasn't just talking Romany hocus pocus, after all.

I'd bought a hammock with my credit card whilst at the festival and Jim suspended it between two walls in his house when we got back. It was a huge Mexican hammock in which we could have both slept extremely comfortably, had it not been for Jim's cats clawing at our bums through the fabric from beneath, clearly thinking it was some kind of hammock/arse game provided purely for feline entertainment.

Jim was often taking me on day trips but this meant I often felt guilty about leaving the ferrets, so when he suggested visiting his mate in the Forest of Dean, I decided it was time that Verity Ferrety and Jarvis had a holiday too. His friend Pat lived in a caravan on the edge of the forest amidst breathtaking countryside. (I was secretly hoping Pat was called Dean and that this was indeed his forest!) I'd had the bright idea to bring along the hammock, so Jim suspended it between two large trees and we took it in turns to loll about in it and enjoy the spectacular views. It was a huge hammock, probably large enough to house an entire Mexican family, which meant we could all fit in. It was fun with three of us, more romantic with two and even better on your own.

As soon as we'd arrived, Verity and Jarv had immediately begun scooting about in a woodpile near the caravan, frolicking amongst the logs like, well... ferrets. In fact, they were enjoying their freedom in the fresh air and countryside so much that it soon became apparent that, having just been liberated from a windowless room in South London, it would be cruel to make them spend their entire lives shut indoors. They found a source of water under Pat's caravan between playing and lapped at it. I placed their food under there too.

Pat said we could sleep in the bender – a shelter made from sapling

CHAPTER 9

wood bent into a dome shape and covered in tarpaulins – and we happily accepted. We crawled in on hands and knees. Inside it was dark, cosy and womb-like and I slept well, curled up against Jim, despite the ferrets crawling over me in the night. They'd got used to sneaking into bed with me when I lived at my parents' house, where they used to nestle into the snug crooks behind my knees. In the morning, they were gone again – off cavorting in the woods. Pat had taken a real shine to them, and made a fuss of them and they seemed to like him too. He was living in the caravan temporarily as he worked on a stone cottage he owned down the hill. He was renovating it using original materials, so progress was slow and time-consuming.

Somehow word got out to the local farmer that there were a pair of rampaging ferrets on the loose and he suddenly materialised in order to reprimand me, worried that they would kill his chickens (the ones he was planning on killing). I told him not to worry as they'd been raised solely on vegan food and didn't know what a chicken was, let alone what one tasted like. I told him they would be more likely to play with the chickens than eat them. The farmer refused to be pacified. I dared not tell him that Verity had already disappeared.

Before leaving for home, I took Pat's number and said I'd ring to see if Verity had turned up and, if so, would come and collect them. Pat was happy to have a couple of wriggly nutters for company, so I left the Forest of Dean ferret-less. I'm ashamed to say that I never did get V and J back. I lost Pat's telephone number for months and, by the time I found it again, my life had changed dramatically and I decided it was too late to collect them. I figured they'd be happier where they were. I did feel guilty about dumping them on Pat though. The things you do when you're young.

During the summer, back at the squat in Bermondsey, Jim and I often took walks along the backs of the houses onto a disused railway track that was slowly being reclaimed by nature. Jim pointed out an abundance of evening primrose flowers: lanky and butter-coloured. The flowers only open their petals in the evening, hence the name. There were also millions of blackberries growing wild – the hedgerows were swollen with fists of the bulbous purple fruit. When life gives you blackberries, make blackberry jam. Or blackberry wine. Gallons of it. Since beginning a relationship with Jim, I'd also developed an interest in wild food and nature and I'd bought a book about making wine from natural ingredients, so I decided to give it a go. I persuaded Yasmin, Rupert and Len to assist and between us we managed to collect enough fruit to make five gallons of organic blackberry wine. This was in 1986, when organic produce was barely even a thing. Not like it is today when you can even buy organic condoms.

One of the other squatters, an American girl named Annie, heard about my wine and fell in love with it. She offered to sell it for me as she obviously recognised that there was a potential market for organic homemade wine, and very quickly she sold the lot. An entrepreneur would have taken this and turned it into a lucrative business model, with a turnover of £1 million pounds in the first year of business, eventually selling their line of hand-pressed organic wild-blackberry wine (no need to mention that it was made in Bermondsey) to Waitrose and winning Woman of the Year awards several years in a row. Sadly, I'm not an entrepreneur and none of that happened. I will not be appearing on *Dragons' Den* any time soon.

When I wasn't missing out on perfectly good opportunities to start my own viable wine business, I would lie on the roof of the house, sunbathing. Between the roofs, some of the handy tenants had constructed a roof garden from old scaffolding. To reach the roof garden you had to climb a ladder, James Bond-style, and once there you could idle away a sunny afternoon amidst an old bath that had been inexplicably placed there and amongst a fairly serious marijuana forest. I didn't smoke weed but the others were all 'connoisseurs'. It was a great place to bask in the sun, chilling out, and we'd often hear the faint patter of helicopter blades high above us. The helicopter could be seen and heard hovering in the same spot almost directly above us every day.

I got to know Rupert and Yasmin really well, so when the latter asked me to accompany her to Greece for the summer, I naturally nodded in affirmation and started thinking about punk bikinis. Rupert's mum lived in Greece and he was already out there. Yasmin

CHAPTER 9

wanted to join him but preferred not to travel alone, so I selflessly stepped up to the mark.

Yasmin managed to persuade me to travel with her on the 'Magic Bus'. It was a journey so long and soul-destroying that the magical part was that anyone ever arrived with their sanity intact. The Magic Bus departed from King's Cross in London and crossed several countries, including what was then Yugoslavia, Bulgaria, Italy and France over a period of what seemed like weeks. It was actually three days but I'm exaggerating here for dramatic effect. Passengers slept on the bus although it did stop every few hours to allow its near-demented travellers to stretch what was left of their atrophying leg muscles, visit the toilets, buy repugnant bus-station food, seriously regret travel decisions and change drivers. They were like old school buses with bad suspension, uncomfortable seats that didn't recline even a millimetre and no air conditioning. If you were hot, you had to open a window. People took turns lying down in the aisle in sleeping bags on the hard floor just to get something that resembled kip.

Having endured this interminable journey (and back) once in my lifetime, I can safely say that I will never do it again. Other than the fact that most of the passengers just about managed to retain their sanity, there was nothing fucking magic about the Magic Bus.

To make matters worse, Yasmin chatted for almost the entire journey, although in all fairness she was telling me about Paros, the island we were heading to, and teaching me some basic Greek, so it was no hardship. *Parakalo*.

I'd left Jim at home as he'd begun to annoy me, although I forget why and I needed a break. I said if I missed him too much, I'd send a letter and he could come out to meet me. I was away in Greece for about six weeks, which was a slightly shorter time than the journey seemed to take.

Arriving back at the squat in Bermondsey, I was in for a shock. I had told my sister, Dawn, that if I wasn't back from Greece after six weeks then I probably wasn't coming back, and asked her to kindly move my possessions out of my squat. She had taken me seriously and, despite sending a postcard saying I was heading home and NOT to touch my stuff, it hadn't arrived in time.

Not only had all my possessions been moved, Dawn had given the man with a van my TV and record collection as payment for helping move my stuff! None of which I had agreed to. I never did get the TV back but, thank God, I eventually managed to get my prized records back.

Jim was ecstatic to see me, and hugged and kissed me, like I'd been away for six months, not six weeks. (Perhaps the 'magic' bus journey had actually taken as long as it felt it had?)

Many of the other squatters had moved out whilst I was holidaying in Greece, as there had been a drugs raid. The helicopters we'd seen hovering over the gardens Sweeney-style really had been police surveillance and had spotted the verdant dope orchard we were cultivating on the roof. Many of the drug dealers were either busted or had panicked and skedaddled. As my flat had been stripped of my belongings, I stayed with Jim for a short while and then moved back to my mum's. I spilt up with Jim not long after that. Greece had changed me and I felt like I'd outgrown the relationship.

One morning I had woken up to Jim looking down at me, grinning. He was making love to me while I was asleep. I freaked out. It made me feel weird and reminded me of more sinister times when I hadn't been in control or had a choice. I decided it was time to be single again.

Chapter 10

A punk in Paros

After three months, I mean days, of laborious travel on the Magic Bus, Yasmin and I arrived in the scorching hot climate of Greece. I was feeling happy and carefree and Yasmin was a great travel companion. I didn't mind that she talked incessantly for what seemed like the entire duration of the journey, as she was good to be around, knowledgeable about the country and even spoke some of the language.

We hadn't pre-booked accommodation as Yasmin had assured me that we would be able to stay with a friend of hers when we got there and that we could rent a room together and everything would be fine, oh yes, just fine. She would get a job and I would have a holiday. I had my tarot cards with me and some silver jewellery left over from my market-trading days that I planned to sell. I could always find people who wanted their cards read so I wasn't too worried about money. I had enough for a week and an open ticket to take me home on the hell bus whenever I wanted to leave.

We arrived in Athens in the late afternoon and made our way to the port of Piraeus. I fell in love with Greece immediately. The heat, the rolling countryside, the clusters of white buildings, the culture... everything was so completely unlike England.

We waited at the port eating *tiropita*, delicious pies made with flaky pastry and filled with goat's cheese, as we waited for the ferry to whisk us off to the island of Paros. It was an eight-hour crossing, which felt like nothing after the coach journey. The boat was busy and the crossing was rough in places. Other passengers were drinking the local brandy, Metaxa, either to blot out the journey or to keep them calm during rough swells, or maybe just because they could. A stranger handed me his bottle and I gratefully took a sip. Metaxa and I were going to become very good friends, I decided.

The ferry docked and we watched as all the other passengers were greeted by coaches and instantly whisked away to their pre-booked hotels and apartments. We had no such luxurious arrangements so, after sitting forlornly like lost luggage whilst everyone else disappeared to their presumably luxury hotels with showers and clean sheets and balconies, we tracked down a cabbie. It was one o'clock in the morning and we'd been travelling non-stop for the best part of four days. Although, if there had been a best part, I failed to recall it. All I wanted was the opportunity to sleep for an eight-hour period, lying horizontally, in a bed, and to remind my body what warm water felt like.

The cab journey was long and I lost track of time. I couldn't see much in the moonlight but I could smell foreign land and pine trees and wild herbs combined into a delicious exotic fragrance that I was unaccustomed to. Bermondsey smelt of traffic pollution and dog poo. I leaned my tired head back against the seat, closed my eyes and listened to the cicadas boisterously chirping.

Eventually we arrived in Naousa, a small fishing town. By now I was dead on my feet. Actually, I was dead on every part of my body. My eyelids were so heavy that it was painful to keep them open. I felt ready to collapse and was prepared to do that pretty much anywhere if a bed didn't magically materialise very soon. Yasmin was admirably still managing to summon up energy from somewhere and left me sitting outside a closed taverna while she went to find the friend who was apparently putting us up. The doorway of the taverna was just beginning to look exceptionally comfortable when she returned. She had managed to track down her friend, and pretty soon we were both crashed out on the floor of his apartment. You don't realise how comfortable a floor can be until you've been imprisoned in an upright position for several days. It might have been a cold stone floor, but to me it felt like I was kipping at The Ritz.

We woke to a characteristically beautiful hot Greek day complete with the kind of azure sky that English people only ever see on paint swatches. We meandered aimlessly into the town to find ourselves an apartment or room to rent. The clean narrow streets were too narrow for anything bigger than a moped. Bright red geraniums and fragrant basil grew randomly in large recycled olive tins, while shocking pink bougainvillea – which I of course loved – clambered confidently up and over everything, contrasting

CHAPTER 10

with the sterile whiteness of the walls. It was certainly no Morden. Everywhere I walked there were cheeky, underweight street cats roaming the streets looking for morsels and waiting for an opportunistic fish head to be tossed their shabby way.

Yasmin and I shared a room for the first few days, before I was 'encouraged' to find a place of my own. Bizarrely, pretty much as soon as she and Rupert were reunited she decided to split up with him, after travelling halfway around Europe, so that they could be together, although the presence of a tall blond Swedish bar owner may have had something to do with her decision. Anyway, it soon became clear that I was cramping Yasmin's style as, no sooner had she parted company with Rupert, she was attaching herself to a Swede with rock-band hair and painfully tight jeans.

Yasmin immediately found some casual work in one of the restaurants, helping to prepare the food. She had worked on the island during the summer for a few years, so knew quite a few other workers who did the same, returning year after year to spend the long hot summers in the Greek islands, drinking cheap beer and splashing about in the water, instead of signing on in South London. I quickly made friends with many of the people she introduced me to, which was just as well as she was too preoccupied with her blond wavy love life to pay me much attention. Which is understandable. I'm sure I'd have done the same in the same circumstances. I was grateful for the new friends I'd made though, as it meant I didn't have to rely on her much.

I had an amazing six weeks being a tourist and lazing about on the beaches like a languid cat. During the afternoons I would often potter about in the boutiques in the town. Naousa was at that time still charming and relatively undiscovered. Most of the tourists were Italian and German, with a few English people. The place attracted artists and craftspeople, which lent a bohemian vibe to the place that I was comfortable with. Photographers and painters would set up makeshift galleries along the outer walls of shops, where they exhibited their pictures of local views and typical Greek vistas.

Naousa is built around a small harbour edged by restaurants and bars, whose lights glittered charmingly once it was dark. Late at night, you could hear the tiny fishing boats chugging away into the seemingly obsidian sea and, in the morning, the fishermen could be found sleeping along the harbour or in their boats whilst their nets dried. Freshly caught squid were suspended from washing lines, glittering wetly in the sunshine. Clearly the Greek fishermen knew all about pink glitter.

To keep myself going it was obvious I needed to earn, so I used to spread a shawl out on the floor by the bus stop and display my silver jewellery left over from my Camden Market Electric Ballroom days, or offer tarot card readings, either there on the ground or in one of the nearby tavernas, in exchange for food, drinks or a little cash.

It was a beautiful and simple life and so different from what I was used to. I forgot my worries and felt like I had the space to start discovering who I really was, without the always-looking-behind-you mentality of living in a big stinky city. The good thing about travelling is that you have the opportunity to leave your history behind you. You can pretend to be anyone you want to be and there is no one there to expose you. For the first time in my life, I felt totally free and with absolutely no one to answer to. I could do exactly as I wished without fear of being judged. Paros was like going home. I imagined that this is what a proper home would truly feel like, rather than the one I had had in Morden or anywhere else so far. I felt so welcome and at ease there. It was an incredible experience.

The new friends who I'd made also worked on the island, either in bars or restaurants, and would therefore stay up until the early hours of the morning, and sleep late. We would meet in a cafe in the afternoon and take turns buying a bottle of Metaxa. Then we would hang out until midnight or beyond, taking advantage of the balmy evenings and sipping on the cheap Greek brandy. It was divine being able to sit outside all night without getting cold, listening to the sea gently slapping against the sea walls, whilst the moon's reflection fidgeted on the water's surface.

As a testament to how relaxed and comfortable I felt in my Greek home, my psychic abilities increased dramatically during the time I was there. I was reading the tarot every day, either for myself or for others. I was in one of my favourite bars one day when an Irish woman who'd heard I could tell fortunes requested a reading. I went back to my room to get my cards and the image of The Moon tarot card popped suddenly into my mind. The Moon card can symbolise deception, the hidden or illusions.

Chapter 10

I returned to the bar, where the woman was sitting with a man I assumed was her boyfriend or husband. They bought me a drink and I asked the woman to shuffle the cards. The first card I laid on the table, interestingly, happened to be The Moon. I smiled to myself and laid out a further nine cards in the Celtic Cross spread. I proceeded to tell the lady the meaning of each card. At each interpretation, she shook her head and said that I was wrong, and insisted that we should reshuffle the cards and begin again, as they hadn't been shuffled properly. Strange, I thought, as that had never happened before: the cards are usually right. Nevertheless, to be obliging, I gathered up the cards and passed them to her so that she could reshuffle them.

I began to lay down the cards again. The first card I placed on the table was, yet again, The Moon, and the next three cards were identical to the previous ones that had been picked and were all in exactly the same positions. She was stunned. Her male friend was stunned. I was stunned. That has never happened to me before or since. The odds of it happening are ridiculously high. I explained to her that those were the cards for her and that they obviously wanted to be there and tell her something but, yet again, she rejected my interpretation. I didn't know what to say as in my experience the cards were usually accurate, but she was insistent that this was not the case.

Suddenly, her male friend butted in, apologetically: 'I don't know why she's saying no, because everything you are saying is absolutely right.' They had a few words between them and eventually she admitted that the cards were right for her. I don't know why she was rejecting my reading. Perhaps she was scared of something or in denial. Anyway, I got paid.

I got the feeling that I was the first punk who had ever washed up on Paros's shore. I had vivid Tango orange hair, which earned me an incredible amount of attention. The local kids were in awe of me and my flaming locks and would shout hello and wave frantically as they went past. The adults were less convinced and didn't really know what I was or how to approach me. I would often turn my head to look at something, just as several Greek heads all turned away, thinking I hadn't noticed them staring. I mostly enjoyed the attention as no one took any notice of crazy hair colours in London anymore whereas, in Greece, people would build up the courage to come and touch my hair – which was a bit invasive, but I guess they thought I was an alien.

I was also a strict vegetarian, but Greece – especially a remote Greek island – struggled to understand the concept of vegetarianism in the 1980s. I therefore lived almost entirely on Greek salads, which fortuitously I learned to love, despite being suspicious of this new-fangled feta cheese and olives business when I first washed ashore.

But much as I loved Greek salads, a punk cannot live on feta cheese, olives, cucumber and tomatoes alone. It shouldn't have come as quite such a shock to me that Greece was mainly full of Greek food, but it did. Coming from the UK, where we've compensated for our lack of interesting traditional food by importing cuisines from every corner of the globe, I somehow thought it would be similar. I soon learned that most Greek restaurants serve the same selection of dishes, most of which contain meat. And even when they advertised 'Greek Special Ties', they were generally serving the same 'special ties' as the restaurant next door. So stumbling upon a taverna that sold something as exotic as a jacket potato was like discovering buried treasure. On rare occasions, I'd spot a restaurant serving pizza – PIZZA! – the luxury of which cannot be overstated. If you've ever travelled, as a vegetarian, in a country that doesn't recognise the concept of vegetarianism, you'll know exactly what I mean.

After six weeks in Greece, I was obviously fluent in the language. Are you lying, Gail? Yes, I am. I did, however, know how to say 'yes', 'no', 'thank you', 'slowly', 'excuse me', 'I love you' (which I sadly didn't get the opportunity to use, apart from to a bottle of Metaxa), 'two beers' (I definitely got the opportunity to practise this one), 'spinach pie', 'cheese pie' and an entire phrase that meant 'can I have a souvlaki without meat?'. So I felt like I was pretty much 50 per cent of the way to fluency. I mean, what other words are there?

A souvlaki is a type of Greek kebab, in which spiced meat is rolled into flat bread. Asking for a souvlaki without meat is like ordering a hamburger without the burger; or buying an album and asking for it without the vinyl; or purchasing a bus ticket but asking for it without the journey. How I wished I'd done that. It's kind of like asking for a souvlaki but without the souvlaki.

The first time I asked for a souvlaki sans meat (in fluent Greek),

CHAPTER 10

the vendor appeared to stop breathing in order to stare blankly at me. Greek tumbleweed suddenly appeared and, well, tumbled in front of the restaurant. This had never happened on the island before. Eventually, the vendor managed to compute the strange data I had supplied him with, and the world started spinning again. He asked me if I was Jewish, assuming that nobody would voluntarily abstain from meat consumption unless it was for religious reasons. I explained that I wasn't Jewish. Then he had a sudden coin-drop moment and clearly thought that I was too poor to eat meat, so very generously slipped a few chips and salad into some pitta bread and charged me the equivalent of 16 pence.

When I visited the same restaurant the following year, vegetarianism had obviously been explained to him and his prices had risen accordingly. I once stumbled upon a severed cat's paw near his eatery, so I was very glad that I was vegetarian and hadn't been eating kitbabs.

My new friend Metaxa, the local drink of choice, had been linked with many people leaving the island with alcohol problems. As far as I was concerned, Metaxa was cheap and potent – which ticked both boxes in my slightly unsophisticated criteria at the time. On one occasion, I somehow managed to drink just the brandy out of a glass of Metaxa and Coke. It must have floated on the surface of the drink. When I showed the glass of remaining Coke to a few people, they instantly branded me a witch. Perhaps all that time spent on the Magic Bus was beginning to pay off, I thought.

I kind of compounded the witch thing as I always wore lots of jewellery, with rings on every finger and copper bracelets etched with Celtic designs. I wore them for psychic protection but, to the untrained Greek eye, I must have appeared a little witchy. Especially on a small island where they didn't know what vegetarianism was. I'm not sure the bracelets worked, but I guess if you put your intention into a piece of jewellery, that intention or belief will give you some kind of reassurance.

The good thing about knowing a few people on the island was that I got the low-down on all the characters, both agreeable and unsavoury, and knew who could be trusted and who couldn't. I was warned about one man in particular, a balding middle-aged man who fancied his chances with the younger girls and liked to boast to his mates that he'd bedded them which, considering his appearance, seemed altogether unlikely. I mean, Metaxa is strong but...

In my experience of being a young girl, baldness and/or middle age were not generally top of the list of desired qualities in a sexual partner. Anyway, Freddy liked to show off about his sexual exploits (which is often a sign that they never happened in the first place) and had no qualms about damaging a girl's reputation, so long as his sad mates thought he'd managed to do sex on a girl. Round of applause for Freddy. I've lost count of the number of Freddys I've met in my life. Every girl has fallen victim to a Freddy or two and his fantasy fucks. Telling people you're a millionaire and being a millionaire are really quite different things. What they must truly think of themselves when they lie alone in bed every night I can't imagine.

So one night I was in a bar alone, when I became the focus of Freddy's next conquest; real or imaginary, it didn't matter to him. Freddy unctuously sidled over to my table and started a conversation. It all began innocently enough, but then he asked me to go to another bar with him. I'd been warned never to be seen alone with this predatory old twat or walking out of a bar with him, as this would magically transform into tales of him 'giving me the time of my life'. I declined his generous proposition, saying that I was fine where I was and would be leaving alone. Of course, being the kind of man Freddy was, he tried to persuade me to go with him, despite me giving him absolutely no indication that I was interested in him, other than a little polite conversation as I didn't wish to appear rude. His persuasion technique was really subtle. At first he tried to sweet-talk me but, as soon as he realised I wasn't as easy as he'd hoped, he became less subtle and more and more verbally aggressive in his approach.

I shut my eyes, trying to ignore him, to block this horrible little man out of my sight. I had been taught psychic protection exercises and tried to enclose myself in an invisible bubble of protective light, but then a very strange thing happened. I became extremely aware that, on a psychic level, Freddy was trying to penetrate my thoughts and concentration. I psychically saw his arm reach into my energy field, trying to assault me. I mustered up all my psychic power to throw his arm away and a power struggle on the astral plane ensued between us. It took all of the psychic strength

Chapter 10

that I had and I was genuinely amazed by, yet simultaneously fearful of, this man's strength and capability.

To onlookers it would have looked like a young girl with extremely orange hair trying to ignore an extremely unattractive man in a bar. But I had to summon up what strength I had to push away his lecherous arm. I opened my eyes. Freddy stared at me. He seemed to be in shock. Surprised at my strength. He sneered at me as I walked out of the bar alone, leaving him to be mocked by his pack of male friends for having failed to pull me. Not that men like Freddy would let that stop them making up stories about a girl.

As I left the bar in the cool night air after another broiling day, I suddenly felt painfully drained. My inner psychic ninja was exhausted, and I could barely walk (and my friend Metaxa was not to blame on this occasion). Luckily (thank God for small islands), I ran into Paulo and Ellen, whom I'd met when I first arrived. Paulo was half British/half Greek and Ellen was Dutch. When they saw the state I was in, they rushed to my aid. I tried to recount the psychic set-to I'd had with Freddy but wondered if I was making sense or if they believed me.

'You need to go and see Amy,' said Ellen. I'd met Amy previously – an elegant older English woman, with beautiful long grey hair that she wore piled up on top of her head. But I had no idea why they were taking me to see her at this time of night.

'Oh my god! What happened to you?' exclaimed Amy as she threw open the door to us. Paulo and Ellen explained how they'd found me, seemingly drained and powerless and barely able to walk. Amy placed her pleasantly cool hands upon my wrists. 'You've been sucked empty,' she said. 'And your bracelets – they've lost all their energy! What the hell did that bastard do to you?' I explained what had happened and Amy listened intently. I clearly didn't have to worry about her not believing me.

'Don't ever let that bastard near you again,' she said angrily, after I'd recounted the psychic battle. 'You are a young witch and you need to take care of yourself, OK?'

I looked up at her, startled. I generally didn't tell people I was a witch, as I knew most people would think I'd been eating the wrong berries and I feared ridicule at best, persecution at worst.

When I finally left the island, six weeks later, it was the lovely Amy who escorted me all the way back to Athens in order to keep me safe from what she called the kamakis – Greek men whose aim is to conquer as many foreign women as they can, and then boast about their conquests to their male friends. We have a word for these people in English too: wankers.

I had other bizarre experiences whilst I was on the island. One night I was at Matt's Bar, which was about to close down at the end of the holiday season and therefore all the drinks were extra-cheap and the measures dangerously generous. I was embracing Greek culture by playing backgammon with a friend, when I looked up and noticed two English-looking guys enter the bar. One had long dyed-black hair and fingers dripping with heavy silver rings. He looked exactly like a guy who'd dated Sian when I was in the Lost Cherrees but I discounted this as we were on a remote island, eight hours from the Greek mainland, and with 320 days of sunshine a year, not exactly your typical holiday destination for pale-skinned goth types.

I carried on playing backgammon but, moments later when I couldn't resist looking again, I recognised some of my own ring designs hanging off his fingers.

'I'd recognise those rings anywhere!' I shouted.

'Gail!' Nogbad exclaimed, spinning around, instantly recognising me. We hugged each other, had the whole 'small world/can't believe it' convo, and he introduced me to his friend. We spent the rest of the night imbibing copious amounts of cheap booze and catching up. Sadly, they were supposed to be leaving that day but their ferry crossing had been cancelled due to rough seas, so I offered them shelter in my room for the night, as they'd already checked out of their accommodation. They were grateful for this as, later on, a gale hit the island. By the morning, the storm had passed and they were able to catch the next ferry. It had been lovely to spend time with someone I kind of knew.

Even stranger things happened to me while I was on the island. One incident still haunts me now. It may sound strange, but I swear it is completely true and, if you've read this far, you've probably realised that I'm the kind of girl who attracts unusual experiences like a non-smoker attracts cigarette smoke. (Which, as a non-smoker, always happens to me!)

Chapter 10

When I was younger, I would often experience what I believe were memories from previous lives. In one of those past lives I had been a slender and attractive woman with long brown hair. I recall that I wore long skirts and had lived in either a cave or perhaps a hollow carved out from a hill. Along the mud shelves were jars of herbs and potions. Maybe I was a wise woman or perhaps a shaman or witch? I had been aware of this past life since I was around nine years old, although I'd never discussed it with anyone as I knew it was a tad strange and I didn't want to be branded a weirdo, or considered mentally ill or banned from watching TV.

One of the strangest recollections I have of this pre-Gail existence is of being an incredibly powerful woman who was protected by two black dog-like slaves with long pointed ears and scarlet eyes. There was definitely a mistress-and-slave dynamic between me and the beasts and, oddly, some kind of sexual sensation that I find difficult to explain. Maybe it was an attraction from the beasts to their mistress? Or perhaps I was a mad kinky bitch in another life?

As I got older, the memory of this 'flashback' (for want of a better word) had faded and I'd started to wonder if it was less of a memory and more of a figment of the imagination of a bored and creative nine-year-old. As I say, I'd never spoken about it to a single soul.

Right, so one night whilst sitting with friends outside one of the bars in Naousa, I was introduced to a young man and his girlfriend, both around the same age as myself, i.e. in their early twenties. Both were English and we soon got chatting whilst paying homage to Metaxa. Suddenly, I was aware of the man locking eyes with me. Everyone else in the bar seemed to carry on talking around us, totally unaware of any weirdness.

'I know you,' the guy said slowly, and I could feel his eyes boring into me, reaching deep into my psyche. And it wasn't just the Metaxa talking. As I met his gaze, I had a sudden flashback to this same past life in which I was a hot and powerful wise woman.

'Describe me,' I said, challenging him.

Smiling, he began to describe me exactly how I would have described myself, including the long skirts I wore, his eyes keeping their hold on mine the whole time. As he spoke, it was as though everyone else at the table was blocked out. They were caught up in their own conversations, unaware of what else was going on around them. It was just me and him sharing an extremely strange moment.

'Now describe me,' he said, reciprocating the challenge whilst still holding my gaze with a wrench-like grip. This was more difficult, I thought, tuning in but not convinced I would be able to 'recognise' him. Then, with a sudden jolt, an image appeared of one of the dog-like beasts I'd visualised before. My eyes quickly opened.

'Well?' he said.

How do you explain to someone you've never met before that you think they might have been one of your two doggy slaves in a previous life, now reincarnated in human form and sitting in front of you? On an island. In Greece. There's no easy way.

'I can't,' I said, shaking my head. 'I'm too embarrassed.' I could feel my cheeks flushing red with embarrassment.

'Try me,' he persisted. It felt like he already knew exactly what I was thinking and could see into my mind's eye. I took another slug of medicinal brandy for Greek courage and thought, what the hell? What did it matter if he laughed at me? It's not like I'd ever have to see him again and there was no one else listening.

'OK,' I said slowly. 'So. Well. You were a dog-like creature, like a slave to me, but there were two of you. You had long pointy ears and red eyes and you followed me everywhere.' I expected him to dissolve into guffaws, but instead he was silent. With a deadly serious look on his face, he undid his shirt buttons and pulled the fabric aside to reveal quite a nice body, oh and a tattoo of... a black dog-like beast, with pointy ears and red eyes – exactly how I'd remembered. Well, as you can imagine, I was spooked to fuck and a chill shot through my spine like an injection of freezing water. There was no possible sensible explanation for what had just happened. My skin was covered in gooseflesh and I was lost for words. Taking in the fact that one of my dog slaves from a previous lifetime and different dimension was sitting in front of me on a remote Greek island was quite a task.

More bizarrely still, having renewed our connection, my new canine friend was instantly interested in taking up the role of servitude again, despite the fact that his poor oblivious girlfriend was sitting next to him. How's he going to explain this to her, I wondered? 'Hey

Chapter 10

darling… this is Gail. Now don't take this the wrong way but she was my mistress in a previous life when I was a dog slave, and…'

I got up to stretch my legs and to get some more brandy from the supermarket. 'I'll come with you,' said Rover eagerly, and I could swear he was panting. His girlfriend shot him a be-daggered look. 'Now I've found you again, I don't want to let you out of my sight,' he said as he caught up with me. I felt extremely awkward as I reminded him that we were in different lives now and would have to carry on in this life living apart.

Rover wanted me to stay the night in his room, with him and his girlfriend. I politely declined as it had all got a little bit too weird for me, which is saying something. I made sure that I didn't run into them again after that night and, about a year later, I heard that he had overdosed on heroin and died. I was saddened to hear the news. I also heard that his girlfriend had dumped him when they'd arrived back in England. That bit of news hadn't surprised me after the way he had treated her when he'd become fixated with me.

I had arrived on Paros with £50, a return ticket home, my tarot cards and jewellery to sell. The money I had made from the readings and from selling the odd piece of silver kept me going most of the time, but I was also offered the occasional cleaning job. I cleaned the fountain in front of one of the hotels. I only earnt five quid and ruined a skirt worth about that much in the process. Still, I could buy another one from Kensington Market when I got back home. We were all wearing fringed hippie skirts in those days. I also spring-cleaned the apartment of a woman who owned a jewellery boutique, who not only gave me some drachmas but prepared a massive lunch of salad, cheese and macaroni – which was the most I'd eaten since I'd arrived. All in return for a little bit of sweeping and dusting. I'm sure she was completely capable of doing the cleaning herself, but I think she'd kindly taken pity on me.

The drachmas were a godsend as I had been worrying about money and wondering if it was time to go home. In fact, I was down to my last 50 pence. Before I got the job, I had been walking along the coast road with the sun warming my back. I'd relaxed and counted my blessings, reminding myself how lucky I was to be in such a beautiful place. Something would turn up, I told myself. As I walked back to my apartment, feeling grateful for everything around me, Paulo,

Ellen's boyfriend, approached me and told me about the cleaning for his boss. 'You see,' I said to myself, 'have trust, something always turns up.'

But six weeks later I really was running out of money. I still had my return ticket but it was late September, which meant the end of the tourist season. Much of the island would be shutting down soon and so there would be no tourists to read cards for. I also needed to get home to sort out my place in Bermondsey. And Jim would be wondering what had happened to me too. So I made the decision to go home.

Amy kindly escorted me back to the mainland and delivered me safely to Rupert's house in Athens. He'd got bored on Paros after splitting up with Yasmin and had gone back to Athens. However, Rupert and I had had a bit of a row one night on the island. He'd drunkenly told me that I was full of my own importance because I could do tarot readings and I'd been in the Lost Cherrees. But he'd still said I could stay with him if I needed to, while I waited for the next Tragic Bus home.

The next bus was due to leave in two days' time, so I decided it would be best to keep out of his way as much as possible and not cause any trouble. He showed me the outside shower in the courtyard, which other families shared. It was cold, but I welcomed the chance to get clean after the eight-hour ferry crossing. Then he made me some beans on toast yet barely spoke to me. I don't think I've ever been so happy to see baked beans. Before or since. I hadn't had English food for so long and could probably handle not eating feta cheese for a few months.

The next morning, I went to check out the times for the bus. I had a map that Rupert had lent me and I happily made my way through a bustling food market selling pungent herbs and plump fruit. I weaved through cobbled streets to a large square, where I found the bus timetable. Mission accomplished, I decided to hang around and absorb the chaotic Athenian atmosphere, which was so different to that on Paros. I also felt it would be better for everyone if I stayed out of the apartment for as long as possible.

I drifted around the square, browsing in the small shops and boutiques and enjoying the buzz of the city. A young man called me over in French, asking if I knew where a particular road was. My French is appalling but

Chapter 10

I tried to answer him to the best of my ability. He laughed and asked if I was English. He was Arabic and on holiday visiting his brother who lived in the street he was trying to find. He invited me for a drink. I shrugged. Why not? I was at a low ebb having left the island and because I felt awkward around Rupert.

Anyway, we chatted for a while and then he invited me back to his brother's place. *No Gail, no!* I can almost hear you saying. I don't know why, but I went along, not really caring about the consequences. When we arrived back at his brother's place, he introduced me and they began a heated conversation in Arabic, stopping momentarily to ask if I could understand them, and then carrying on in Arabic when I said no. After a bit more bickering, the brother left.

My new acquaintance showed me to the bathroom, where he said I could have a hot shower. Most of the showers on Paros had been cold, so access to hot water was a real luxury. When I came out, we started to talk. Then he kissed me, running his hands over my skin. I had allowed a complete stranger to pick me up on the streets and take me back to a strange place. I had no idea where I was and was now allowing him to touch me. I no longer seemed to care about myself. I was completely emotionally detached and allowing my body to be used by a stranger, for his pleasure, in ways I had never allowed anyone to use me previously. I just didn't care anymore. I felt worthless. I felt like I didn't have a choice.

'I think you don't enjoy it,' he said, after realising I was unresponsive and, to my astonishment, he stopped what he was doing which, under the circumstances, was a pretty noble thing to do. He was right: I wasn't enjoying it. I was indifferent.

I quickly got dressed and left. I realised I didn't know where I was and started to wander the streets. The Arabic man had given me vague directions to get back to the square but I'd obviously taken a wrong turn. I asked a lorry driver, who wrote directions down for me. Except the directions were in Greek and didn't involve the words 'cheese pie', 'please', 'thank you' or 'souvlaki but without the meat'. I tried to match the directions he'd given me with the street names but the Greek alphabet was really intent on making things difficult. I eventually found my way back to the square and reluctantly sauntered back in the direction of Rupert's, dreading his lack of welcome. It was already late by this time. Then I looked up and saw

Rupert coming towards me. He stood out from the crowd with his long black dreadlocks, pale skin and thin frame all dressed in black. Oh great, I thought, I'm the last person he wants to see.

Suddenly he spotted me and came running towards me. 'GAIL! GAIL!' he yelled, and as he reached me he threw his arms around me, and gave me a squeeze. That, I was not expecting. 'Thank God I found you. I was so worried,' he exclaimed and I realised that, incredibly, tears were trickling down his cheeks.

Rupert had my passport in his hand and proceeded to tell me that he'd been so worried about me being alone in a foreign city and gone for so long that he was on the way to the police station to report me missing. Talk about absence making the heart grow fonder.

'I thought you hated me. I didn't think you wanted me around,' I told him, stunned.

'Don't be silly. Let's get some wine. I'm so glad you're safe.' He smiled, and we went back to his to drink wine.

I kept quiet about the Arabic man.

Rupert said he had trouble sleeping so, as I'd learned a few massage techniques from a friend back home, I gave him a back massage. He was very lean and I could feel every bone through his skin. He soon fell asleep (thanks to my great massage skills. And a litre of wine), and I crept quietly into the other bed to sleep.

Note to self: there are many men whose intentions are honourable.

The next day, I was on the Magic Bus heading home.

Chapter 11

Sarnies, drugs and Peckham

After one had returned from summering in the Greek islands, one moved back to one's parents' house in Morden, yet again. Crap.

I got a call one day from my friend Pete, who told me that the sandwich bar he was working in were looking for part-time staff and were paying the wages cash in hand, which was illegal and handy as I was still getting Enterprise Allowance money from running my own small business, and it wasn't much. I was familiar with sandwiches and liked eating them, so I was already qualified.

My hair was now shocking pink. I'd encountered discrimination in the past at job interviews because of my coloured hair, but I decided to give the sandwich bar a try and rang the number Pete had given me.

'I'm ringing about the vacancy you have. I hope you don't mind me asking, but are you colour-prejudiced?' I asked boldly.

'No. Why?' came the manager's puzzled response.

'Because I've got pink hair,' I told him. I didn't want to travel all the way to Blackfriars to be rejected solely on my stunning looks. I'd spent enough time on public transport recently.

'We like a bit of colour around here,' the manager said. 'But if any of the customers complain, then you'll have to go.' So I started working at Scole's – a chain of designer sandwich boutiques owned by an Austrian guy.

I began by buttering bread using a palette knife, spreading the margarine on and then removing it again, leaving just a suggestion of marge. That was my main job: just standing in the same spot, buttering a mountain of bread for hours. My tertiary education was beginning to pay off. Another facet of the role was carrying peeled avocados, which had been waiting in a bowl of water and lemon juice, to stop them turning brown, to the sandwich makers. I'd never seen avocados before (this was the mid-'80s) and they reminded me of slimy legless frogs – it was months before I plucked up the courage to actually try one.

There were a few of us crammed into a tiny kitchen, frantically buttering, slicing and assembling sarnies for rude businessmen. No one complained about my hair, which was a blessing, and I survived my first few weeks. Before long I was promoted to serving and making sandwiches. I was a fast worker and the boss liked me. I soon got jobs for my friends too, so that Scole's was mostly staffed by people with strange hair.

Most of us were working there to fund other projects, such as bands and artistic pursuits, and there were a couple of guys who worked as go-go dancers in Heaven, the gay nightclub in Charing Cross. They were wild characters – one had a shaved head to which he'd affix coloured corn plasters. He was heavily influenced by Leigh Bowery, the outrageous and notorious club animal and fashion designer from New York City. He showed me a fantastic 1950s-style dress he'd constructed entirely from blue-and-white-striped Tesco carrier bags.

'Look at me! Look at me!' he'd squeal and we'd all turn to see him standing there modelling a hat that he'd crafted out of iceberg lettuce leaves – and that suited him too. He was the only person I've ever met who could look good in an iceberg lettuce hat! There was another guy, Vince, who was a professional ballet dancer. He was in charge of creatively arranging the sandwich platters for the meetings and conferences of big corporations such as Goldman Sachs, Reuters and Lehman Brothers (we weren't far from Fleet Street). I don't think the stuffy executives had any idea about the scruffy and colourful individuals who had prepared the sarnies they consumed whilst discussing mergers and acquisitions and yearly forecasts – or whatever the fuck they talk about.

A friend of mine, Chris, who was the drummer in the band Hagar the Womb, got a job working with me as a delivery boy. Chris was one of those human dustbin types who can eat continuously and never gain even an ounce in weight. One day he saw a load of leftover lettuce about to end its life in a dustbin. He ran to get a carrier bag and took the lot home. I think we must have fed half the London punk

Chapter 11

population with leftover sandwiches whilst we worked there. When I worked in the Liverpool Street branch I used to fill a box with the leftovers and leave them on the steps of the church around the corner, so that the homeless could help themselves.

My, by now, best friend Caroline's boyfriend, James, also became one of the delivery boys, along with Veg, the bass player from Hagar the Womb. I think it was definitely the punkest sandwich chain in London – every business needs a USP. The delivery boys used to skive off after a delivery and have a sneaky pint and a fag in the pub before returning to base and would usually pinch a couple of sandwiches from each platter before they reached their destination, rearranging them carefully so that no one would notice. There's nothing like a sandwich-shaped gap to signify a missing sandwich.

One day, James came into work with a three-inch cut on his chest. Caroline had rung me the night before. Their relationship had been volatile for a while and she had taken to drinking neat gin straight from the bottle with a straw when we went out, which was not the behaviour of a happy soul. She'd previously trashed his flat in a rage, smashed his guitar and stuck rubbish on the walls with Sellotape, including shoe insoles, all of which she thought was hilarious.

When she rang me this time her mood was deadly serious. I can't remember if she was accusing him of seeing someone else or just ignoring her, but she'd opened her pencil case and pulled out the Stanley knife blade she kept there for sharpening her eyeliner. She'd slashed his chest, enough to break the skin but luckily not deep enough to warrant a trip to A&E. She was extremely remorseful and James had forgiven her. So when James came into work the next morning, I fully expected him to say nothing about the incident.

However, it soon got back to me through the sandwich grapevine that James had told the other delivery boys that he'd been attacked the night before by a trio of black blokes. I was furious. How dare he make out that black men had attacked him, the lying racist bastard! And probably just because he was too embarrassed to admit he'd been attacked by his girlfriend. I told the boys the truth, and although they never said anything to his face, they laughed at him behind his back.

He'd even cut the neckline of his T-shirt lower to show off the scar. What an attention-seeking, lying poseur!

Besides the punks, Scole's was home to Den, a homeless alcoholic who slept under a railway bridge and would wash in the toilets when he came into work. Then there was 'Studs', a very quiet and unassuming guy. He lived in a squat in Peckham and sold a little speed, which didn't quite gel with his geeky image. At that time, like many punks, I used to partake of the odd dab of speed when I went to nightclubs, so Studs's second job didn't bother me.

I was having a tough time at home again in Morden as both my parents were drinking heavily and arguing frequently, and this time they couldn't blame my ferrets. Studs mentioned that there was a spare room in his squat in Peckham if I wanted it so, despite knowing that Peckham was a dodgy area, full of run-down council estates and tower blocks, I decided to take him up on his offer and trolleyed me and my stuff over there sharpish.

Peckham was so rough that even the postmen worked in pairs for fear of being mugged. What great items of value muggers thought they might plunder from the sack of a postman who delivers mail to depressing tower blocks in squalid estates in one of London's shittiest neighbourhoods, I just don't know.

Studs's squat was in a 1960s-style block of flats. The kind of constructions you find all over England, which were ugly even when they were new and which haven't aged elegantly. I think the architects' brief must have read something like 'cheap and soulless', and I think they did a pretty good job of achieving that.

The squat consisted of two bedrooms: one was mine, while the other belonged to another girl with an almost newborn baby, and Studs slept on the sofa in the living room. A few weeks after I moved in, the girl with the infant moved out as she'd cunningly realised that a room in a squat with a drug dealer on an estate in Peckham was probably not the best start to life she could provide for her baby and wisely moved back to her parents' place.

It might surprise you to discover that my room had a second-hand mattress on the floor, fitted as standard. I brought my keyboards, of course, but I rarely tickled their ivories much anymore. I had an old

Chapter 11

ex-Post Office pushbike which, as I recall, my dad had given me, and which, unlike the poor neglected keyboards, did get a lot of attention. It was black and sturdy with no gears and I'd been using it to cycle from Morden to Blackfriars and back again every day, clocking up 15 miles each way, meaning that I now had concrete calf muscles like strongman Geoff Capes.

Studs's flat was a council flat just behind the Civic Centre off the Old Kent Road of Monopoly fame. I was living in a location that featured in Monopoly. And that was where my excitement about living in Old Kent Road, Peckham began and finished. I had never been a fan of South London, and Peckham was a place of little, if any, charm or character. It also had a reputation for being the biggest shithole in London. Which is saying something. London has some very beautiful areas, and it has some right bloody dives. No one would volunteer to live in insalubrious Peckham, so I guess I must have been pretty desperate to get out of Morden to have taken up Studs's offer.

The squat itself was in a reasonable condition, with hot and cold running water and heating. It was on the fourth floor and benefited from the luxury of a lift. Which actually worked.

I knew before I moved in that Studs dealt a little speed but had no idea that he was actually the local methadone and heroin dealer too. He really didn't seem the type – he was even-tempered with shiny long blond hair and glasses – completely failing to resemble any character from *Trainspotting*. I guess that's how he got away with it. By not being very Irvine Welshy.

Little naive me soon realised that what I'd assumed was eczema all over his arms turned out to be track marks. It's a good job I didn't get round to buying him some E45 cream for his 'eczema', as I'd planned to do.

Studs himself was actually a sweetie and we would often stay up for hours talking shit, assisted by the dabs of speed he'd let me have for free. He'd often offer me dabs in the mornings too. No wonder they thought I was 'the fastest sandwich maker' in the South.

The downside of living with a drug dealer was the constant knocks on the door from his druggy punters. At first he would go to the door and perform his transactions discreetly without allowing the punters into the flat. I don't know whether this was to try to protect me from what was going on or maybe because he just didn't want me to know the extent of his dealing but, as time went by, his standards slipped and I'd often come home to discover some very dodgy-looking strangers sitting in the living room. Studs would be nowhere in sight, having left the punters waiting whilst he went to his own supplier. I had no idea who these people were and I would try and initiate a bit of small talk, as I figured no one would stab me to death once we'd discussed the weather, but really I felt very nervous, and would will Studs to return soon with all my might. I also didn't like the fact that my bedroom door was unlocked while strangers were in the house, both while I was in it and out.

I'd got into making homebrew from kits and made a couple of gallons of wine and an entire barrel of beer, which was awful – and unfortunately there was a lot of it. When I'd lived in Bermondsey, as well as making the blackberry wine, I'd had a go at brewing cider, but a clearly confused wine fly must have sabotaged the batch (it only takes one) and it tasted like cheap table vinegar. Even the local crusty, who boasted about his cast-iron stomach and superhuman ability to drink anything so long as it had an alcoholic content, was unable to drink my vinegar cider. So that shut him up.

The maturation of the beer and wine coincided nicely with my birthday, so naturally I decided to throw a party. Three friends – Sharon, Doc and Marina – took me to the Dew Drop Inn in New Cross so that we could have a few sharpeners to invigorate the brain cells and get us into the party mood. As luck would have it, my cider was spiked with vodka and before long I was barely in control of myself. Every time I tried to stand up, the rest of my body tried to lie down, regardless of how far away the floor was.

My friends generously spread the word that I was throwing a party and some people we vaguely knew tagged along with us back to the flat. One of the partygoers was a six-foot four-inch Irish guy with blonde spiky hair, who tucked into the free beer straight away. He loved it, which was just as well as no one else did, and started decanting it inside himself in large quantities.

A little later he staggered into the living room, where Studs was sit-

CHAPTER 11

ting peacefully with his mates smoking spliffs and listening to Queen records. 'What's this fucking shite?' the now drunk-on-vinegar Irish giant bellowed, and demanded that the record be changed to something more punk. Studs's friends left, having had their peaceful night ruined somewhat by an intolerable man who stank of chips. One of the guys who left was a motorbike despatch rider I'd recently started dating. I never saw him again after that. I guess he was appalled by my drunken behaviour and choice of friends. I can't blame him, looking back.

Having upset Studs's friends, the Irish guy then went out onto the balcony. I thought it was to get some much-needed fresh air, but very quickly Marina came running inside in a panic.

'Gail, come quick!' she urged breathlessly. 'That Irish bloke is threatening to throw my boyfriend over the balcony.' Which wouldn't have been so bad if we hadn't been on the fourth floor.

Rushing outside, I found that the Irish guy had a tight hold on Marina's boyfriend and was indeed attempting to shove him over the balcony wall. I was getting more sober by the second, so I grabbed hold of the Irish guy's arm and pulled him backwards, making him release his victim.

'Do you know him? Is he a friend of yours?' he asked me; I could see that his eyes were having trouble staying focused.

When I said I did know him and, yes, he was a friend, the Irish guy straightened himself up, apologised and slowly staggered out the front door, as if absolutely nothing had happened. The rest of us watched open-mouthed while poor Marina's boyfriend stood clutching at his beating heart, realising what a lucky escape he'd just had. None of us knew this guy and we had no idea if he really would have thrown someone off a four-storey balcony, but we were all shaken up.

As time went by, Studs's standards slipped and it really concerned me that strangers were often left in the flat when he was out. I worried about my own personal safety and fretted about my possessions being stolen. I didn't have much apart from my precious keyboards, but I guess that's the point – they were all I had. I couldn't even leave food in the kitchen because one of Studs's 'clients' would invariably eat it, regardless of whom it belonged to. Studs, meanwhile, never seemed to eat. His diet consisted of the three main food groups: drugs, roll-ups and Special Brew.

He'd wake up after crashing out on the sofa and open a can of Special Brew for breakfast, and would then proceed to drink can after can, punctuated by roll-up cigarettes. The ashtrays overflowed and the carpet was covered in fag ends as we had no Hoover, although sometimes I went over it with a dustpan and brush.

One day, after I had come home from work, there was a knock at the door. Studs went to answer it and took the man into the kitchen, out of my sight. I wondered what was going on, as they were there for some time and I could hear shouting. I wasn't sure whether to go and investigate but the man came into the living room and surveyed the mess.

'How can you live like this? You live like pigs! You should be ashamed of yourselves,' he sneered. He then pointed at the TV. 'Whose is that?' he demanded.

'That belongs to someone else. I'm borrowing it,' Studs replied.

'What about that?' the man said gruffly, pointing at the stereo.

'That's mine. You can have that,' Studs said nervously as he unplugged it and handed it over. Studs and the man then went into the kitchen.

After he'd left, Studs came back into the living room and I noticed his mouth was bleeding. The man had threatened him with a knife in the kitchen. Studs must have owed him money for drugs. He often gave people their supply on tick and he was the one who'd lost out. He couldn't afford to pay his main supplier and one of the heavies had been sent round to deal with it. Studs could have been seriously wounded or a lot worse.

That episode shook me up but not all of the addicts who came to our apartment were stereotypical smackheads; many of them were extremely ordinary and perfectly nice, able to hold down jobs and keep up a smart appearance whilst feeding their habit. The heroin and methadone users started hanging around the flat and I got to know a few of them. They were just normal people, not the stereotyped losers portrayed in the media.

Eventually, a couple of them started jacking up in front of me,

Chapter 11

as they didn't want to wait until they got home to load up. At first it was all done out of my sight, but soon they asked if I minded. Polite smackheads, at least. In a way, I found the whole process somewhat fascinating and almost ceremonial. The spoon laden with brown powder, gently heated above a dancing flame, watching as it transformed into a bubbling liquid. The drawing of the liquid into the syringe and the gentle flicking of the barrel of the syringe with the fingernail of the middle finger in order to remove any bubbles that remained in it. Then the application of a tourniquet around the arm, the drawing out of a small amount of blood from a prominent vein with the needle, which was then mixed with the heroin or methadone. Next, the needle sliding gently into the skin, and finally the mixture being injected back into the user's vein. Usually they would leave just after injecting, but often a couple would go into the empty second bedroom and pass out on the mattress in a blissed-out state in order to enjoy their trip, wherever they went. It was really a good job that the girl with the tiny baby had moved out.

I got a vicarious sense of what it must be like to take a heroin hit, but it concerned me that I was becoming too accustomed to these scenarios. Seeing people shoot up in my living room had become normality. I was becoming desensitised to Class-A drug use. I had never tried heroin or methadone but I was scared that I might one day decide to try it for myself. And I didn't want that to happen. Not to me.

I finally decided that I'd outgrown living in a drug den the day I came home from work to find Studs comatose on the sofa having spent the day imbibing cannabis and marinating himself in Special Brew. He was barely able to reciprocate when I said hello to him. I'm not even sure he realised that I *had* come home. He certainly didn't forewarn me that there was someone else in the flat.

I went to go to the loo and was surprised to find that I couldn't open the door. It was locked from the inside. I called out to Studs and he drowsily explained that there was already someone in there. They'd jacked up and fallen asleep on the toilet. I was horrified. I really couldn't go on living in this chaos. The man, a complete stranger to me, eventually regained consciousness and managed to remove himself from the toilet, but I had to hold onto my wee until he did.

I looked around the place. The drug-dealer guy was right: the place *was* disgusting. There were beer cans everywhere and ashtrays that had overflowed and jettisoned their contents over the floor. I was living in a drug den. I realised that this was not the life I wanted for myself. My squatting days were over.

Luckily, a bedsit had come up for rent through a girl I knew in Dalston, Hackney. Her parents were loaded and had bought her a brand new yuppie flat to live in while she studied at art school. Upstairs in the flat was a bedsit that they wanted to rent out. It was more than I could afford but I took it anyway. I was desperate to get away from Peckham and start a new life. I'd had enough of living in dismal conditions. Because I was on the Enterprise Allowance scheme, I was entitled to housing benefit but the housing benefit rules meant that I could only get paid up to a certain amount. Although I could get a low rent paid, I hadn't rented anywhere previously because I didn't have enough money for the obligatory deposit. Thankfully, as I knew the girl, she let me move in without putting down a deposit. Even if I could only afford to stay there a couple of months, at least I would be away from the drug den.

Marina came to help me move. She was the only friend I had at that time who had a car. Actually, she was the only friend I had who knew how to drive. We loaded a few of my boxes of stuff into the lift but, as I loaded the boxes from the lift into the car, some of them were left unattended for a few moments. On my return to collect them, I saw two young lads trying to walk off with them. That's fucking Peckham for you! I shouted after them, half smiling at their cheek, and they returned the boxes, apologising profusely. 'Sorry miss, we didn't think they belonged to anyone.' Such charming liars!

Two weeks after I left Peckham, I heard that one of the druggies, a bloke I actually thought was reasonably nice, had copied Studs's door key and sold it to a Nigerian family. A big tough Nigerian man had let himself into Studs's flat one day and ordered Studs to leave. 'This flat belongs to me now. Move!' he ordered. Studs didn't argue but meekly picked up his belongings and moved out. It scared me that had

CHAPTER 11

I not moved when I did, I would have been in that flat and kicked out onto the streets too, with nowhere to go. My parents had made it clear that they didn't want me back in Morden any more than I wanted to go back there. I was determined to climb up a rung of the property ladder and to live independently; and now I had a legal paid-for home to do it in. It might have been only a bedsit – but it was *my* bedsit.

Before I moved into Studs's, I'd started dating a punk called Spring. He was nicknamed that on account of his bounciness and would bounce down the street rather than walk. He certainly had a spring in his step.

I'd met Spring at a gig. He lived in the same council estate as my mate Sharon. The first time I spoke to Spring, he asked me to marry him. We were sat on the floor of the Tube station after a gig and he asked me to meet him outside Brixton Registry Office the next day and we'd get hitched. Spring made me laugh and, the next time we saw each other, we started to go out together.

I soon got Spring a job in Scole's when they were short-staffed. Having introduced so many friends to jobs there previously, the manager asked me if I knew anyone else, so I naturally suggested Spring, as he was in need of a bit of cash. She was shocked, to say the least, when he turned up. Spring was always a bit... well... grubby-looking, with dirty hands and usually a sticking plaster or two concealing some wound or other he'd managed to pick up. He wore 24-hole DMs (Doc Martens – the footwear of choice for the fashion-savvy punks and skinheads about town). One boot had been hand-painted with highlighter-pen yellow-and-green spots, and the other with a completely different design I don't recall. Punks weren't that much into symmetry. He also wore ripped green combat trousers, faded black T-shirts and a distressed black leather jacket (from back when 'distressed' meant you'd worn the shit out of something, not bought it that way and paid extra because it looked like someone else had worn it for you).

Spring was six foot or so, with a matching larger-than-life presence. He had a crimson Mohican haircut that was smoothed back against his head and tied in a ponytail at the back. On meeting him, the manageress blushed, turning the same colour as Spring's Mohican. He really wasn't what she'd been expecting, but she'd already promised me she'd give him a try, so he was put on bread-buttering, the gateway job in the sandwich-making business, for about five minutes at least, before being relegated to deliveries. He didn't last long on deliveries either.

Spring was definitely a character. He was very pleased one day because a tramp had handed him a pound coin, telling him that he thought he needed it more than he did. Many punks would beg for money, but Spring had managed to get money without even trying – from another beggar, no less, who really was homeless. He saw this as quite an accomplishment.

He was always getting himself embroiled in trouble. He had the kind of face that complete strangers just wanted to punch and I saw it happen a few times. We'd get on a bus together and someone would pick an argument with him and, before I knew it, he'd end up in a punch-up and get thrown off the bus. Probably not the kind of man my folks would have wanted for me, but I liked him.

We were doing two's up on my bike one day near St Paul's Cathedral, with me sat on the saddle, whilst he stood up and pedalled. We were happily hurtling downhill when a man in a suit suddenly jumped in front of the bike and demanded that Spring dismount. He began shouting that he was a plain-clothes policeman and that it was against the law to ride with two people on a bicycle. We looked at him, startled, unsure whether he was making it up. The besuited copper in disguise shoved Spring off the bike, so that he whacked his own balls on the bike's crossbar. Strange little things like that used to happen to him a lot. He seemed capable of attracting trouble without even trying.

On another occasion, he turned up at mine about 3am excitedly cradling a bag full of stolen goods. He claimed he'd tried to steal a car and had found the bag inside. He set off happily the next morning to sell the booty having borrowed my chunky bike, which he ended up trashing on the Elephant and Castle roundabout. God knows how he managed to do that but, on this occasion, he didn't manage to thwack his cobblers. My poor bike remained chained to railings for months.

Chapter 11

I couldn't collect it with its broken wheel and eventually the council took it away.

Spring once convinced me to go to Brighton with him for a day trip. The catch of course was that he had no money, or at least none that he wished to squander on train fares, so we bunked the train in London and when we got to Brighton we climbed over a high fence to avoid paying.

We sat on the pebble beach drinking cider, like good punks, and then decided to stay the night, so we squeezed beneath an upturned catamaran and used a Union Jack flag as a blanket. The punk bedding of choice.

Another night, Spring invited me to the cinema, which was strange in itself as it wasn't the sort of thing we really did – I wondered how many walls we'd have to scale to get in for free. He said he would collect me at 7pm. Suspiciously, I agreed, wondering what the catch was. I didn't see or hear from Spring again until two years later. Which was probably a blessing.

Chapter 12

Dalston

So there I was in my own bedsit in a brand spankingly new house that was owned by the wealthy father of a girl I knew, who had decided to invest in this newly built house just off the very shabby Ridley Road Market in Dalston, Hackney. It was a sharp contrast to the rest of the area, which was dirty and run-down. Back then, Hackney was filthy and neglected – an amalgamation of dog-eared four-storey Victorian houses that looked like they could do with a wash and dodgy-looking tower blocks scattered haphazardly along unevenly paved and litter-strewn streets lined with clapped-out old motors. And you should have seen it on a bad day. Hackney has up and come now, gentrification having turned it into one of the most fashionable areas in North London, but it wasn't up and coming when I lived there.

The house itself though was made from clean new yellow bricks and I was the first person ever to live in it. To say that made me feel special, after years of squatting in run-down buildings with mostly dodgy squat-mates, is an understatement. I felt like the Queen of England. And my bedsit was at the very top of the house – the penthouse if you will. It was clean and new and fresh. It was tiny, but comfortable and, best of all, it was mine. I had a lock on the door, my own bathroom and toilet and a kitchenette. And I didn't have to share them with anyone. Peace and privacy. One's corgis would even have approved. Priceless!

And I had a brand-new bed delightfully encased in fresh new linen. From Habitat, no less. No second-hand mattress of dubious parentage on the floor. This was posher than anything I'd previously lived in, my parents' place included. It was the antithesis of living in a squat. I relished the smell of the new cotton bedding and loved the clean white walls, like a housewife in a Daz commercial.

The kitchenette was separated from the single bed by a small venetian blind, giving me barely enough room to cook something without the blind touching my bum, although that could have been considered a perk in itself. There was a two-ring hob and a small fridge that did its best to keep me awake at night with its gentle humming. If you've ever tried to sleep in the same room as a fridge, you'll know what I mean. And it was situated a foot away from my head. It was like being an extra in *Eraserhead*.

I had everything but the kitchen sink. No, I mean I really didn't have a kitchen sink. In order to wash up I'd have to fill a washing-up bowl from the bathroom sink, put it in the bath and kneel down. But what did I care at that time? I felt like royalty. Plus, to compensate for the lack of a kitchen, I had a bathroom with a normal-sized bath, for which I treated myself to some posh bubble bath, knowing that no one else was going to use it but me. I was feeling pretty fucking special.

The toilet broke the first night I was there. I'd invited four friends over for a house-warming party to celebrate my arrival in the upper echelons of society. I had more than four friends at the time, but I didn't have enough house to warm them in, so four friends it was. And it turned out to be a blessing as the toilet cistern couldn't cope with its new role and started to leak. It got repaired the next day but I was castigated and told not to overuse the toilet again. Just how one goes about overusing a toilet, I was never really sure.

Jane, whose dad owned the building, also lived in the house. Her bedroom was beneath my bedsit and she shared her living room and kitchen, which were both good sizes, with a boy from her college. Annoyingly, he was only charged £15 a week rent and had a massive room, yet I was charged £65. In those days, £65 a week was quite a high rent, even in London. Now, it wouldn't get you the last remaining corner in an old skip parked on the Cally Road but back then it was a decent amount of money.

One of the conditions of me moving in, which in retrospect I should have been wary of, was that I had to sign an agreement which stated that I wouldn't go to the Fair Rents Panel, where they could legally fix the rent at a fair price for the accommodation being rented. I signed the document, eager to move in, but took it to the Fair

CHAPTER 12

Rents Panel anyway, who told me that the document itself was illegal. Hackney Council would only pay £60 of the rent for me, as I was on the Enterprise Allowance Scheme, so I had to make up the other £5 from my part-time cash-in-hand job at Scole's.

I lived almost entirely off leftover sandwiches during this period. And, being vegetarian, that limited my diet further to cheese, avocado (even if they did remind me of slimy limbless frogs) or a cheese-and-slimy-limbless-frog combo. Despite one's private cooking facilities, I didn't take advantage of them very often. At the end of Ridley Road, there was a 24-hour bagel bakery that I often ended up in. I think my diet at that time must have been mostly gluten with a side order of cider at a ratio of approximately 76:24.

I still spent as much time as I could at gigs and parties and frequented rock clubs like the Astoria or Busby's on Tottenham Court Road in the centre of London, mostly with Cindy, who I'd stayed friends with. Our musical tastes had changed somewhat and we'd started to frequent a pub in Wardour Street, Soho called the Intrepid Fox or, as everyone called it, 'the Fox'. The Fox was full of goths and metalheads; most people wore black and had alternative or gothic make-up and hair. The walls and ceiling of the Fox were plastered with tour posters from the likes of Motörhead, Guns N' Roses, the Black Crowes and the Red Hot Chili Peppers. The chandeliers in the upstairs bar were made out of an assortment of items, such as old syringes, dismembered Sindy dolls and a mishmash of other weird or gruesome stuff that had all been painted matt black. The bar staff seemed to have been selected for their bizarre appearance rather than their ability to pour a pint, and there was a time when they all modelled black-and-red rubber fetish wear. It turned out that they were advertising one of the local sex shops.

The music was generally so loud that you couldn't hear the person next to you speak, meaning that they would have to scream in your ear, which makes you wonder why we didn't just stay at home and listen to music very loudly. I think this experience – combined with many years of going to extremely loud gigs and playing in punk bands, which meant standing near massive speakers – didn't do me any favours. I would often come home with my ears ringing and hearing a whistling noise that would last for a few days afterwards, which I thought was normal.

Post-punk had become alternative, meaning the alternative to mainstream, although so many so-called alternative people seemed strangely judgmental to me. If you dared to dress outside of what was considered cool within the subculture, you were ostracised by the very people who were supposed to think it was cool to look different.

I still made my own clothes from time to time, still with my mum's faithful old portable sewing machine. It was 1987 and tight Lycra leggings were in fashion so, being the rainbow personified that I am, I'd made myself some bold leggings from wildly psychedelic Lycra I'd found at Berwick Street Market. I wore them proudly to the Fox, only to discover a group of people all dressed the same as each other who were staring at me and making rude comments intentionally within earshot. 'Oh my god! What IS she wearing?' I heard one girl say, as she stared right at me. Ironic coming from alternative people who wanted to be different from the mainstream! Shame they weren't able to act differently to the mainstream too.

Upstairs in the Fox was for the 'elite' only and you had to show your elite membership card to gain entry. Looking back, I'm not sure that this was much different to the way in which the trendy mainstream poncey clubs we all despised functioned, except that here the clientele all wore black and the music was heavier. There are cliques everywhere.

Some of the girls we knew had jobs in the local peep shows in Soho. One started off 'modelling' lingerie apparently but, after a few months, went on to work 'the slots'. I've never been to a peep show because I don't have testicles but the girls told me all about it. Gullible men paid decent sums of cash to look through a slot at a badly paid stripper and, as soon as their money ran out, the slot slammed shut. At this point, the only way to get the slot to reopen was to ply it with more money. Sad really. The girls had to encourage the men to part with as much cash as possible by prolonging their strip or by using other sure-fire winners, like simulating sex with another girl or using a vibrator. One girl told me that she got reprimanded for using the vibrator too soon, as you had to wait until the men had parted with

Chapter 12

a certain amount of cash before you 'pulled tricks' that might finish them off. Some of the girls we knew from the nightclubs wore similar clothes for clubbing to what they wore for their peep-show jobs. They figured that they were wearing skimpy clothes anyway, so why not get paid for it?

Like me, most of my crowd and the people around me were drinking very heavily and regularly and using speed to help stay awake at nightclubs, as the days (or nights) of clubs closing at 3am were long gone. One of my favourite clubs was called Slimelight, and was near the Angel Tube. It was a piss-take of the more famous and more mainstream Limelight Club in Central London. I managed to get into the Limelight once, but it was exceptionally boring. The Slimelight was much more up my goth alley.

The Slimelight would open after the pubs had shut and stayed open until 7am. No one could stay awake that long without a little pharmaceutical help. Those who couldn't afford or obtain speed took other stimulants, such as Pro Plus caffeine tablets. They gave me palpitations, so I stuck to drink and the odd dib-dab of speed if anyone should offer it to me. I rarely bought it myself.

The loud pumping music in the Slimelight seemed to travel right through your bones. It was heavy industrial goth, punk and rock. Inside, the club was filled with a thick suffocating fog of cigarette smoke and dry ice, which meant that you couldn't actually see the dance floor. Lots of very pissed and drugged-up young people wearing restrictive clothing and unable to actually see – what could possibly go wrong?

I would often fumble my way across the dance floor to the toilet or bar, edging along slowly in case I bumped into anyone; and then, as the dry ice settled, I'd realise there was actually no one to bump into anyway. Dry ice was a good way to make a club look busy when in fact it was empty.

A typical Saturday night round about then would consist of meeting my old *Sounds* penfriend Cindy in the Fox to get merry on cider or snakebites, stopping off in Piccadilly Circus for a bean burger at Burger King and to use their toilets to reapply make-up and style hair and then getting the No. 38 bus to the Angel for Slimelight.

Soap the Stamps, Jump the Tube

One night, while Cindy and I were negotiating a pea-souper of dry ice and fag smoke, we were approached by a guy with a red Mohican who must have been six foot four and who was with another shorter guy with dyed-black spiky hair and a pierced nose. They introduced themselves as Joe and Chas.

I quickly got chatting to Joe, who was a despatch rider (a different despatch rider to the one I had dated in Peckham) and who liked to talk about bikes. He said he had a huge Kawasaki 1100cc bike. I'd developed a passion for motorbikes when I'd gone to Greece with Dylan when I was 19. He'd hired a motorbike and taken me on the back. We rode without helmets, the wind in our hair as he negotiated hairpin bends along beautiful mountain paths with amazing vistas over azure waters. I was instantly hooked.

I talked to Joe about motorbikes for most of the night and he came back to my bedsit in Dalston after we left the club. He convinced me that we could walk back to mine as it wasn't far from Angel to Dalston, but I think perhaps he meant by bike as it seemed to take hours. Actually, it DID take hours.

I dated Joe for a while and he helped me procure my very first motorbike, which was a rather humble MZ 125cc. I bought it second-hand from a lady who advertised it on a card in the window of Burwin Motorcyles on Essex Road. It had done just a paltry 400 miles, so was practically new. MZs weren't a popular make and the bike itself was, well, strange-looking, which made it cheap. It was a two-stroke, and a kick-start, and was pretty much considered the Lada of the motorbike world. I didn't give a fuck about bike snobbery. It was bright red and clashed really well with the psychedelic leggings I'd worn to the Fox that night. I absolutely loved it.

One night, during one of our conversations that wasn't completely centred around bikes, Joe revealed that he used to have a Mohican similar to Chas's and had worn a shirt with the Subhumans skull icon on the back. He said he'd seen the Lost Cherrees play a few years ago and I was sure that I'd seen him before, as the description sounded really familiar. I told him that I used to write to people via the *Sounds* music paper and he said he did too. It then suddenly dawned on me that this Joe was the same sexy Joe with the Mohican who I had writ-

Chapter 12

ten to years ago. The same Joe that Perry had stolen my phone number from. He was very shocked when I relayed what had happened with Perry to him, and was glad that they'd not remained friends after he'd left the building they'd both lived in. We wondered if fate had intervened and brought us together after all.

Joe revealed that he had just split up with his wife. They lived together in North Kensington and he was waiting for her to move out. It also turned out that she was seven months pregnant with a baby Joe. He told me he didn't want anything to do with his ex or the baby but I didn't think he would feel like that forever. In my heart, I knew he would be curious about his child when she was born and it was possible he would get back together with his ex-wife for the sake of the baby. I felt I'd be with him until that happened.

I stayed in Dalston for less than a year as the bedsit literally started to fall apart around me. Shelves came crashing down, showering me with books, and I got the blame for putting things on the shelves that were too heavy. So what you're saying is, don't put books on the bookshelves? The landlord, Jane's dad, said he would be round the next day to fix the shelves but I said that wasn't convenient for me as I had already made other arrangements.

The next day, I was happily crimping my dark-purple shoulder-length hair when I became aware that the door handle was turning. I looked up just as Jane's dad came into the room, without knocking, uninvited. I told him it was rude not to knock because I could have been undressed, in the bath or in bed and that I was busy and could he come back another time? He ignored me and started drilling right next to me so that the drill dust fell into my keyboard between the keys. I was furious and we had a blazing row, after which I decided the best course of action would be to move out. I didn't want this rude man letting himself into my room again. I didn't feel safe. And they were either dramatically overcharging me or dramatically undercharging the other tenants.

A friend of mine said that there was a room going in her shared house in Tottenham and there was no deposit to pay, which was lucky, as I didn't have the money for one. I handed in my notice for the bedsit and Jane's dad took the news badly of course because I said

I was moving out in two weeks. I was meant to give at least a month's notice and he was worried about not being able to find the next tenant to rip off within a fortnight, so he decided to charge me for damages that I hadn't incurred. There was a little wear and tear, but nothing serious. He was a horrid man and I really felt sorry for Jane, who was stuck with him as her dad. I ignored his request to cough up money for damages and moved out. Fuck him. And anyway, Chapter 12.5 is next.

Chapter 12.5

Extracts from my diary of 1988

6 JANUARY 1988

Got up early this morning. Lippy from the sandwich bar invited me to his place for a traditional German meal. I've never tried German food before and I can't wait to try sauerkraut. He wants to hear me sing as he needs a backing singer for his band.

Lippy persuaded me to come to the Pyramid club tonight even though I'm skint. First, I popped in to see a couple of the other guys from the sandwich bar at their flat in Elephant and Castle. The boys were getting ready to go out too, and caking their faces with loads of make-up. Lippy joined us later, dressed as a cowboy. On the way to the club, we bumped into some other boys in make-up who kept staring at me – one in particular. Puzzled, I ignored them until the one who had been staring the most, came up to me and said, 'Aren't you going to speak to Spring's brother then?'

How bizarre! I haven't seen Phil, Spring's brother, in ages, but my Tarot cards did reveal I was going to bump into someone from my past! Phil told me that him and Spring had had a massive row and now live in separate parts of London and that Spring had been run over. (Shit like that is always happening to Spring.)

The sandwich bar boys had got us free tickets to get in and free drinks vouchers. I went back home to Lippy's but stayed in the spare room. I was so tired, I could have slept on bricks.

8 JANUARY 1988

Full of flu today but still went to work at the sandwich bar. Dosed up on chamomile, honey and lemon, and rubbed Tiger Balm into my temples and forehead. Lippy invited me over to his place. I sat at the front, upstairs on the bus, on the way to Lippy's and there were only two other men on it. I asked one of the men if I was on the right bus to Angel. He said yes, but I was sure it wasn't. When we got to Mildmay Park, the man I'd asked stood up and came to sit next to me. *Fucking Typical* – an almost empty bus and he had to come and sit right next to me. Hadn't he heard of personal space! Told him not to wind me up, and got off the bus and got the next one. Totally pissed off. I've not travelled alone for ages and now I am reminded why I don't.

Got to Lippy's but didn't mention the weirdo on the bus. Did some singing and played some keyboards with him. He recorded my voice and I was surprised it sounded alright despite not having sung for over five years.

POP WILL EAT ITSELF
UNIVERSITY OF LONDON UNION (ULU)
15 JANUARY 1988

Started the day by buying a personal stereo (a Walkman) with graphic equaliser from Tempos. Now I can have music wherever I go. It was just £17.99 and the last one in the shop. I also treated myself to a pair of black stilettoes. Not sure I will be able to walk in them as I've become used to wearing men's flat boots as they are more comfortable and fit my big feet better.

Went to Pop Will Eat Itself later. The union was unsurprisingly full of drunk students. The drinks are amazingly cheap. The support bands were boring but the place was packed. I tried to dance with a couple of mates when Pop Will Eat Itself came on, but it was too rough and sweaty so I gave up. It was a great gig though.

Missed Cindy – we'd arranged to meet at The Intrepid Fox but I was delayed and didn't make it to the St Moritz club either, in case she wasn't there either. I went home and was listening to the Walkman at the bus stop but I could still hear a loud drunk who was staring at me and going on about the 'thing' in my nose, saying, 'There's a girl

CHAPTER 12.5

at my office with a thing in her nose! Who are you all working for? That's what I want to know...'

MUM'S 50TH BIRTHDAY PARTY
16 JANUARY 1988

Dad threw a surprise party for mum's 50th at their social club. I'd spent the day cutting out some fabric so I could make a jacket and skirt. I might sell it when it's made as the fabric is a bit too boring for me. Cindy asked me to come to The Intrepid Fox and the St Moritz night club after my mum's party. (Cindy had a spare ticket for me for the Full Tilt at the Electric Ballroom last night, but I missed her by five minutes. Typical!)

Mum's party was full of people her age and I was the youngest one there. I couldn't think of anything to talk about and got bored of being asked the same questions about where I was living, if I was working, did I have a boyfriend, and other conventional tick boxes.

Made the most of the free booze and decided to stay the night at Mum's instead of clubbing. Dad was banned from drinking whiskey as he was pissed enough on the beer. Mum's best friend confided in me that Mum is back to secret drinking at home. I wish she hadn't told me because now I feel responsible for Mum and I don't have the energy to look after her. I think she needs to get help. I'll have a chat with my sister about it.

17 JANUARY 1988

Mum's birthday. Woke up at 7.30am. and dashed back to Dalston, having stayed the night in Morden. I was just in time to grab my stock of jewellery and rush off again to Camden Market. Debbie, Cindy's friend, was on the bus and said she was doing the stall with us, which was a surprise as Cindy hadn't mentioned it. She's made brooches from bits of an old amplifier. None of us sold much and still had the stall rent to pay – but at least it was divided three ways. Cindy didn't sell anything at all so she's going to try to sell the rest of her stuff down Carnaby Street tomorrow as she is desperate for money.

25 JANUARY 1988

Worked at the sandwich bar and Lippy says he wants me to make him and his mate some jackets that they can wear on stage.

Vince thanked me for bringing him a fish slice on Friday. He's thrown a party and everyone had to bring a fish slice (an implement for picking up cooked fish, not a slice of fish!). He ended up with about 30 fish slices. He's going to keep the best ones and give the rest away.

I met one of Cindy's flatmates, Mork, who'd been at the PWEI gig a couple of weeks ago, and she gave me a compilation tape she's made me with PWEI, New Model Army, the Mission and Sisters of Mercy on it. She also gave me a book on dreams. (Two other people have given me dream interpretation books – must be trying to tell me I sleep too much or live in a dream world!) She also gave me a Cancerian bookmark, which was beautiful and I didn't have the heart to tell her I'm a Leo.

Went to see Fatal Attraction at the cinema with Cindy. It was packed. Great film.

5 FEBRUARY 1988

The area manager at work gave us a talk about cleanliness today. She said a bloke had bought a sandwich yesterday and there was a drawing pin in it and he's eaten it. All his mouth was ripped up and he's been rushed to hospital. Unfortunately, he works for the papers and wants to write a story about it. We are in deep shit. Everyone has had their bonuses stopped. How can someone eat a drawing pin without realising it? Everyone felt really bad and guilty. The drawing pin must have dropped off the noticeboard into the shredded lettuce below. Today the lettuce was moved.

CHAPTER 12.5

Went to visit Mum in Morden and found some old letters from Dave the keyboard player in Adventures in Colour. Has it really been six years since I was in that band?

3 MARCH 1988

12.21am. I've just returned from the Fulham Greyhound pub after seeing Loop, the Junior Manson Slags and Bastard Kestrel. Keith Goldhanger, who introduced me to Deb (Lost Cherrees), is now in Bastard Kestrel. It was great to see him and Deb and her sister Catherine. They are all looking well.

Work was hideous. I nearly walked out. Wanted to tell all the customers to fuck off. I've had enough. In the end, I asked the manager if I could do deliveries instead as I am bound to crack soon if I keep working like a fucking robot. He said 'Ok!' Great!

6 APRIL 1988

Now working at the cycle courier job. Glad to have left the sandwiches behind. Was sent to the wrong address and wasted 20 mins at the wrong end of Holborn. Some twat went into the back of me as I was on my way home. The back wheel is bent and now wobbles when I cycle. I'll take it to a bike shop for repair tomorrow, my hands and face are black from London grime.

26 APRIL 1988

Went to the motorbike shop in Dalston lane (Jon's Scooters) to find out about motorbike courses in Hackney. The despatch riding on a bicycle is killing me. Cindy suggested I try cleaning jobs instead as I could make £3.60 an hour doing that.

27 APRIL 1988

It was raining which meant I got soaked doing the courier work. However, there was more work than usual, which was handy as it's pay per drop, meaning you only get paid for each letter or package you deliver and not an hourly rate. I popped into the sandwich bar where I used to work and was offered a free sandwich but then, on seeing the boss, I was then asked to pay for it in case my mate got in to trouble.

I popped into the hair dressing wholesalers for some plum hair dye but they were out of it, so I bought midnight blue instead. I've some red rose dye at home, so if I mix it with the blue, it will be the right shade of purple I'm wanting.

I got back to the office at work at 6pm. I was soaked through and my feet were squelching. By the time I left at 7pm, it had stopped raining. My wages were a measly £56 for the week.

4 MAY 1988

Dreamt about letters last night. Got to work just after 8.30am. and was given 13 letters to take to SE1. Delivered them all before 11am. I still haven't got my wages, so the boss lent me £20 and asked if I was coming in tomorrow. I said yes, so long as I'm not knocked down on the way home or on the way there in the morning.

So what happens on my way home? Yep, I get knocked down! Some prat in a red car decides to turn left into a place called Wilmington Square, in Clerkenwell, just by the pub. I couldn't brake properly in the wet weather, so I yelled to the driver and he braked but was still in my way! I tried to follow the car round rather than crash into him but still managed to crash into his wing mirror. I landed on the pavement in a crumpled heap in front of the stationary car. I was so shocked, that I just lay there for a few moments and the bastard driver didn't even come out of his car to see if I was ok!

Shaking, I got back on my feet and shouted at him. I wrote his

CHAPTER 12.5

number plate down and he wrote down the courier company number from my despatch bag. Luckily the bike was ok but I have bruises on my leg and a few lumps are now appearing. The driver moaned about his expensive wing mirror. I couldn't believe the selfish prick! I told him it was lucky it was just a broken wing mirror. My leg could have been broken – or worse! I told him if he'd been using his precious mirror, he would have seen me and not turned, so he clearly didn't need it anyway!

LORDS OF THE NEW CHURCH
THE MARQUEE CLUB
12 MAY 1988

Managed to get a ticket to Lords of the New Church tonight. I knew the doorman and he said he's often seen me cycling around Mayfair as he's also a van driver during the day. Small world. The band were brilliant and played my favourite songs – 'Russian Roulette' and 'Dance with me?' Ended the night by going to the Intrepid Fox and then the Kit Kat club. Must remember to eat the Kit Kat they give you – last time, I left it in my pocket and it melted. A mate was on the door and said I could get in free if I said my name was Rose, which was handy as I was skint and didn't have enough to get in *and* buy drinks.

26 MAY 1988

Started the night in The Intrepid Fox. The midget jewellery seller was there. He came over and asked us if we wanted anything. I said no and as I went to pick my drink up, my hand brushed something cold. I looked down and saw the midget had his dick hanging out. At first I gave him the benefit of the doubt and thought he'd forgotten to put it away after a pee. Then he said to Cindy, 'See anything you fancy?' I told her to look down, and he walked away. We saw his dick sticking right out – full on boner! Yuk!

STAR RIDER MOTORCYCLE COURSE
6 AUGUST 1988

Despite getting up early this morning, the MZ (motorbike) took ages to start. Joe had to do it for me in the end. First he took me to get some petrol. I was really nervous so he took me to the Star Rider course. Escorting me on my little MZ125 while he was on his big fuck-off Kawasaki. I was half an hour late, but they still let me join the class. I passed the test! Joe was amazed – he couldn't believe it and neither could I! I was really proud of myself.

Chapter 13

Tottenham

I moved to Tottenham with mixed feelings. I was glad to be away from Dalston and onto the next adventure but Tottenham wasn't one of London's most attractive areas. My new place was in need of renovation in 'a rapidly up-and-coming area', as an estate agent might describe it. I'd call it a right dump. The house itself was OK but, like Peckham, Tottenham had a reputation for being an extremely rough area. Plus we were located a stone's throw from Tottenham Hotspur's football ground. However, we weren't near the high street or any of the other main trouble hot spots. On Saturdays, the local shops would close early if there was a home match and coppers on horseback would patrol the streets.

My room was large, with a double bed in it, for a change, on the ground floor. I was sharing with Mary and her boyfriend Sean, although after a few months they split up and he moved out. Mary was much shorter than me, well most women were, but Mary was MUCH shorter than me. She came up to my shoulder. She wore ankle-length hippy skirts in flowing fabrics and her long natural brown hair was crimped. I told you, crimping was big business in the '80s. We were all doing it. Hair crimpers to the '80s were as hair straighteners are to the current day. Except men crimped too.

Nic also lived there. He was a goth with long dyed-black crimped hair – which was pretty much the only goth hairstyle throughout the '80s. He often layered it and backcombed it glam-rocker style, which was becoming a thing. Nic bedecked himself with heaps of real silver jewellery and wore a nose ring as well as several earrings in each ear. He often wore jeans and a faded denim jacket and big loose shirts undone at the chest. He was a lot of fun and often made us laugh. He had painted his room black and was the only tenant with a lock on his door. Nic was like a Russell Brand prototype.

My own hair was shoulder length by this point, and I had dyed it purple while I was in Dalston, but I'd become fed up with the purple dye coming off on everything, including my motorbike helmet, pillows, hairbrushes, boyfriends, wallpaper, my own face, passers-by and neighbours. I wore chunky silver rings on every finger but soon found that motorbike gloves got caught on them so I'd had to take the more intricate ones off. Was I becoming old and sensible? Luckily, no. I still managed to wear a massive ring that was so big it concealed half my hand. It was made from silver and was in the shape of Neptune, the god of the sea. Neptune's fishtail curled round my finger and he held a trident aloft. I also wore an eyeball ring that I'd bought from The Great Frog, a high-end alternative jewellers off Carnaby Street, where lots of rich and famous alternative personalities, such as Lemmy from Motörhead, bought iconic pieces and paid large amounts of money to have items specially commissioned.

The eyeball ring was made with a resin eyeball set into silver, with snakes as eyelids. It used to unnerve people as the eye was so realistic. The jewellers used 'real' fake eyeballs bought from ocularists and from the medical industry. My ring was superb.

By now it was 1988. Both men and women in those days, in the circles I moved in at least, wore spandex leggings and blouson shirts with loud designs. I was still riding the MZ but I already had my real eyes on something more powerful, having successfully passed my bike test. I didn't like the plastic Japanese bikes that were so prominent on the roads. The Japanese bikes were often snobbily referred to as 'Jap crap'. I favoured classic British bikes, although there was no way I could afford to buy one and I wasn't mechanically minded enough to keep one on the road either. I wanted something made of metal, all shiny chrome like the custom bikes I saw in *Back Street Heroes* magazine, which I now bought on a regular basis in order to quench my burgeoning thirst for all things bike.

So, I put my thoughts out to the universe that I wanted a more powerful bike and that the keyword would be 'cheap'. A short time later, I mentioned to an aunt that I was after a better motorbike. She immediately told me that my other aunt and her partner had an old bike they wanted to get rid of, and that they were on the brink of

CHAPTER 13

taking to the dump to be scrapped for metal. A phone call secured me a classic collectible 1970s ex-racing bike – a Suzuki GT500. It was still in working order and I was told that, if it passed the MOT, it was mine for free! My aunt, Annette, and her partner, Jim, were in their forties and had decided they were too old for motorbikes, which is insane – so long as I can fit the crash helmet over my rollers and squeeze my varicose-veined legs into leather trousers (with an elasticated waist) I intend to still be riding bikes into my eighties and beyond.

I fell in love with the bike the moment I saw it. I didn't care that it was Japanese. I'm not racist. It was metal and chrome and perfect. In fact, it looked very similar to a British bike, so really, I got exactly what I'd petitioned the universe for. Thanks uni baby. When I said 'cheap' I hadn't meant free but, hey, thanks for listening! I couldn't believe my luck and was amazed at the effectiveness of putting my thoughts out there and making a quick call on the psychic telephone. Using the psychic telephone – or 'cosmic ordering' I believe the more popular term is – is much like prayer: you might not know who it is you are asking for help, but trust that your request will be heard and acted on in some way. It works for me.

The Suzuki turned heads wherever we went, although probably for all the wrong reasons as it was a two-stroke, which was unusual for a big bike. Oh, and because it was extremely loud. Oh yeah, and because thick trails of black smoke spewed from both exhaust pipes. People could hear me coming from half a mile away and, if they didn't hear me, they could see me. Or smell me. Or my bike, at least.

I often had truckers pull up alongside me when I stopped at traffic lights and lean out of their cabs in order to compliment my bike. A few even offered to buy it off me as it was rare and collectible, but I refused to be parted from it, even if bits did sometimes drop off on long runs. I promised myself that one day I would do it up and restore it to its former glory.

One drawback of my beloved bike was that it had to be kick-started, not like modern bikes with their fancy electric ignitions. The kick-start pedal was high up and, because of my rheumatic knee, I would have to lift my leg into position on the pedal with both hands and then force my leg down to start the engine. It must have looked odd. I told you we turned heads.

However, when it started, it had a deep throaty roar that transformed into a purr of contentment. Bill the witch had taught me about totem animals and psychic protection, so I would visualise a proud and fierce lioness on the back seat (wearing a helmet, of course) protecting me as I rode and looking after my bike when it was parked.

Before Mary's boyfriend Sean moved out he owned a Vespa and his friend, Saucy Jon, often visited on his Lambretta. After Sean moved out, Jon lived on our sofa for a while. He earned the name 'Saucy' Jon because he would go up to girls in nightclubs and use the line, 'Hello, you're a bit saucy!' to chat them up. He'd follow this with a come-to-bed Essex wink and some cheeky banter – and that was often enough to ensure he didn't go home alone.

Whilst he was inhabiting the sofa, Saucy Jon decided that he would sell his Lambretta and buy a Triumph instead. He came back one day as excited as a puppy with a squeaky ball and announced proudly that he'd bought a Triumph Bonneville. 'Let's take a look at it,' we enthused and watched bewildered as he brought the bike into the kitchen. In a series of boxes. Subsequently, over a period of months, he set about lovingly restoring it. In our kitchen. But fair play to him, he was meticulous and did a fantastic job of painstakingly putting it back together and in full working order. I couldn't even do a Rubik's cube. Once it was in one final bike-shaped piece, he polished it to an incredibly high standard that made all the other bikes parked outside our gaff look shabby in comparison.

Saucy Jon had started to come to the same nightclubs as us and would park his bike outside Full Tilt Club on Friday nights at the Electric Ballroom in Camden and ask the bouncers to keep an eye on it. He would always bring a spare helmet in case he got lucky with a lady, although I'm not sure most women give a fuck what car or bike a man drives or rides. But 'Bonnies' *were* considered the third coolest bike you could possibly have, after a Harley Davidson and a Chopper.

Once inside the club, Saucy Jon would stand in the middle of the nightclub floor by the bar, holding both helmets and wearing a big grin whilst he surveyed the territory to see if any ladies had noticed

CHAPTER 13

that he was a bike owner. Personally, I'd chain my helmet to my bike, or leave it in the cloakroom, but then I wasn't trying to pull birds.

I did get a huge thrill out of being a female biker, though. There is a sense of power and pride in being able to control a big bike. Women were still considered the weaker sex in a lot of ways and it was assumed that they could only handle small bikes, mopeds or bus passes. In fact, it was mostly assumed that women couldn't ride bikes at all and just rode pillion on the back of their boyfriends' bikes. Wearing high heels and a bikini. Men would be surprised when I revealed that I rode a 500cc. I got a huge kick out of riding my bike and an even bigger one when I turned up at bike festivals dressed head to toe in black leather with a hot man as my pillion passenger (although not wearing high heels and swimwear).

Joe was with me on my 23rd birthday when I decided to get my first tattoo. I'd wanted one for a couple of years but hadn't found a design that I liked enough to commit to for the rest of my life. I wanted a fairy but couldn't find a tattooist who would lower himself to draw a fairy on me. Ridiculous, I know. In those days, tattoos were mainly carried out by men who were either mean-looking skinheads or burly and hirsute bikers in dodgy-looking back rooms. So drawing a fairy on a girl would have severely damaged their credibility. I mean, how would they ever live it down? Sebastian had taken me to a tattooist's at the Elephant and Castle when I was 21, but the two massive skinhead tattooists covered in really bad tattoos and whose knuckles were grazing the carpet grunted at me and said, 'We don't do fuckin' fairies here!'

Joe had told me about Lal Hardy in Muswell Hill, who'd been featured in several tattoo magazines and was quite happy to tattoo a fairy on my arm, because I was a girl and I was paying him and he knew that drawing a picture of a fairy would in no way alter his sperm count or make him a homosexual, if that's what the other tattooists were afraid of. In fact, Lal already had a fairy tattoo in his portfolio, so he was obviously no stranger to tattooing fantasy figures if that's what his paying customers requested.

It was my first-ever tattoo and so I braced myself as the design was transferred onto my skin. I had no idea what amount of pain I was about to endure. It was a hot day in July and not much air was circulating in the small studio. Lal started the tattoo gun and said he would start by doing one of the fairy's antennae so that I could gauge the pain. I was surprised that it felt more like being tickled than scarred for life with a vibrating ink pen. Thankfully, tattooing had evolved somewhat from the days of thick lines gouged into the skin with a spear by a Neanderthal to fine lines using much more sophisticated equipment, although I think you can still find the former operating tattoo parlours throughout England, if you so wish. Just don't ask them to do you a fairy, though.

We were all very AIDS- and hepatitis-aware back then as the AIDS breakout had only happened a few years previously. I therefore checked that a new needle and inks were being used. I didn't have to worry: Lal was the consummate professional and now has many celebrity clients who let him draw on them. Back in the summer of 1987, there was Lal, tattooing my arm and warning me that the closer the needle got to bone the more it would hurt. I would have adopted the brace position if he hadn't been using my arm to tattoo on, but fortuitously there is not much bone close to the surface on the upper arms, and the discomfort was bearable.

I was right in the middle of thinking how goddamn brave I was being and what a fearless 500cc-bike-riding hardcore Amazonian I was, when I decided it was a good time to take a peek at the work in progress. There was the needle of the gun carefully drawing permanent lines on my young plump skin, leaving a small rivulet of my fresh blood that Lal wiped away with a tissue. I watched my blood and the ink combine and then a thought popped into my head. Why is someone mutilating me? Why the fuck am I paying someone to do this to me? Call me weird but I don't even like pain.

I looked down again at my smearing blood and the emerging design and I suddenly started to feel very faint and asked Lal to stop. I went outside for some air and took some big breaths. When I returned, Joe teased me about my low pain threshold (oh he who will never give birth to a baby) and Lal leapt to my defence, saying he'd

Chapter 13

had many big strong blokes completely pass out while having tattoos and that I shouldn't feel embarrassed.

Eventually, my fairy was finished. In hindsight, I should have designed my own tattoo for uniqueness, but this one was cute. She was naked with perky breasts and long flowing hair, caught mid-flight. She cost me 25 quid. Pennies now, but a fair old sum at the time.

When my dad saw my tattoo, he tried to pass judgment, until I reminded him that he himself had a tattoo. My mum immediately said that people would think I was 'one of those girls'. What kind of girls did she think they might think I was, I queried. 'You know,' she replied, 'one of the girls in the porno films. They all seem to have tattoos.' When I asked her how she had managed to glean this fact, she realised what she'd said and smiled a little awkwardly before admitting to having seen the odd one or two... out of curiosity, of course.

A while later, I felt ink-lined to once again pay someone else to draw indelibly on me and make me bleed. This time I chose a lion's head to represent my star sign Pisces. OK, that was a joke. I'm a Leo. The lion's head image I chose was surrounded by a flurry of what looked like clouds. I wasn't entirely sure that I wanted the clouds but then the tattooist informed me that the clouds wouldn't cost me any extra so, always one to take advantage of a bargain, I thought fuck it: free pain! Someone was offering to hurt me for an additional 15 minutes and they weren't going to charge me extra for doing so – how could I resist? I was proud of my new 'tat' until I showed it to a work colleague and he said, 'Why is the lion wearing a bubble hat?' Indeed, the blue clouds could easily have been mistaken for blue bubbles. I was mortified.

Around this time, I was still wearing a lot of black but my image had morphed from punk to rock chick – biker jacket, cowboy boots, miniskirts, etc. I still embalmed myself in as much make-up as I could legally fit on my face before being arrested for impersonating a clown. Except when I was on the bike. Make-up and bike-riding really don't mix. When you put your helmet on your slap is perfect, but when you take it off, you look like an ancient map of Shanghai.

I started going to more rock-oriented clubs, such as the Astoria in Tottenham Court Road and Busby's next door (both now demolished). Here they would play rock and metal. A lot of the folk from the '80s punk scene had also gone down the hard-rock route as punk itself had kind of 'dyed' out. I also used to meet my gang of rock and biker friends at a place called the Elbow Room on Tottenham High Street. There was a tiny space out the back with a water feature consisting of a waterfall and several live goldfish. One night, one of our crowd had the bright idea of emptying an entire bottle of washing-up liquid into the water feature to see what would happen. Erm, duh! Surprisingly, the washing-up liquid began frothing over the sides of the water feature, moving towards the door like killer foam in a B-movie. Sadly, but not really surprisingly, all the goldfish died and when the landlord found out who was responsible he barred the individual.

Quite right – fucking idiot. There's a 'comedy' T-shirt I've often seen that says 'Instant arsehole – just add alcohol'. Yeah, that.

Our pad in Tottenham seemed to be the kind of place that attracted friends for a weekend but who'd then proceed to stay with us for months. Steph was one such person. She had separated from her boyfriend and moved onto the sofa for a few months while she sorted herself out. By then, Saucy Jon had moved into a real proper bedroom with his own walls and doors and a bed and stuff. Which is lucky, as I'm not sure the sofa was big enough to accommodate two full-size inhabitants.

One day, Nic announced that he had some free tickets for Stringfellows nightclub in London. Peter Stringfellow was, and still is as far as I'm aware, a sleazy businessman from Yorkshire who owned strip clubs and nightclubs throughout London. He has bleached-blond hair and is permanently slightly/very orange and looks like a cheap magician in a working men's club up north.

We dolled ourselves up to the nines although, to be honest, we were all so congenitally scruffy that we'd be lucky to be awarded a six. We assumed that we looked like unconventional rock stars but the bouncers at Stringfellows were less convinced. We weren't orange, middle-aged or flashing our credit cards and car keys about like the

CHAPTER 13

rest of the clientele, for a start. But we did just about manage to get in, mainly due to our nerve and because we already had tickets.

Wine was free from the bar before ten o'clock, which was precarious when you lived on the breadline. We took advantage of the fact by taking it in turns to grab as many glasses as we could, and stockpiling them for post-10pm usage. Needless to say, we wound up each downing about two bottles of on-the-house red or white. Having each sunk enough wine to tranquilise a small horse, we decided it was time to hit the dance floor. I have a vague recollection of me and Nic being reprimanded for swapping shirts in the middle of the dance floor. The bouncers pounced on us, and informed us that we must keep our clothes on, which was more ironic than an ironicky thing as Stringfellows was a strip club known for its pole dancers in skimpy, if any, underwear!

After we returned, our table had been cleared and we had been replaced by a well-dressed couple sipping champagne, with a bottle resting in the ice bucket and a martini glass filled with olives. The typical clientele of Stringfellows. As recompense for the theft of our table, I pilfered their olives.

Steph and I left, coincidentally not long after the free booze had run out, because not only could we not afford the extortionate prices charged at the bar but, quite frankly, this type of 'ambience' and the clientele repelled us. We staggered towards Trafalgar Square on a quest for a night bus. Steph was having trouble walking. Poor people and free alcohol is never a good combination, so we rested on a nearby wall. I was appalled by the number of men who came over to try to chat up Steph, as it was obvious she was extremely drunk. That incapacitated young girls are seen as such an easy target for unprincipled and predatory men makes me feel quite ill. These creeps were still coming up to her and asking her name and generally behaving like sleazy predators. The girl could barely stand!

We managed to make it to the right bus stop. The Tottenham bus eventually approached – *hoorah*, I thought, but then Steph became momentarily conscious just as the bus arrived and insisted she wanted to go back to her own place in Sydenham. When I tried to convince her to come back home with me, she refused and became belligerent.

SOAP THE STAMPS, JUMP THE TUBE

There was no way I was letting her go back home on a night bus on her own in her state, with all those arseholes hovering around. Oh the joys of friendship.

I even tried tricking her into getting on the Tottenham-bound bus with me but, just as the bus pulled up, she opened her eyes just enough to see it was a Tottenham bus and absolutely refused to get on it. Eventually, a bus to Sydenham materialised but Steph was unable to coordinate her legs enough to step onto it so that the bus driver refused to take her. Even the police had come over to check she was OK. An hour later, we finally managed to get on a bus. A Sydenham bus. I resigned myself to escorting her safely. Steph was leaning on me, comatose.

When we got off the bus, a kindly stranger offered to help me. I was glad of the help, and we were able to support her between the two of us.

The guy said he knew exactly where Steph's road was and we started limping slowly in that direction. After a while, everything suddenly began to feel unfamiliar. I'd been to Steph's a few times and I'd never taken this route. Instinctively, I knew we were heading in the wrong direction. Luckily, having handled a big motorbike for a few months, I had upper arms like He-Man, and was able to manoeuvre Steph back in the right direction, and away from the dark and deserted streets that the man was deliberately trying to take us to, for whatever motive.

The bloke still had his arm around Steph's waist and was refusing to let go, insisting that I couldn't manage her on my own. In fact I couldn't, but I didn't want this sick weirdo to know that. He refused to go away as I steered Steph towards her flat and I was aware of him groping Steph's arse. For fuck's sake.

I began to pray that Steph's estranged boyfriend, Ray, was at home and that the stranger wouldn't force himself into her flat and try to rape or attack us. Or worse. Steph realised she didn't have her keys on her and would have to wake Ray up to gain entry to the flat anyway. It was about four in the morning by now. As luck would have it, as we turned into her street, Steph regained consciousness a little.

'I hope the boys are home,' I said to her, loudly, trying to scare the

Chapter 13

stranger off. Maybe if he thought there were other men around he would back off and fuck off. He asked which house it was. I could see Steph's and Ray's motorbikes parked outside the flat.

'The one with all the bikes!' Steph slurred, hoping to give the impression we were mean bikers. She banged on the front door and, thankfully, Ray answered it. Steph stumbled in and innocently thanked the guy for his help, completely oblivious to anything that had happened.

The weirdo took one look at all six foot or so of Ray and made a hasty retreat, disappearing into the night. Apparently, he only liked easy targets. Steph had absolutely no memory of anything that happened that night, but I vowed never to get so drunk again and to always remain in control.

While I lived in Tottenham, I had a small accident on my MZ motorbike. I was just passing through Turnpike Lane, looking hot and Mad Max all in black, and the traffic was moving slowly. The car in front of me was creeping along at a pace that would make a snail look hasty, and I didn't realise it had actually stopped, as no brake lights came on. By the time I realised that I also needed to brake, it was too late and I whacked the car's rear bumper. I put my feet on the floor to steady myself just as the bike bounced back and forced the foot peg into my Mad Max–style motorbike boots. The boots were built more for fashion than practicality and the metal plate dented inwards, forcing one of the studs into my leg. I was stunned and so dismounted and wheeled the bike to the kerb in order to settle myself down, as I was a bit in shock, and to check for injuries. The car had already driven off, completely oblivious to the fact that I'd just splattered against the back of it.

As luck would have it, I had dismounted right outside a chemist's. I sat on the kerb and took my boot off to check I still had a foot and a few other things. A woman came out of the chemist's and asked if I was OK. I told her my leg was numb and she said that I'd better come into the shop to have it looked at. There was no visible damage apart from a bit of redness but my leg was rapidly swelling. She sprayed it with some kind of magic swollen-leg spray that she said would help bring the bruising out although, to be honest, my leg looked like it was having no problem performing this function all by itself. It was busy doubling in size, like I'd accidentally drunk some kind of leg-specific Alice-in-Wonderland potion.

The girls from the chemist's had heard the bang as I hit the back of the car (unlike the actual driver) and had come out to check I was OK, bless them. They encouraged me to go to the local hospital for an X-ray and said that they would keep an eye on my bike for me. By the time I arrived at the hospital, my left leg had grown exponentially from knee to toe and was turning a colour I'd describe as aubergine meets mauve. There were no breaks or fractures but there was internal bleeding and bruising and I was told to keep an eye on it to make sure it didn't get infected. Assuming that an infection would lead to amputation, I assured them, as they bandaged me up, that I'd keep an eye on it.

A few days later I was due to go on holiday with my mum and my sister, Dawn. Mum had heard me enthuse about the Greek island of Paros with such affection that she'd asked me to take her there on holiday. Dad had recently left her after years of cheating on her and she was now regularly drinking very heavily. Dawn had also recently come out as a lesbian, which had caused family tension.

Mum packed a massive suitcase, which contained a huge bottle of vodka and a massive jar of Nescafé coffee. She was worried she'd be unable to find vodka or Nescafé on a Greek island, despite my assurances that we were only travelling to another part of Europe, and not actually back in time.

Mum had booked an apartment for us on the other side of the island in close proximity to a lovely beach, but with little else unless you wanted to take a bus to another part of the island. Sadly, the holiday was mostly a disaster, with a recently separated boozy mother moaning about my father the whole time – which was understandable. And a lesbian sister who constantly expressed a dislike of men in general. And me with a large and painful aubergine where my leg should have been.

The 'apartment' my mum had booked turned out to be a room with three single beds squeezed next to each other with an en suite shower

CHAPTER 13

and loo. There was barely space between the beds for my normal leg, let alone the other one. I had the middle bed and had to contend with my mother's awful, incessant snoring, made worse by steady consumption of vodka. I took to sleeping with my Walkman headphones on and the Sisters of Mercy lulling me to sleep.

Mum was not happy in general. Obviously she was suffering emotionally after the break-up with my father, but she was also used to a more luxurious life, with all the facilities. Not only were we all crammed into one room, there was no kettle and no plug sockets anyway. Meaning she'd lugged a kilogram of Nescafé across the continent for nowt.

Things worsened with there being a lack of eateries and shops in the area, but the biggest problem by far was that there were no dartboards. Mum was a keen darts player and couldn't believe that anywhere would be lacking a simple dartboard. She dealt with her misery by befriending the giant bottle of vodka and found some other English people, also in their late forties, who she could hang out with.

After drinking heavily one night (most nights actually) my mum launched a verbal attack on me, telling me how much I must hate her to have brought her to such an awful place. But it was she who had selected the town and booked the accommodation. My sister tried to defend me, but Mum wouldn't hear of it and then accused us of ganging up on her. It was really miserable. We'd all been hoping for a nice holiday and it was all going pear-shaped. Mum ended up storming off in a vodka mood, with my sister shouting after her. Lovely.

The next day we travelled to Naousa, the town I usually stayed in on Paros, and met up with my friends Paulo and Ellen. Mum soon cheered up as she had new people to talk to, people to whom she wasn't related. Paulo and Ellen were such a nice couple and helped her feel more at ease.

I showed them round the pretty harbour and we ate in one of the local tavernas. Mum agreed that Naousa had much more to offer than Pisa Livadi, where we were staying, and that we'd have enjoyed a much better holiday if we'd stayed in Naousa. Like a good daughter, I managed to resist the temptation to say *I told you so.*

Chapter 14

Toys and love

Having worked at the sandwich bar for a couple of years, and feeling like I really knew and understood the finer intricacies of the sandwich, I decided it was time to find myself a full-time job that didn't involve sliced bread. To start with, as I have already mentioned, I worked briefly as a bike courier. My calf muscles were already like those of a rugby player having cycled from Morden to Blackfriars and back – a round trip of 30 miles – every day to work at the sandwich bar. I rapidly learned the names of the main London streets and areas and, after being trapped in a sandwich bar for two years, I enjoyed the job. I was outside all day with the wind in my vivid purple hair. And all the poisonous chemicals in my lungs. The cycling was getting me super-fit; meanwhile, it felt like the pollution was killing me. I may as well have smoked 40 B&H a day.

The stripy tights I wore beneath my knee-length leggings earned me the affectionate nickname Pippi Longstocking with the controllers in the despatch room, although it's a nickname that only lasted six weeks, as my courier days came to a grinding halt one day when I collided with a car turning left into Wilmington Square off Rosebery Avenue in Islington. Little did I know then that I would be living there less than a year later. I decided to look for a safer occupation instead.

Scouring the newspapers for something that would involve less potential death but no sandwiches, I noticed an advertisement for a toy tester in Wembley. I had visions of myself playing with teddy bears and Star Wars figures, so I naturally applied and was offered the job.

On my first day I was taken to the toxicity-testing department, and placed in a laboratory where I was issued with a white lab coat and some plastic safety specs. It was like being in '70s TV puppet show *Joe 90*, but without the strings and jittery limbs. My job was to scrape the paint off toys such as die-cast metal cars or teddy bears' eyes with a sharp scalpel blade (this is probably against the law now but, at the time, teddies still had no rights). I then had to force the paint scrapings through a small metal sieve with a fine mesh and then weigh a pre-determined amount of the resulting powder into a test tube. The test tubes were then ready for the chemists to test the paint by adding artificial stomach and saliva solutions in order to gauge the levels of heavy metals, such as barium, arsenic and mercury, that might be ingested. The other people who also did my job were imaginatively known as 'scrapers' and seemed to be at the very bottom of the jobs hierarchy. The sieve was cleaned with neat acetone in-between each paint sifting, so once again I was working with harmful solvents. If any toys failed the tests they would go for retests. Which can be very stressful for a teddy bear, especially the younger ones. The company was part of Trading Standards and they issued certificates authorising the use of the CE mark and other international safety standard stuff.

One perk of the job was that we could take the tested toys home if they weren't too mutilated. Sometimes it was just kinder to put them to sleep. I would often arrive home with a disabled teddy that had lost the use of an eye or, in more extreme cases, had an eye completely removed (without anaesthetic). I would give many toys and teddies to Bill the witch's little nieces, who thought I was clearly the best adult in the world as I was an endless source of expensive but physically impaired toys.

My friends soon found out what I was doing for a living and threatened to report me to the Teddy Bear Liberation Front for the practice of soft toy vivisection. I couldn't blame them. I was maiming teddies for money and, what's more, I enjoyed it.

I soon made other friends in the job as I would get bored with sieving metal filings and wander off into other departments for a cup of tea and a bit of a chat. From making friends elsewhere, I began to be offered other goods to take home that had survived the testing: a free bicycle, a skateboard, an iron, a hairdryer. It was like *The Generation Game* but with conveyer-belt prizes that had slipped through quality control. And with a lot of cuddly toys.

I often found myself at the back of the building, where the mechanical engineers tested furniture and other heavy goods. It was interesting how

CHAPTER 14

they devised machines to simulate a bum constantly sitting on a sofa and gauge the resulting wear and tear. If they'd needed a bum to sit on a sofa for extended periods of time, they only had to ask. I had one that was very fit for purpose.

The people who worked there were a good laugh and the men in the mechanical department took a shine to my bike. They would help me fix things on it when it went wrong and one guy showed me how to fill a dent in my petrol tank and respray it, whilst another tried to teach me the guitar, but it turned out that my fingers weren't 'stretchy' enough. Which in some ways was a relief.

I was so bored of scraping eyes (already desensitised to the cruelty) and sieving metal filings that I tie-dyed a T-shirt under my desk. I must have been a nightmare employee. When people left their jobs, they were told they could return to the company if things didn't work out for them elsewhere. The same was said to me, but I got the impression that they didn't actually mean it. I'd been toying with leaving in order to focus on making and selling clothes, so that's what I did.

By now I'd become skilled at reading tarot cards and so I decided to go along to a spiritual centre in Wood Green in North London that had advertised that they were looking for new readers. I had only ever read for family and friends and a handful of strangers in Paros, and I was now ready to spread my psychic wings further.

When I arrived, it instantly became obvious that I was the youngest card reader there, by about 30 years. The man who ran the centre showed me to a table and said that he would send over a couple of people for me to give sample readings to and, if I was any good, I could stay.

The first reading I gave was to the organiser's wife and seemed to go OK, but the second was to an elderly man with a head of white hair and a matching moustache. I asked him to shuffle the cards and then I nervously laid them out. I was surprised as many of the gentleman's cards were love cards. Surely this man was too old to have a love life, I thought. However, I dutifully read the cards and tuned into one particular card – The Queen of Pentacles. I began describing a lady approximately seven years younger than him with short red wavy hair and pale skin. The man nodded. Suddenly a woman's name popped into my head.

'I'm hearing the name Rene or Irene,' I said to the man.

He sat back in disbelief and suddenly produced a wide smile. 'Her name is Renee, it's a French name, but I wouldn't expect you to have got that. Yes, Rene or Irene are the English equivalents,' he told me.

I was chuffed to smithereens. I'd not 'heard' names before or experienced anything outside the traditional meaning of the cards. Based on the gentleman's feedback I was invited to stay, and in fact to come along every Saturday if I wished. The rent for the table was £5 for the day and each reading was £5, no matter how long it took. I was soon busy doing readings for the general public, building up my confidence and making a little extra pocket money.

For my 24th birthday I decided to throw a party. I had seen an old mate at a gig the week before and told him about the party and word had soon spread. One person, Smoky, showed up with 10 Swedish guys he'd just met in the pub. Thankfully they were all a good laugh and, in the morning, I woke to find various Swedish bodies strewn around the house. It was like waking up in Ikea after the apocalypse. One was even managing to sleep on the stairs. I mean, how the hell does one sleep on stairs?

It was at this party that I met Steve (a new Steve). A tall guy with dark hair that was cropped short and spiky. He was wearing a T-shirt that sported a punk band logo (probably the Dead Kennedys). I was instantly attracted to him. His chat-up line was that he had two pet rats and they wanted to meet me. How the hell could I refuse?

Our first date took place at the iconic Marine Ices Italian ice-cream parlour in Chalk Farm not far from the old Oddities Market, which had since closed down. I took him on the back of my Suzuki. He was nervous to start with but soon realised that I wasn't a complete maniac and could actually ride a bike.

Steve lived with a couple of other mates, in a flat above a kebab shop in Hackney. The two guys he lived with were involved in an organisation called Class War and one of them was arrested and subsequently sent to prison during the infamous poll-tax riots a year later, in 1990.

Steve worked as a gardener for Hackney council. He introduced me to

Chapter 14

the joys of Tangle Twisters ice lollies. Iced confections were definitely a theme for us.

One day we were walking back to my place in Tottenham when we saw someone's possessions in the front garden. As we approached, I saw that there was a cheque book flapping about in the wind. I went to investigate and quickly realised that it was actually mine. And so were the rest of the possessions. Steve and I gathered up as many of my belongings as we could carry.

Inside the house, the landlady was going absolutely berserk. She had given us notice of eviction but three of us hadn't found anywhere else to move to so we had appealed for another couple of weeks. My housemate Mary advised me to call the police as she was conducting an illegal eviction.

I walked into the kitchen, to discover Saucy Jon sitting with his latest female conquest, acoustic guitar slung around his neck. In-between strumming chords, he was scoffing chips as if nothing out of the ordinary was happening. He looked up as I entered the room and stopped playing guitar for a second.

'Hello Gail,' he said cheerily. 'Want a chip?'

I was incredulous that he had sat calmly eating chips and drooling over this unknown girl whilst the landlady had thrown all of my belongings out of the house and into the front garden, where anyone could help themselves to what they wanted. No, I did not want a fucking chip. Part of the reason the landlady was so furious was because Saucy was living in the house without actually paying rent.

I took Mary's advice and called the police, who arrived swiftly. The landlady quickly transmogrified in front of the law from a howling dervish into a perfectly reasonable polite and smiling woman. She lied to the police, saying that she was moving back into the house and that's why we had to leave. The police said that I could legally stay and that, if she wanted me out, she would have to take me to court.

After the police left, the landlady went into the bathroom and pulled all the wallpaper off the walls, filling the bath with shredded paper, as she tried to make the place as uncomfortable and unwelcoming as she could for us. There was no way I wanted to stay in the house with such a nutter. I'd lived with enough of those already.

Steve gave me a big hug and said I could move in with him. His room was barely big enough for him and his pet rats, but he was happy to have me there and his flatmates were agreeable too. There wasn't enough room for my possessions, so I ended up dividing my stuff between three different friends in separate locations. It was several years before I was reunited with all my stuff in one place again. During which time I learned that it is horrible not having control over your own things or a secure permanent roof over your head.

Two months after meeting Steve, he told me he was going on holiday and, of all the places in the world he might have been visiting, he was going to Greece. Not just to Greece but to Paros – *my* island. I told him all about it and I must have seemed very enthusiastic as he invited me to go with him. Next thing I knew, I was on the ferry back to Paros!

This time, we stayed in the harbour town of Parakea, which was a different kettle of Greek fish to Naousa altogether – a tourist party town where you could find English food and cheap shots, and sadly many English tourists to go with them. But at least I didn't have to live on feta cheese alone or order a meat dish with no meat.

But the holiday was huge fun and I realised that I was developing very strong feelings for Steve, which will make you wonder why one day, whilst we were playing a game of chess outside a taverna in the hot sun and drinking a couple of beers, I answered no when Steve asked me if I would marry him.

The reason I said no was because I didn't really consider his words to be a serious marriage proposal, as we had barely known each other two months. And anyway, I thought it was a hypothetical question, as he had asked *would* I marry him rather than *will* I marry him.

So we didn't get married but we did treat each other to new tattoos. Steve had the logo of the Alternative Tentacles record label tattooed on his arm, and I had a merman across my shoulder and back. It was a design in a tattoo magazine that I'd fallen in love with. The tattooist had a massive octopus tattoo across her back that she had designed herself (the tattoo, not her back). I imagine she didn't do the tattoo herself. That would have been impressive. Or disastrous. She gave my merman a brilliant body and fishtail, adding muscles and sexy long hair. I also had a smaller merboy, called a sea squitling, tattooed above the merman, from a design by the artist Patrick Woodroffe.

CHAPTER 14

Steve never asked me to marry him again.

Chapter 14.5

Extracts from my diary of 1988 – part II

JANE'S ADDICTION
CAMDEN PALACE
27 SEPTEMBER 1988

Nic persuaded me to come to Camden Palace with him. He said Jane's Addiction were a glam band, but they turned out to be reggae meets Nick Cave, meets Bauhaus. Crap!

Before we went out, I read Nic's tarot cards. I predicted he would meet a girl with long dark hair whom he already knew and although he wouldn't take her home that night, he'd arrange to see her again. Later, at the Camden palace, Nic was talking to a girl he knew with long dark hair [hey, we were all goths back then!] and he arranged for her to ring him next week. Yay! My prediction came true!

23 NOVEMBER 1988

My motorbike is refusing to start again!

Cindy and I went for a job interview in a restaurant in Mayfair. She said it was a glorified waitress job. The restaurant was well known for its poshness so we smartened ourselves up a bit, although Cindy still had her four nose rings in and I just had my one.

The restaurant looked cosy and friendly and the girl on reception seemed nice. She took us downstairs to fill in some application forms, then we had to go back upstairs and wait on some expensive leather chairs for an interview. We waited ages and eventually an old man came up and asked us if we were waiting to be interviewed, and what as. He disappeared back downstairs and came back with our application forms and said, 'Sorry.'

I didn't know what he meant so I said, 'Oh, I'm Gail Thibert and this is Cindy Jones,' and he replied 'No! I mean you can't have the jobs! I can't take you as this is a high class restaurant!' Bloody cheek! Who the hell did he think he was? He told Cindy that her hair and nose rings weren't suitable, so we both just walked out without another word to the offensive old man. He could have bloody told us we didn't look the part before we filled out four fucking pages of fucking application form.

On the way home, we popped into Tower Records and the Limelight and picked up application forms for jobs there. We had to get buses home as the tube was on fire at Oxford Street and the station had been evacuated. Took two bloody hours to get home. Not a great day.

NAPALM DEATH
BRIXTON CANTERBURY ARMS
9 DECEMBER 1988

I'm glad I took a cab to deliver some cakes from the sandwich bar (yes, I'm back there again) and not the tube. I heard a 17-year-old boy was stabbed to death at Holborn tube station. Taking the cab meant I avoided the tubes and walking into this incident.

I met Sharon later to go to the gig in Brixton. We saw a phone box cordoned off and a big pool of blood. Yuk! I've always hated Brixton because stuff like this happens there a lot.

10 DECEMBER 1988

Went to Wood Green with Saucy Jon and Mary on the bikes. Sorted out a TV and video rental deal for £15.98 per month. We need to return on Thursday to secure the deal and make a payment.

The landlady came over and criticised the mess the garden was in – the same mess it was in when everyone first moved here. What did she expect? Us to be landscape gardeners in our spare time? She wants

CHAPTER 14.5

to put our rent up to £45 per week or rent out the living room. I'm sure she can't do this. Me and Nic will go to legal aid for advice.

I met Cindy at The Fox later. A fight broke out suddenly and I was knocked to the ground and trapped under the two men who were fighting. I ended up with a bruised face, a cut lip and bruised elbow. My necklace snapped and I was covered in beer. I was really shaken and crying with shock. Cindy took me to the toilets to calm me down and repair the damage.

THAT PETROL EMOTION & WE ARE GOING TO EAT YOU
TOWN AND COUNTRY CLUB, KENTISH TOWN
13 DECEMBER 1988

I've always liked That Petrol Emotion and they didn't disappoint tonight. I first saw them when I was about 17, with some penfriends I'm rarely in touch with these days. WAGTEY are a friend's band, formed from old members of Hagar the Womb, so a double treat tonight.

GAYE BIKERS ON ACID & LESBIAN DOPE HEADS ON
MOPEDS
BOSTON ARMS, TUFNELL PARK
15 DECEMBER 1988

A brilliant gig! Bought a Gaye Bikers T-shirt that said 'Make way for my motorcycle, baby!' Thought this was appropriate since I passed my bike test and now have a bigger bike. The bands were great and I danced all night although it was rough down the front, so I stayed towards the middle where people were still dancing but I was less likely to get bruised.

Chapter 15

Tottenham - part II

Mary had expressed an interest in squatting before we were ejected from the Tottenham gaff. Her new boyfriend Tony lived in a squat and she liked the idea of the lifestyle, along with the obvious appeal of not paying rent. She had never squatted before and decided she'd definitely like to give it a try. I'd really had quite enough of living in squats but living in rented accommodation hadn't been that much better either, so I agreed to get a squat with Mary and Tony.

We had already tried to open a squat in a four-storey Victorian house in one of Hackney's quieter residential streets. One of the basement windows was slightly open, so we were able to clamber through without having to break any glass or force any doors. Once inside, we discovered several sack-loads of unopened mail by the front door, so it didn't take Columbo to work out that no one had lived in the property for some time. We set about cleaning the place up and filled 22 bin bags with rubbish. We found even more mail in the basement, all stamped with an HMP address, so again it didn't take Columbo to realise that the last occupant had probably just been released from jail.

I claimed one of the downstairs bedrooms in which there was already a single bed with a decent-looking tiger-pattern throw, which I liked. It would be company for my tattooed lion in the bubble hat, I reasoned.

In the next room, scattered on the untidy floor, were strips of tin foil and half-burned candles. Clearly someone had been using the place as a drugs den.

Mary and Tony took a room at the top of the stairs. We were feeling really quite pleased with ourselves, having discovered such a good vacant property in a nice quiet street. We took it in turns to remain in/guard the house. The law at the time allowed squatting but the house had to be occupied at all times, in order to claim squatters' rights. If the property was discovered empty, we could be evicted or the property could be boarded up, which would then make it illegal for us to re-enter the building. We had a rough idea of our squatters' rights and knew that any evictions had to be carried out properly through the law courts. This was a long, drawn-out process, which meant we could remain in the property for several months whilst all the legal bumf was sorted out.

One day, before I'd even had a chance to move my belongings from Steve's flat, I heard a sound coming from the very room I had earmarked for myself and my lion with the bubble hat. I opened the door, just as several youths in hooded sweatshirts were climbing through the broken window. I protested that this was already our squat, but there was just little old me standing there, and probably not looking very scary. Mary and Tony were upstairs, oblivious to what was going on below. The youths laughed in my face and then locked me out of the room, saying it was now theirs. I felt powerless and a bit scared. I really liked that tiger-print throw.

My heart was pounding as I dashed up the stairs to alert Mary and Tony. We went down to confront the youths and tried our best to reason with them. Clearly they had discovered the house first as it was their drug paraphernalia we had found. They said we could stay in the house, but this was their place for doing drugs and as long as they could still use one room for that, we could have the rest of the house, which was fairly obliging of them, I suppose. They could have got very nasty.

But there was no way any of us wanted to share the house or any potential home with a bunch of drug-taking/-selling delinquents. I'd learned the hard way, in Peckham with Studs, how untrustworthy and volatile druggies can be. I needed a secure home, not a drop-in centre for junkies.

A few days later, I returned to the house with Mary, only to discover that Tony had gone out leaving the squat unoccupied and therefore unguarded. The housing association who owned the property had come along just at the right time and, finding the house empty, had smashed the toilets, leaving just a waste pipe in the ground and nowhere for anyone to 'go'.

Chapter 15

This was a new tactic employed by property owners to discourage squatting. Instead of going through a lengthy and expensive court process that could take up to six months and still not end in an eviction, they hired heavies to smash the toilets, sinks and baths, rendering the property uninhabitable, and impelling squatters to move on. It's a tactic that worked for people like myself who liked to use a proper toilet and sink, but some of the die-hard squatters remained in derelict properties and used the garden or a bucket, or sometimes the local pub toilet, in order to conduct their business. Personally, I couldn't live like that.

It was Lewis and Marie, friends of Steve, who came to our rescue. Lewis had recently moved in with Marie, and said we could move into his old squat in Stoke Newington, Hackney. Tony, Mary and I agreed to have a look and Lewis showed us around a run-down house in Beatty Road, just off the main high street.

Reluctantly we surveyed the empty house, with its graffiti-daubed walls and dodgy floorboards. Lewis chirpily handed over the keys, although they weren't strictly necessary. If you wanted to gain entry you could open the front door from the outside by standing with your back against it and giving it a swift kick like a grumpy foal. It didn't make me feel particularly secure.

The living room had an open fireplace, the back wall of which had been painted black to conceal fire damage. There were large windows but they were filthy. A blanket hung across them like a makeshift curtain, although very little light would have penetrated the mucky windowpanes anyway.

The place was extremely filthy and full of rubbish so we set to work cleaning it, jettisoning all the trash and making it immediately more welcoming by painting over the graffiti with clean white paint.

It was like that scene from *Calamity Jane* where the two women fix up a ramshackle cabin while singing 'A Woman's Touch', except Doris Day was played by me with black hair and the other bird was performed by Tony.

I took a large upstairs room that was close to the second bathroom. One was living in an abode with dual bathrooms! The bathroom contained a porcelain Victorian high-level cistern, which was lovely.

Except you had to be careful when you flushed it as the heavy cistern was loose and it was only a matter of time before I flushed the bog and was instantly knocked out by a plummeting vintage cistern. I also had to be a bit careful when walking from my room to the bathroom, as some of the floorboards were rotten and precarious. If I'd put one foot wrong I'd have landed in the lounge.

There was also a large room on the top floor, above mine, which our friend Veg was going to move into. We went to inspect the room and I spotted what I thought were wires poking through a hole in the ceiling but, on closer inspection, were, to my horror, the little feet of a poor dead pigeon. No one was brave enough to deal with the deceased pidge, so it remained there decaying. The room also contained an old mattress covered in dubious stains, next to which were a number of used condoms that contained strange red fluid, which was possibly blood but we really weren't too sure. Nor were any of us that enthusiastic about identifying the fluid.

I don't think Veg ever stayed there but he liked to call it his room, so he had the option to stay if he was ever stuck in the area and wanted to sleep in a room full of rotting birds and used and bloody condoms.

Not long after moving into the squat, I was chatting to Mary in her bedroom one day when I realised I could smell gas. I called the emergency gas service, who quickly came and discovered a leak in a pipe in Mary's room, right next to her bed, where she had been sleeping for the last week and where she'd been happily puffing away on cigarettes. We were both mortified when we found out she could have blown us up when lighting a fag or, worse still, fallen asleep and never woken up. The gas supply was turned off immediately and we were advised to ask our landlord to get it fixed. It must have been obvious to the gasmen that this was a squat. After all, who would pay money to live in the kind of conditions we were living in? Of course, there was no landlord and we couldn't afford to get it fixed ourselves. So now we had to live without gas, which meant no heating and no hot water. Fuck!

At least the cooker was electric, so we could cook and boil a kettle for hot water to wash with. When autumn arrived, we bought cheap paraffin heaters, which pumped out lots of condensation but only

CHAPTER 15

managed to provide heat over a two-inch radius. The house was freezing, so Mary and I would often put our two heaters together in the front room and huddle near them under blankets to keep warm, like a pair of medieval serfs.

We would go to Steve's house when we needed to immerse our bodies in hot water, or to the house of his friends around the corner, who also squatted but were doing so in considerable luxury compared with us. We were truly grateful for that. Mostly I would stand shivering in front of the sink and perform a strip wash, as I didn't want to keep imposing myself on friends' bathrooms.

To start with, it was just me and Mary rattling about in this great big house full of eerie spare rooms, but a friend of a friend called Lianne soon moved into the room above mine.

Lianne was tall and slim with woodland-green spiky hair, and she decorated her room with arty pictures that she'd snipped from magazines. She was pretty and sociable and we all had a laugh on the rare occasions we bumped into each other in the big and otherwise empty old house. Occasionally we'd go to the local pub, which was called 'Rumours', which made it sound like it should have been a nightclub on the teen soap *Hollyoaks*. Lianne quickly renamed it 'Traumas', as it was the place where we would convene after a particularly bad day, a shit week, an awful month or something worse.

One day, I was flicking through my prized collection of *Back Street Heroes* custom-bike magazines when I discovered, to my absolute biker-chick horror, that several pictures had been ripped from the magazines. LIANNE! I banged up the stairs in a right mood to confront her about it but, even more infuriatingly, she couldn't see what all the fuss was about. I wasn't OK with people entering my room without my permission, let alone boldly vandalising my cherished bike magazines. I could see some of the pictures already pasted to the wall behind her. Clearly, there wasn't a lot I could do about it now, as I could hardly stick them back in the magazines. She hadn't realised that I was collecting the mags, *apparently*. Might have been nice if she'd asked before wielding her big spiky-haired fucking scissors about in someone else's room. Harrumph.

When I moved out, I also discovered that my rare Tourists album had somewhat magically vanished. The Tourists were the band that Annie Lennox was in prior to forming The Eurythmics and I've never seen a copy of that album since. It had been one of my favourite records and had disappeared in a puff of smoke. These are the hazards of sharing accommodation with others. Often, people have no respect for each other's belongings and space. In Tottenham, one of my housemates admitted to using other people's toothpaste and then blowing the tube back up to conceal their heinous dentally related crime. I clearly remember using my bubble bath and shampoo on numerous occasions and dumbly wondering why the consistency seemed inexplicably more watery than when I'd first opened them. Was some strange chemical process taking place? Or was I sharing my home with thieving bastards? I hate sneakiness. If anyone had ever asked to use my stuff I would have said yes, so it really wasn't necessary to go all covert and steal from me. There was enough Matey for everyone to have a bubbly bath.

My friend Cindy knew an Asian lad called Sunny who heard that we had an empty room and asked if he could move in, saying that his dad had thrown him out and he had nowhere to go.

'Why did he throw you out?' I asked cautiously, thinking there might be a good reason.

'I set fire to the house,' he replied matter of factly.

Ah, that could be a good reason, I thought to myself. The last thing we needed was a bloody pyromaniac moving in. I told him that, very sadly, all the rooms had already been taken by non-pyromaniacs. We had no room for a psycho. Been there, done that, T-shirt bought, lesson learned, book written.

While I was with Steve, my friends Sharon and Doc invited us to the infamous Treworgy Tree Festival in Cornwall. Sharon and Doc were going down in their recently bought camper van and encouraged us to join them, saying that the festival was free and that they would save a space for our tent next to their camper.

Steve rode pillion as we set off on my lovely Suzuki, weighed down by panniers bursting with camping gear. It was a seven-hour journey and Steve confessed to falling asleep a few times so I was worried sick that he might fall off on one of the motorways. I imagined suddenly

Chapter 15

seeing his black-clad arse receding into the distance in my wing mirrors, rapidly getting smaller and smaller as he disappeared off down the motorway, still asleep.

A few hours into the journey, through some spectacular countryside and doing 'the ton' (that's biker-speak for 100mph. Oh yeah) whenever I could get away with it, the sun started to go down. I put my headlight on but, after a while, it suddenly went out again. I turned it on again, it stayed on for a few minutes and then went out again. Oh rats! – I was only driving in the dark without a bloody headlight. Luckily, by then we were off the motorway and on the country roads approaching the festival. I crossed my fingers that we would make it to the festival before darkness really set in. I kind of needed the headlight to see and be seen.

Eventually, we saw the festival signs and the queues of cars lined up to get in. I took great joy in overtaking the massive line of cars and got near the front on my nifty machine. The headlight failed again so I switched it off to save the battery, but a policeman saw me and told me to turn my headlight on. I switched it 'on', hoping and praying that it would actually come on and – huzzah! – it did and we managed to get past the copper before it died again. I managed to dodge various cops and stewards on our way in, switching my headlight off and on again as needed, hoping that the battery wouldn't die completely and leave us stranded in Cornwall.

Somewhat bizarrely, clearly with skywards help from the great god of fluke, we managed to find Sharon and Doc in the dark, despite not having mobile phones, mainly because no one had bothered to invent them yet, which was slightly slack on their part. We put our humble tent up in the space that Sharon and Doc had left, next to their van, but it was deeply furrowed ground. I didn't have an airbed and felt every single lump and furrow beneath me. Even though the ground seemed quite even, by the time I lay down, it felt like someone had sneaked some rubble, a couple of sharp pointy rocks and a few spanners beneath the tent. Steve was OK: he was so slim that he slotted snugly (and smugly) between furrows and didn't even notice that it was uncomfortable. Grrrrr.

Before we went to sleep, we had a few drinks and bumped into some other people we knew, who told us that the festival was being shut down by the local authorities as the water supply was contaminated. People had been using the water to make up feeds for their babies and the babies were getting dysentery. The toilets had overflowed and were so disgusting that people were lining up to use a nearby field in order to do their business in front of an audience of bemused cows. The whole situation was pretty disgusting. By the morning the field was littered with used toilet paper, which must have been nice for the cows. So we packed up again and headed home, a less stressful ride in the daylight, without the need for the headlight. Not my best festival experience.

I was so pleased to get home to a proper mattress and a flushing toilet, even though I'd only had to rough it for one night. Although Beatty Road has to be the worst place I have ever lived, it was still infinitely better than the furrowed ground/dysentery field festival. I had been applying for housing association accommodation for several years and kept praying that something better would be offered to me soon. Like my own place at an affordable price, for example. However, despite having been on the waiting list for yonks, my chances of being rehoused were still slim. Priority was given to ethnic minorities, refugees, recovering drug addicts, alcoholics, the disabled and single mothers.

You also had a better chance of being rehoused if you were gay, which is strange as I'm not sure that being gay belongs in the same category as having a heroin addiction, fleeing a war-torn country or having an extra mouth to feed. For one thing, the average gay man is supposed to earn more than the rest of us. They clearly hadn't heard of the pink pound back then. In fact, sadly, being gay was still very much an underground thing, and people were still victimised, beaten up and persecuted for being openly gay. Landlords would often refuse to house people if they were gay, black or unmarried. Times were changing, but they were changing slowly, and there was still a definite hangover from a more Victorian past. Anyway, I was neither black nor gay and, after my experiences in Tottenham and Dalston, I was reluctant to rent privately again. I didn't want to be at the mercy of a private landlord who could make me homeless at any moment

CHAPTER 15

and charge me a premium rate for the privilege. I was already living on my nerves after so many negative past experiences.

It was around this time that I split up with Steve. I am not exactly sure why I broke up with him, looking back. It was probably a combination of immaturity and an inability to nurture proper loving relationships. I was also still enjoying my new social life at the biker clubs and pubs. Despite craving stability, I also rebelled against it. Typical me. My own worst enemy.

Buuuuut… as luck would have it, someone told me about a housing association that had plenty of houses and was taking on people who were Irish or had Irish connections. I have no idea why being Irish or slightly Irish was deemed a suitable criterion for cheap housing, but who was I to quibble? And don't you know that me very own grandpaddy was from the Joyce family to be sure and, faith and begorrah, my great-grandmother herself had come all the way over from Ireland, so she had. I wondered whether this qualified me and rang the association to enquire. I was in luck and was posted an application form – and I didn't even have to put on a really fake Irish accent either. It was crazy but there were so many housing associations with bizarre criteria in those days. It was acceptable for an association to only house black people or lesbians or black lesbians or everything but black lesbians – whatever niche they decided really. Anyway, I had finally found a housing agency whose criteria I just about matched and so I returned the completed form.

And wouldn't you know, a month later I was offered a house in West Harrow. A lovely suburban house with bluebells in full bloom in the garden, birds chirping happily in the nearby trees and a distinct lack of roaring traffic. Even the air seemed cleaner. It was like an oasis in the desert of my chaotic life. The front garden was beautiful and the house was secure and stable-looking from the outside. It had none of the homeless comforts I was used to, such as a collapsing roof, graffiti-plastered walls, fungus-encrusted curtains, dead-pigeon light fittings and drug-dealing housemates. Yet I liked it. I decided to move there, marking a much-needed fresh start to my so-far fairly unpredictable, and some might say unlucky, life.

It was a four-bedroom house. The other rooms had been saved for Mary and Veg, who had decided not to move in as it was too far away, but I accidentally failed to pass this information on to the agency. Plus I hoped they would change their minds and move in with me. Another woman whom I hadn't met yet had been allocated a room in the house and had already staked her claim to the biggest room, putting her stuff in there like a German holidaymaker waking up at 5am to spread their towel on the deckchair closest to the pool. So I chose the downstairs bedroom, which was actually the only room with any form of heating, apart from the living room.

I wasn't entirely enthusiastic about going without heating again. I'd only got one arse, and that had already been frozen off at Beatty Road. Plus it was a lovely room that was both clean and carpeted – two concepts I'd rarely encountered (with the exception of my parents' house). Plus I had patio doors that allowed me to bask in the sunshine during England's predictably tropical summers. OK, but at least I could bring my motorbike round the side of the house onto the patio and park it there safely.

I was so excited to have a fresh start that I went out and bought myself some brand new bedding and, on the first night, slept on the floor wrapped in my new double duvet as, yet again, there was no bed or mattress. In fact, there was no furniture at all. One of my workmates, on hearing that I was moving house and had no bed, offered me a single bed for free and, not only that, she said that she and her husband would deliver it to me at the weekend. It was such a beautiful gesture, I actually cried. That's right, like a baby. Having slept on second-hand mattresses, often found on the street or of no fixed previous owner, on the floor, here I was getting a mattress and a bed base from someone I knew.

Before I had that first night's sleep, I spent several hours in the bath preparing myself for the moment of luxury when I slid my clean body between clean new sheets. My new bathroom was in immaculate condition, and had a thing called hot running water. *What be hot running water?* I thought to myself. Having been without a bath and hot running water for about a year, I ran the bath and soaked until the ingrained dirt was released from my pores. The water turned brown

CHAPTER 15

from all the muck I hadn't been able to scrub off just by strip-washing in cold water standing next to a sink. I was like one of those rescued dogs from RSPCA films that are found living under a pile of rubbish and are then bathed and taken care of and suddenly transform into an adorable little puppy. All I needed now was a nice family to come along and adopt me and show me what real love was.

I had the house to myself and, believe me, I made the most of it. I ran the bath again about an hour later and had another bath, just because I bloody well could. I watched the hot running water spew from the tap as if I was a small child witnessing a miracle. I felt like I had won the water lottery. I could now have a bath whenever I liked. I lay there in the luxurious warm water, feeling safe and warm whilst I waited for my new family to come and pick me. Then I remembered that I wasn't a dog and climbed into my clean new-ish bed beneath brand-new bedding and a new duvet and slept like a motherfucking princess.

I had a work colleague who was looking for somewhere to live and, as Mary and Veg hadn't claimed their rooms, I suggested he should move in and pretend to be Veg. It worked well at first, but he kept forgetting to call himself Veg in front of the other tenant whenever she made a rare appearance. We pretended that it was his nickname and that he didn't always use it because he used his real name, Patrick, instead.

Despite having a full-time job and a low rent, I still didn't have much money. I didn't really get to know West Harrow too well as I wasn't there for long. I never stayed in any one place for long. It was a weird place. Before I realised that there was actually a proper super-market in the neighbourhood, I thought the only shop that sold food was a nearby Indian wholesalers. I would therefore buy gigantic bags of rice and lentils and cook rice and lentil dhal with fresh coriander and Indian spices. It was tasty, nutritious and filling, and best of all it was cheap.

I was finally reunited with my possessions, which had been living in various ever-tolerant friends' attics, cupboards, garages and spare rooms. I didn't have a record player for my vinyl collection but I had my keyboards so I 'played' along to recordings of Skids and Faith

No More. I never did learn how to play chords and stuck to playing punk-style, i.e. using one hand.

Despite being out in the sticks, luckily my new pad wasn't far from the Tube station and there was a night bus that dropped me a five-minute walk/stagger away, so I could still continue to go clubbing when the urge took me, which it usually did.

West Harrow was certainly way posher than the last few dives I'd 'lived' in. Although, in fairness, most places were – I had lived in some particularly grotty areas. Much like Morden, West Harrow was a green suburb with tree-lined streets and well-maintained houses, so there was a sense of familiarity. But also like Morden, it was as boring as fuck. There was not much on offer socially, especially for a young woman who was used to having the throbbing metropolis at her fingertips. So, despite my idyllic suburban surroundings, I still found myself heading into London to see friends, go to gigs and get my fix of glittering city lights. Plus, not many of my friends exhibited any desire to travel all the way to Harrow to see me, even though I had bluebells growing in my garden, hot running water and everything.

It was not long after splitting up with Steve that I realised I had made a mistake in letting him go, so I invited him to my new bluebell-encrusted suburban love nest to see if there was any hope of reigniting the relationship. To my delight, he agreed to come over, all the way from Hackney. Stupidly, however, although completely in character, I had the foresight to go on a brutal clubbing night beforehand and had managed to get way more drunk than was strictly necessary. So poor lovely Steve, having made the epic journey from deepest darkest Hackney to West Harrow, was greeted with a bleary-eyed and probably slightly smelly young woman who was sweating cider and could barely string a bunch of syllables together, let alone entice him sexily into her boudoir (with brand-new bedding) like a smouldering vixen. After an afternoon spent watching Miss Stinky-and-Knackered fall asleep on the sofa, he let himself out of my house and I didn't see him again for a very long time. I felt like such an idiot. I have since washed and cleaned my teeth.

Chapter 15

After just a couple of months, I was offered a room in a house in King's Cross, bang in the centre of London, and I didn't even have to pretend to be a black, drug-addicted, lesbian architect from Fife. I was on the horns of a dilemma: uproot myself once more and move into a shared house with no heating with a bunch of complete and quite possibly mad strangers in smelly and run-down King's Cross; or remain in pretty, tranquil West Harrow, where the air was sweeter than wine and my room opened onto a lovely garden ripe with perky bluebells. So I moved to King's Cross. I wasn't one to let common sense get in the way of an exciting life.

After I moved out, Patrick, who was still impersonating Veg, got found out thanks to the other girl kindly grassing him up to the housing association, which was lame because he was no trouble at all and was paying rent. They called me at work and, thankfully, after scalding me a bit, they allowed him to stay, maybe because he actually was genuinely Irish, complete with a proper Irish accent and everything, and he had been a good tenant who had always paid the rent on time. I bet the relationship between him and the girl who grassed him up was really pleasant and harmonious after that.

I was becoming increasingly reckless. I met a friend of Cindy's at a nightclub and told him I was moving out. He said he would be interested in moving in as he was living in Tent City in Hackney and that it was cold and people stole from him. I felt for him as I knew what it was like to live in an unstable environment, to be cold and to have one's possessions taken. I introduced him to Patrick and they seemed to get on fine. Patrick said he was happy for this guy, who I'd only met once, to move in, so long as he paid his rent and a share of the bills, which the man agreed to do.

Soon afterwards, the man moved his girlfriend in too and then, one day, after Patrick had given him money to pay the electricity bill, he did a runner and was never seen again and, strangely, neither was the bill money. Oops. Ironic considering he'd complained about people stealing from him in Tent City.

Chapter 16

Wilmington Square

Pedigree was the name of the housing association that owned my next residence in Wilmington Square, King's Cross. Ironically, their houses were literally a mishmash of rooms, which seemed to have one thing in common – that they were held together by a combination of damp and excruciatingly bad, outdated decor. Pedigree? Mongrel, more like.

Prior to being rehoused, I attended an interview at their offices in North London, to make sure that I was black, lesbian and architect enough, or something like that. Following this, I had to meet my potential housemates in order to ascertain if I was black, lesbian and architect enough for them. Luckily for me, I clearly ticked all the black, lesbian and architect boxes and soon moved into a room in an impressive-looking, four-storey Georgian house in Central London. It was good to be back in the old smoke. Fuck bluebells.

Wilmington Square was just off Rosebery Avenue in now-very-fashionable Clerkenwell, but the address was classed as King's Cross, and at that time – the late 1980s/early 1990s – it was a part of Islington that was shabby and neglected and full of immigrants and poor people. All of the run–down properties had been sold off to housing associations because the council could no longer afford to maintain them. The square consisted of many regal Georgian houses arranged around a beautiful public rose garden, and it wasn't difficult to imagine how beautiful the area would have been a century ago when each of the houses was home to one family and their servants. It was all very Mary Poppins. Now, most of the houses were privately owned and, sadly, were split into flats. From the outside, the properties still looked dead posh with their imposing facades. The square attracted sunbathers during the few days of English summer and roving drunks at night, regardless of the season.

It was a fantastic location, just a short walk to King's Cross, Farringdon and Angel Tube stations. Directly behind the house I lived in was a disused swimming pool, which soon got converted into more flats as property prices rose and the population of London expanded at an incredible rate. There were also a few council flats, and the old Peace Centre, which had been home to many an anarcho-punk back in the day. It was already long gone by the time I arrived, and was soon turned into the Amnesty International building and, later, into a children's nursery.

Just behind the square was the lovely Amwell Road, known locally as Amwell village, as it really did retain the feel of a rustic little village full of interesting shops, including an old-fashioned watch and clock repairer with a huge old grandfather clock in the window; a bespoke handmade-shoe shop; and an old-fashioned dairy shop, which seemed to be permanently closed, which had a display of vintage milk bottles in the window. After I moved out, some seven years later, Shane MacGowan from the Pogues opened a pub there called Filthy McNasty's where live bands played despite the 'venue' being slightly smaller than a fairly small living room.

I was also close to Exmouth Market on the other side of Rosebery Avenue, which was also home to a shabby bric-a-brac market during the week and on Saturdays, if you were lucky, and if anyone could be arsed to trade. Weekends were like a ghost town. The market vendors used old-fashioned wooden barrows that could be wheeled away into a nearby street and stored for the night at the end of the day. Exmouth Market, and the area around it, has now been taken over by what have now become known as hipsters but it was nothing like that back in the '80s – just a fairly overlooked and authentic part of London. It was nothing special. Not a beard, man bun or slate place mat in sight.

My first impression on entering the big house, my new home, was that it was in the middle of being decorated. There was no carpet in the hallway and the cold, bare floorboards looked like they were waiting patiently to have their old paint and varnish stripped off before being repainted. And it looked like they'd already been waiting a fair time. The lofty hall and stairwells were a strange mix of beige and cream. When I say a strange mix, I mean one colour finished abruptly

CHAPTER 16

as the other began. I believe there's a reason why such a painting effect never caught on. It looked like a decorator was due to arrive any minute to finish off the job. I kept expecting to see a man in overalls suddenly appear with a large cup of weak tea in one hand, a packet of Rich Tea biscuits in the other and a folded-up copy of the *Sun* in his back pocket. Not that I'm suggesting that all builders eat Rich Tea biscuits, of course.

There were also big cracks in the plaster and the original wooden sash windows were badly fitted or had shrunk over time, making them about as effective at keeping draughts out as an umbrella would be at keeping you dry whilst swimming. In the winter, I taped cling film to the windows in an attempt to keep the draught out – who needs double-glazing? The extra-wide front door had been designed in order to allow the fashionable ladies of the era, who wore pannier dresses or crinolines, access during more genteel times. It was wide enough to allow three people wearing contemporary clothing in, side by side, in less genteel times.

The house also had original black railings topped with angry-looking spikes and it still had a coal bunker, which would have been in use less than a century ago. There was even an original iron ring in one basement room for tying an animal to. It must have been an amazing property back then. Such a shame that so many proud and impressive old buildings had been left to decay.

Other tenants included Bruno from the Dominican Republic who had skin as black as tar, and his partner Kim from Manchester. And Keith, a bass player in the well-known psychedelic band Here and Now. I say 'well-known' but I had never heard of them, although it turned out that they often played festivals and many of my friends were impressed when I said I lived with a member of the band. (I eventually heard some of their stuff a few years ago, over 26 years after moving out, and kicked myself for not having listened to it earlier.) Keith owned a Persian cat called Gabby, which often sported dreadlocks due to a lack of brushing (and not because it was into Bob Miaowley and the Whalers). I didn't really see that much of Keith as he was most often shut in his room.

There was also a film-maker called Trevor who wore a spacious overcoat, which was fashionable back then. In my imagination, Trev's room housed hundreds of metal film canisters, as he was often seen carrying them. It was highly likely that he carried the same few around with him all the time, I suppose. Maybe he wasn't a filmmaker at all? Maybe he was using the metal canisters as a cover for some dark and dodgy dealings he was doing...? Or maybe Gail has seen too many psychological thrillers and Trev was actually a filmmaker? He did once leave a chicken carcass in the oven for a whole week, after cooking a roast for friends. By the time we managed to locate where the dreadful smell was emanating from, the chicken carcass was crawling with maggots. He was very apologetic, as he knew I was vegetarian, which meant I wasn't always overly enthusiastic about finding dead animals in the kitchen, either with or without maggots.

There was also Nisha, an Indian lesbian, who was modern and stylish and sold medical supplies by phone for a living. She had a parrot or cockatiel or something called Cyril and an equally stylish girlfriend who would visit her often. Nisha's room was always pristine. She had stripped the original oak flooring and polished and varnished it to a high shine. Her bed was raised on tall stilts so that she could fit her dress rail under it.

The house was divided into sections: I was in the top section and shared a kitchen and bathroom with Nisha and Trev. They were lovely people. I couldn't have asked for better housemates.

My own room was OK but, in comparison to Nisha's, it felt a bit drab. I was the last one in, so of course I got the shittiest room. That's how it worked.

I was still working in the toy-testing job performing insidious operations on innocent teddies' eyes, and some of my workmates kindly helped me to move in. I was lucky to have such support as I didn't have a car of my own. The triffid-like plants that I'd been nurturing in the staff kitchen were finally able to come and live with me. I hardly had any furniture, so my meagre possessions lived on the floor. Again, there was no central heating but there was an old-fashioned gas fire in my room. Thankfully, bills were included in the low rent, which was just as well because, in the winter, the draughty old win-

Chapter 16

dows meant the fires had to be kept on all day and night, even after I'd gone to the expense of putting up peasants' double-glazing.

Shortly after moving in, I went to the Slimelight club in Angel, which was now just a short walk away! I got chatting to a young gentleman by the name of Stuart, who was several years younger than me and into an alternative lifestyle. He had long black crimped hair, and wore a silk scarf as a bandana in the manner of The Cult's Ian Astbury. He was wearing a green army shirt with the sleeves rolled up and tight black trousers. Everyone on the punk and alternative scene used to wear tight stretch black jeans, which were mostly bought from the same stall in Kensington Market. Stuart and I clicked and I ended up inviting him back to mine, where we stayed up chatting until 4am. Eventually, as I was so tired, I fell asleep in my clothes while he carried on talking. He prodded me awake a couple of times and then gave up and fell asleep too.

I started to date Stuart. Despite seven years' difference in age between us, we got on well and he made me laugh. Girls like that shit. He taught me not to take myself so seriously. He had a habit of borrowing my clothes and, annoyingly, they often looked better on him than me. And I often wore men's clothes anyway as they fitted me better.

Stuart still lived with his mum but was desperate to move out and, within three weeks of seeing each other, he asked if he could move in with me. I was against this, for obvious reasons, but within weeks his mum threw him out anyway and, as he had nowhere else to go, I let him stay with me for a while. I laid down the law and said I wasn't going to be treated like his mum so, if he wanted to stay with me, he had to get a job and learn to cook. I thought that would deter him, but I was absolutely gobsmacked when, the next day, he went out job-hunting and came back with a job offer and a packet of frozen stir-fried vegetables. I watched as he painstakingly followed the instructions on the packet. Bless his heart. However, the housing association's rules were strict and I told Stuart he would have to find his own place to live as soon as he possibly could, as I couldn't risk losing my room and my tenancy with the association. I'd been through too much shit in trying to get a roof over my head and didn't want to blow it. So he dutifully found a place with a male friend of his.

Stuart loved bikes too and I was passionate about custom bikes, so we went to the Bulldog Bash in Kent, run by the Kent Hell's Angels. I strapped my two-person ridge tent to the back of my faithful Suzuki, along with sleeping bags, a change of clothes and a packet of wet wipes (always prepared!). I straddled the bike in black leather trousers and jacket, full-face crash helmet and a wicked pair of knee-length Fieldsheer biker boots in plain black. I still got a kick out of riding a decent-sized bike even if it did handle like an adolescent rhino and corner like a slightly overweight milk float. I was a cautious rider, especially with a pillion passenger, and took fewer risks when I had an additional life to be responsible for other than just my own.

The closer we got to Kent, the more bikers we saw along the way. Other bikers were almost always friendly and would wave as you approached or nod in acknowledgement. The roar of so many engines zipping past when we stopped for fuel was incredible and the low growl of the motors went right through me, into the pit of my stomach and into my groin.

The weekend was lots of fun. Stuart insisted he knew how to ride a bike and persuaded me to let him have a go on mine. I reluctantly handed my keys over and he was soon tearing across the grass and having a whale of a time. He was riding it for a good couple of hours and, by the time he brought it back, the petrol tank was empty and I had to put it on reserve, so we could get to the petrol station on the way home to refuel. I just hoped that a petrol station would appear before the fuel ran out. I was really pissed off, although I secretly admired his enthusiasm.

I didn't stay in a relationship with Stuart for more than a few months. I rarely stayed with anyone for very long, admittedly. I'm not sure what I was looking for really or if I was really looking for anything or anyone. Soon after breaking up with Stuart, I broke up with my job as a toy tester too. It was a mundane job and, despite working with some lovely people, that simply wasn't enough for me. Not to mention the pain I was inflicting on those poor teds. I still had oodles of creative energy that wasn't being tapped, which I found frustrat-

Chapter 16

ing. I had been experimenting with tie-dyed baby clothes and hand-quilted matinee jackets, and reckoned I could make and sell them for a small profit.

The fabric-testing department had tons of discarded fabric samples that were just gagging to be utilised for something, and they kindly donated bags full of the stuff for my new project. The samples were generally too small for most things, but they just happened to be the perfect size for tiny humans. As soon as I had enough cute baby items to sell, I took the plunge and headed towards Greenwich Market in South London. It was just like my old Camden Market days where I had to queue up on a Saturday in order to – maybe, if the gods of trading were on my side – get a pitch for Sunday, which is the most popular day for markets. The market in Greenwich was at least under cover, so trading was still possible even if it shat down with rain – which it often did. I embarked on yet another government enterprise scheme, which meant that my rent was paid and I had a small income even if I didn't sell anything, which gave me a bit of security.

I bought cheap plain-white Babygros and vests from a wholesaler's and tie-dyed them a variety of primary colours, using a bucket in the kitchen. (Even Zandra Rhodes had to start somewhere.) The results were, let's just say, 'different', but the random designs and bright colours were popular with the Greenwich crowd, who were generally more adventurous and had much more disposable income to be adventurous with.

I packed everything into my motorbike panniers and took a small folding chair on the back seat to provide one's arse with a modicum of comfort on the stall. Eventually, after months of being a casual trader, I was allocated a permanent pitch, which put an end to the tiresome business of queuing and meant that I could just turn up and set up my stall. And being a sexy biker chick meant that I didn't have the hassle of finding an official parking spot, which was often nowhere near the market. The Suzuki let me park pretty much where I wanted. I hung the tiny garments from bungee cords and people would coo and point at them and make the little legs of the Babygros dance or walk. I never got tired of seeing that.

Kim, who lived downstairs in Wilmington Square, also made

clothes – although she made clubbing clothes for adults. She used one of the empty basement rooms as a sewing room, and invited me to join her down there. She had an industrial sewing machine, which she let me have a go on, once I'd overcome the morbid fear of sewing my fingers to my wrists, legs, Kim's wrists, Kim's legs, my other fingers and any other such finger/body part combination. With one slip of the foot pedal, any part of my body could have become painfully attached with strong thread to another part of my anatomy. In my fertile imagination, at least.

I still chugged along on my mum's old domestic machine and Kim and I chatted and made clothes with Kiss FM on the radio until the early hours. Admittedly, I hated Kiss FM because all they played was dance music that made my brain jitter, but I didn't complain because it was great to have someone to work alongside who shared my passion for sewing. Kim had taken on a small concession in an indoor market for up-and-coming designers in the King's Road in Chelsea, where she sold her collection, which consisted of velvet shorts and tops with white stripes down the arms – kind of like glamorous tracksuits, but long before glamorous tracksuits actually did become fashionable. The clubbers loved it.

I still associated the King's Road with the original wave of punks that used to hang out there in the '80s, when I was a wee slip of a punk. I knew, and was still friends with, many of them. I would often meet Angel, my old penfriend from *Sounds*, and some of her punk friends there and would laugh as they cheekily charged tourists a quid for taking a photo of an authentic London punk. The tourists would generally be happy to pay, too, but, if anyone tried to get away without paying, the punks would chase after them and intimidate them until they finally gave in and paid up. The King's Road had changed massively over the years and now, in the early 1990s, there were hardly any punks hanging out there. The ambience was unrecognisable with the area's upmarket boutiques and posh restaurants. The King's Road I knew and loved no longer existed.

Soon the recession started to hit and the market was doing badly. The last thing people seemed to want to buy when money was short was quirky baby clothing, so I began to struggle. I was also supply-

CHAPTER 16

ing a couple of local children's wear shops but it was all sale or return, which meant that I only got paid if they sold something, and I only sold a couple of pieces each week. It was soul-destroying, really.

I soon realised that, if I was ever going to get a job doing the sewing I loved, I would need a formal qualification instead of just trying to blag my way in as a self-taught bodge-it artist, even though that had worked for me previously, at the screen printers! I decided to bite the bullet and enrolled on a two-year diploma course in theatrical costume construction at the London College of Fashion, near Oxford Circus. Thankfully, my previous experience of designing and making under my own label of Rubella Rat came in handy at the interview, although this time I wasn't dressed as a fish!

I had started to date Paul, who had previously been the guitarist for Hagar the Womb. I'd seen them play loads of times and had shared a stage with them when I was in the Lost Cherrees, but I'd never really chatted to Paul much. Hagar had disbanded and Paul, Veg and some of the other Hagar the Wombers had started a new band called We are Going to Eat You (WAGTEY), named after a horror film. I went to see them play a couple of times and enjoyed the new sound. They had a female singer called Julie whose vocals were very ethereal. It was a very different sound to Hagar. I already knew Julie through my friend Fiona and from bumping into her at numerous squat parties and gigs. We all shared a love of gin and cider (not in the same glass though! I'm not that rough!). In fact, I had also previously found Julie a job at Scole's sandwich bar.

I'd gone to see some bands at Camden Palace and bumped into the WAGTEY band members. For some reason, I found myself chatting to Paul and realised that I felt very comfortable with him and enjoyed his company. His hair had previously been bleached and cut in a style that hadn't appealed to me so I hadn't paid him much attention, because women are superficial too. But now he was all smiles and his hair was a natural auburn colour. I sipped my beer as we chatted and I couldn't help noticing how good-looking he was, and it wasn't just the beer talking. Luckily, the attraction was mutual and he asked me for my phone number, which I was happy to provide him with. He rang me the very next day and invited me to a party at his house. Hopefully a party for two, I thought.

On the night of the party it was snowing heavily and I couldn't persuade any of my friends to come with me. For some reason, nobody wished to venture out on a cold and snowy London night, take a packed, damp Tube train to the idyllic Turnpike Lane in order to make small talk with a bunch of people they didn't even know and then get a night bus full of pissed wankers back home at 4am. So I went on my own, determined to see Paul again and to get to know him better. I reasoned with myself that there would be a few people I knew when I got there.

My hair was shoulder length and dyed black and I no longer back-combed it – no one did that anymore. So many crimpers must have retired at the end of the '80s that there must be a graveyard for them somewhere. The rock-chick look was in – so I put on a tight black miniskirt, opaque black tights and plain-black cowboy boots. I was feeling good. I got out of the Tube station at Turnpike Lane and instantly began slipping around in the snow like a slightly inebriated baby deer. In cowboy boots. Which I quickly found out were not intended for snowy conditions. Go figure.

I finally managed to slide up the path to Paul's house and rang the doorbell. The door was opened by someone I didn't know and I felt awkward. Scanning the living room full of strangers, I was relieved to spot Paul and was about to make my way over to him when some bloke suddenly appeared and started blurting on about his motorbike, like this would impress me. Which was a nice try but I had one of my own – with a bigger engine – so I really didn't need to be impressed by someone else's engine size.

Thankfully my stalking… errr, I mean plans, paid off and Paul and I dated for three years. He quickly convinced me that I was wasting my time at Greenwich Market, freezing my tits off for a few humble quid. Giving up the stall would also mean that we could spend Satur-days together, so it was a no-brainer really.

Paul enjoyed riding pillion on my motorbike but was soon inspired to get a bike of his own – another Suzuki but a more modern model – a GS500 or something as I recall. He had a car and would often

CHAPTER 16

take me for days out in the countryside. We visited his parents in Hornchurch, Essex, and I spent a few Christmases with him and his lovely family, who were very close and so completely unlike my own.

I soon found that I enjoyed the relative luxury of Paul's car and, while he was getting turned on to motorbikes, I was becoming more interested in cars. The concept of getting from A to B with heating, music and comfortable upholstery was appealing. Motorbike leathers were cumbersome, as was the helmet. Wearing leather also didn't fit in with my ethical animal-loving nature. Helmet hair and make-up that had been redirected to different areas of your face were unappealing, plus you could also talk to passengers in a car without having to shout above the noise of the engine.

So, I decided that I wanted to learn to drive, and read that you could drive a three-wheeler car on a motorbike licence. Paul was absolutely appalled when I acquired a three-wheeler Reliant Regal van, similar to Del Boy's in *Only Fools and Horses*, called Henry. I, however, was extremely proud of my new purchase. But before I could learn to drive Hen, Paul had to come with me to Morden and drive him all the way back to King's Cross. On public roads. In daylight.

Henry's engine sat inside the van, where the gearbox was, so it was actually hard to talk to each other above the deafening noise, although at least we weren't wearing crash helmets. Paul found it extremely funny that Henry was painted British Racing Green and he wanted to paint go-faster stripes down its side. I wanted to paint flames on it like a custom bike – it would have looked fantastic. Henry's top speed was 60 mph but, in reality, if I even approached such a death-defying speed, Henry threatened to fall to pieces like a clown's car.

Reliants were seen as comical by engine-size snobs – as low down in the vehicle hierarchy as you could get, short of a wheelbarrow. Every time we went out in Henry, people would stop and point or laugh, or stop and laugh or stop, point and laugh. But at least it made people happy. Henry was a bringer of joy. And, anyway, what had I ever cared about fitting in?

Still, I'm sad to say that my relationship with Henry didn't last long. He was a pig to drive and I decided that if I was going to drive a car, I might as well go the whole hog (pig? hog? – get it? – oh never mind!) and learn, like a relatively normal human being, to drive a proper four-wheeled vehicle that went slightly faster than a milk float. Which would be a first for me. Being a relatively normal human being was not something I'd ever given much credence to but, all the same, I started to take driving lessons again.

I had failed my test twice when I was a teenager. The test in those days was not so far advanced from the days when it had consisted of a man with a clipboard standing on the pavement, issuing instructions and then sending you around the block. If you managed to reappear without falling out of the car, hitting a wall or killing somebody or something (accidentally or otherwise) you passed the test and could steer two tons of steel, or whatever the fuck cars were made of back then, in public places. I still managed to fail my test twice, however, but I wasn't going to let this stop me from trying a third time.

Another part of the appeal of travelling by car was that I could sing along to music as I drove or was driven. I still really enjoyed singing. I had tried to join a couple of other bands since leaving the Lost Cherrees but hadn't found a good fit. Paul was working as a sound engineer at Southern Studios in Wood Green, which was owned by John Loder, whose remit was to bring US hardcore punk to the UK. He distributed bands such as L7, Babes in Toyland and the Dead Kennedys. He also recorded British punk bands and distributed the releases. John was the engineer on most of the Crass records. Paul got to work with some well-known bands, including Chumbawamba. He had given up playing guitar and being in a band as he had become more interested in the techno scene and he eventually set up Stay Up Forever records with Chris (later to be known as Chris Liberator) and another couple of friends.

I would often sit by the mixing desk listening to songs and albums being recorded whilst Paul worked relentless sound-engineer hours into the early morning. On one occasion, a band called Foreheads in a Fish Tank wanted some female backing vocals, so Paul volunteered me. I was nervous, as I hadn't sung publicly for so long, but I had a go. I was a little off-key to start with but then found the pitch I was looking for. Paul told me that the band had liked my backing, had put

CHAPTER 16

me on the record and would give me a copy when it was out. I was dead chuffed until he told me that they had used the off-key version, as they thought it was quirky.

I was keen to change from being a keyboard player back to a singer, but I lacked confidence in myself, as always. Paul told me I had a good voice but he was becoming more and more uninterested in live bands, especially as he had developed tinnitus.

Through hanging out at the studio and playing in bands I had got to know a lot of people. Kev, who played guitar for Conflict, lived near Paul and they would often go to the pub together. I liked Kev immensely and had a lot of time for him. He had a daughter but wasn't being allowed access to her after his relationship with the child's mother had broken down. He recounted the story to us and it was clear that the situation was breaking his heart. A year later, Paul and I were very sad and shocked when we discovered that Kev had committed suicide.

I lived in Wilmington Square for seven years. Even though I went there thinking it would be temporary, it turned out to be the longest I had stayed anywhere since leaving home. All the same, I had tried hard to get rehoused, as I felt it was time to find somewhere permanent. I'd been moving from place to place to place since I left Morden and I wanted to put down an anchor. I wanted a proper home of my own instead of just a room or a house.

When I was invited to attend an interview at a housing association, I asked Paul if he would like to move in with me. It was almost impossible to get a council house by then, so housing associations were the next-best bet. We attended the interview but Paul had only ever lived in one place since leaving home and had no idea about the amount of aggravation I had gone through trying to get (and keep) a secure roof over my head. The interviewer asked what our needs were regarding future accommodation. We really didn't need anything special so far as I was concerned: I would gladly have taken anything that was offered to me. I could always try to upgrade at a later date but Paul, in his youthful wisdom, requested a place with parking, although now he says he remembers this conversation differently and thinks it may have been me who requested the parking space, so we'll have to agree to disagree about whose fault it was.

My heart sank. The idea of housing association flats is that you apply if you are on a low income and can't afford to rent privately. We both fell into that category, but Paul did work. I just did a few tarot readings from time to time. One of us joked that we had a lot of vehicles. Surprised, the interviewer asked how many we had and, before one of us could stop the other or deliver a swift kick under the table, it was blurted out that we had two motorbikes and two cars. Well, one and a half cars really as the Reliant couldn't really be classed as a car. We might as well have added that we needed stables for all our pure-bred horses and living space for our butler. We were just being honest and didn't realise that having a fleet of inexpensive vehicles would make us look like we had money – which we didn't – and go against us. The lady conducting the interview scowled and asked how we could afford so many vehicles on a low income. I said they had been given to us, which was true of my motorbike and three-wheeler. She then suggested that we sell all of our vehicles to pay for the deposit to rent privately. Even if we had done that, we still wouldn't have raised enough to pay the deposit and a month's rent in advance for private rented properties. And that was that. Our chance to get permanent affordable housing was blown in an instant. I was gutted. I was stuck in a shared house with an uncertain future and no idea how long the tenancy there would last before I had to find a new home again. Great!

One day, myself and the other tenants were contacted by Mongrel to say that they had found someone to occupy one of the empty basement rooms. A meeting was called to interview the new prospective tenant and we gathered in the kitchen, where we were introduced to a Nigerian man called Kyuka, who was seeking refuge in the UK. Throughout the meeting he sat quietly, barely saying a word. We were all lively personalities and didn't feel that Kyuka would really fit in. In the past, with housing associations, people were vetted and the other tenants had a say as to whether they thought they could live with the new tenant. We all felt that there was something a little odd about Kyuka, as if he was deliberately keeping quiet, like it was an

CHAPTER 16

act. However, our objections were overruled and Kyuka was given the basement room, next to the one Kim and I used as a sewing room.

The housing manager at Mongrel then asked us all to donate what we could to help Kyuka as he literally had nothing. I was on my way downstairs to give him one of my saucepans and a sleeping bag when Nisha stopped me and took me to one side. 'Gail,' she said, 'don't you think something's a bit odd, just moving this man in like this? It's not our job to provide for him. That's up to the housing association.'

At first I thought she was just being mean, as I love helping people out, but I thought about it and saw her point of view and decided not to give him anything, as that was the housing association's remit. A few weeks later, Nisha asked me to look at his room with her while he was out. On one of the walls were posters of ridiculously expensive cars such as Ferraris and Jaguars and in a corner of the room (despite there being no other furniture) there was a huge colour TV and a video recorder.

'You see,' she declared, 'one minute he doesn't have a pot to piss in and now he suddenly has a TV and video player.'

About a week later, we were sitting outside a nearby pub when Kyuka walked past with some friends. We all said hello as he passed, but both Nisha and I noticed the expensive-looking heavy gold chain around his neck and the gold rings on his fingers. He certainly didn't appear to be a man who was struggling to purchase his own bedding. 'I'm going to report him,' Nisha declared.

Kyuka also tried to sneakily move another person in without anyone noticing. I was in the sewing room one day, happily sewing away, when a stranger walked in and scared the shit out of me. He stood in the open doorway and asked me who I was.

'Erm, I live here,' I replied sarcastically.

'So do I,' he said. 'This is going to be my room.'

No one had mentioned anything about another man moving in. 'I don't think so,' I said.

He told me that he was Kyuka's brother although they looked nothing like each other. When asked, Kyuka said that his 'brother' was just visiting. It didn't take Kojak to work out that it was all beginning to sound just a little bit suspect.

One morning, I went into the kitchen in my dressing gown and was startled to discover this strange man sitting at the table. I was already suspicious of this guy and I felt uncomfortable with him suddenly appearing in the top part of the house, which belonged to me, Trev and Nisha. Especially as I was wearing just a dressing gown. I told him that he wasn't allowed in this part of the house, but he refused to leave, saying he needed to use the table. He clearly had no boundaries or respect for other people's space or privacy. I didn't believe him. I thought he was just using it as an excuse to snoop around the rest of the house. Everything about Kyuka and his fake bro was suspicious.

A week or so later, Kyuka's fake brother knocked on my bedroom door at the very top of the house. He had a pair of trousers in his hand and wanted me to repair them for him, as he'd seen me with my sewing machine. The fact that he knew which room was mine made me more suspicious still – he'd obviously been snooping. I told him to fuck off and that he wasn't meant to be in the house at all. There was something about this man that made my skin crawl and, from that day onwards, I started to lock both my bedroom door and the door that separated the top flat from the rest of the house.

Everyone in the house was starting to feel uncomfortable and someone reported the Kyuka bros to the housing association. Kyuka was asked to leave and, when his room was checked, there was no sign of occupancy and the TV and video player had also gone. Over the following weeks, there was a stream of visits from electrical-appliance rental companies demanding their goods back due to unpaid rental agreements. Kyuka and his 'bro' had been using the house as a base for scams. About a month later, after this had been happening on an almost daily basis, the police turned up looking for Kyuka & Co too. I opened the door, totally unsurprised, and duly showed them the empty room. We were all definitely glad to see the back of the dodgy duo.

Chapter 16.5

The two special machines in my life

Stitching on an industrial level – the baby elephant. (Note the witchy little helpers)

Vroom vroom! One proud owner of a bike licence – and my beloved Suzuki

Chapter 17

Wilmington Square – part II

Tenants came and left Wilmington Square. Kim split up with Bruno and went back to Manchester. Nisha moved in with her new girlfriend, meaning that I could have her room, complete with shiny floors. I enjoyed the extra space and the view that the room afforded over the square, where I could listen to the same drunk staggering around every Friday night singing *Show me the way to go home.* You'd think he'd have memorised the route after a few weeks. But no.

Admittedly, the windows in the new room were even more draughty and rattled in high winds but, with the extra space afforded by the mezzanine bed, I was able to fit in a sofa and a TV – so it was almost like a mini bedsit.

After three years of dating Paul, and as it was a leap year, I threw caution to the wind and boldly asked him to marry me. He said no because he didn't believe in marriage. In fact, we had never really discussed plans to live together or move forward together in the relationship so, after a few more months, I decided to call it a day. We agreed to stay friends, and indeed we are still on friendly terms today.

Myself, Cindy and Angel had started to go to clubs together. We were now all into the rock-chick phase and wore fancy cowboy boots. We mostly drank in the Intrepid Fox, and clubbed at the Astoria, the St Moritz Club and Busby's. It was the '90s.

Cindy had white-and-pink hair extensions down to her knees, and Angel had yellow hair extensions down to her waist. Not wanting to be a rock chick without a crowning glory – it was all about big hair – I decided to get black-and-brown extensions that reached modestly to my waist. I had always wanted long hair but mine grew very slowly and broke off when it reached my shoulders. Absolutely nothing to do with the amount of bleach and dye, hair products and crimping irons I had exposed it to at all. No, couldn't possibly be that.

By the time my new do was finished I had so much hair that I could barely get my crash helmet on. This left me with two choices: remove the hair extensions or buy a bigger crash helmet. Well, I'd wanted an open-face helmet for eons. I didn't even have any goggles; I just wore a pair of cheap sunglasses to keep the road grit and 120-mph flies and sparrows out of my eyes. Oh the folly of youth.

Angel's friend in New York invited her over but, as luck would have it, she didn't want to go alone, so she invited Cindy and me along. Thankfully, the tarot readings had picked up and I was able to afford the airfare. When we arrived at JFK airport in the middle of the night, the customs guys took one look at the three of us with our ridiculous hair extensions, tattoos, miniskirts and cowboy boots and said, 'Where's your gear?' We looked at each other quizzically, wondering what the hell he meant. We knew there were many American-English words that had different meanings in UK-English, but we had absolutely no idea what 'gear' meant. Did he mean drugs? Were we going to get our bums searched for cocaine?

'Your guitars and stuff,' he said eventually with a smile.

One of the customs guys asked to search my rucksack and found the small velvet pouch that contained my tarot cards, which I take everywhere with me. I told him what they were and his colleague said, 'Oh my wife has some of those. You don't want to be messing with that stuff.' And with that, the tarot cards were hastily placed back in my rucksack, nothing else was touched and we were ushered through customs without another hitch.

We stayed with Angel's friend, who lived in an apartment in Manhattan. We marvelled at the towering tenement buildings with their external fire escapes and the bright yellow taxis and the policemen with guns who we had grown up seeing on TV. It was like being an extra in *Starsky and Hutch*.

I loved New York and took mountains of atmospheric photos of the wonderful city, especially the street art and creative graffiti. Mostly, though, we were night owls, always out visiting rock bars and clubbing until the next morning. We quickly discovered the nearby

CHAPTER 17

liquor store and promptly bought enough wine to anaesthetise a *T. rex*. This wasn't entirely our fault, your honour. Even the wine came in gallon-sized containers. This meant that we had to haul giant bottles of very cheap wine back to the apartment, which in itself was enough to work up a giant thirst.

One night, we went to a very crowded bar and I ended up sitting next to a couple who were drinking a pitcher of beer. That was another thing I liked about NYC: you could buy a massive jug of beer to share with your friends, instead of trying to carry several full drinks through a crowded bar. The couple saw that my glass of beer was running low and asked if I would like some of theirs. At first I declined, as I didn't know them, but they soon introduced themselves and poured some beer into my glass, anyway. You can say no to beer once in an evening, but twice is bordering on the ridiculous.

The woman told me that she was a nurse and that she had had a bad day. She had been called out to attend a shooting incident. On arrival, she had attended to a man who had been shot in the head and whose brains were literally hanging out. I recoiled as she provided graphic details of the colour and texture of the jettisoned brains. I was disturbed, but listened intently all the same. I'd had plenty to drink and found the gory description extremely fascinating.

'Can you believe it?' she said in the thickest New York City accent. 'The man was still alive and he'd had half his brains blown out!'

The subject eventually changed to something less gory as we talked about bands and what we'd been doing since we arrived. I told them that I'd seen a band called Extreme play at a nightclub. Not many people had heard of them at that point, hence them playing a nightclub and not a stadium large enough to hold half the population of the US. I'd heard them on XFM radio back home and really liked what I'd heard so, when I found out that they were playing the club we were already in, I got all excited and tried to get Cindy and Angel to come to the front of the stage with me, but they hadn't heard of them so I was on my own. I was mesmerised by the amazing sound and, of course, by the not-too-ugly singer/guitarist Nuno Bettencourt, who had very displeasing long dark hair and an extremely fit body – which, of course, I found disgusting to look at.

241

SOAP THE STAMPS, JUMP THE TUBE

Back in the bar in New York with my new drinking buddies, the man ordered another pitcher of beer. I offered to pay but they wouldn't hear of it. They said I was a guest in their country and they wanted to show me American hospitality. They also told me that they were going to a gig after the bar shut, and had I heard of The Ramones? Woah! The pioneers of the US punk scene? Of course I had. My new Yank bezzers told me they could get backstage passes to the gig, as they had connections with the security there. They asked if I wanted to come too. I explained that I was with my friends and didn't want to go without them. 'Hey, you can all come!' the guy told me, and I went to find Cindy and Angel to relay the good news.

To my utter surprise they said that they were having too good a time where they were, chatting to our host's mates (our host being Angel's friend, whose apartment we were staying in) and didn't want to go. I was incredulous. How could anyone in their right mind refuse free entry and backstage passes to see The Ramones! In New York of all places! It was a chance-in-a-lifetime opportunity.

'Aw, that's a shame,' the couple said when I told them the news that my friends – two ex-punks – had turned down the incredible opportunity to hear '1, 2, 3, 4...' live.

'Well, you could always come on your own,' the guy suggested.

'Yeah, we'll look after you,' said the woman.

I was very tempted but I didn't want to get separated from the others. I didn't know the area well enough to go out on my own and I didn't know this couple well enough to spend the rest of the night in their company. My loyalty to my friends won over and I declined their offer.

On the way back to the apartment, I told the girls that I couldn't believe that they had declined to see such a famous band, and for free. Cindy had a bit more common sense than me, and replied that if they were really playing, surely our host would have told us about it? It would be in all the papers and would have been advertised for months. I was unsure but, the next day, they checked with our host and he confirmed that he had heard nothing about them playing. It then dawned on me that the couple had been luring me in, like a squid (me) with pink glitter (The Ramones), by being super-friendly

242

Chapter 17

and getting me drunk. They were probably planning on robbing us. I shuddered at what had potentially been a lucky escape. Thank God for Cindy's cynicism.

After 10 awesome days in NYC it was back to London and normal life. Trev decided to move in with his girlfriend and, despite being sad to see him go, I now had the whole of the top flat to myself. I no longer had to wait for someone else to finish having a bath before I could use the loo or vice versa. In fact, there was only myself and one other tenant in the entire house. My surroundings felt tranquil for a change. However, things didn't stay idyllic for long. Of course they didn't.

Debbie, who often drank with us at the Intrepid Fox, had been living in another housing association property at the other end of Islington. She heard that I was living in this huge listed building with just one other tenant and approached her housing manager to ask if she could get a transfer to the house I was living in. Which was fine, except that she did all this without actually speaking to me about it first.

'Gail, I'm going to be moving into your house,' Debbie blurted out one evening when we were in the pub together.

I was shocked that she hadn't discussed it with me first. I felt like she should have asked me how I felt about it before secretly arranging to move in. I felt betrayed. However, she was my friend, so how could I say no to her? I didn't want to damage our relationship; I liked her, but I like lots of people, and that doesn't mean I want to see them every time I go for a wee-wee.

Anyway, move in Debbie did. She took Trev's old room directly beneath mine. It had been left in a bad mess, so I helped her clean it up. I guess someone had to move in sooner or later and better it to be someone I knew and liked than another dodgy geezer like Kyuka.

However, Debbie had inadvertently alerted the housing association to the fact that there were many empty rooms in the house and so they would soon want to fill them all and claim the rent. I felt a bit guilty too. The homeless situation in London was terrible and I, of all people, ought to have known how important a secure and stable home was, yet I was being selfish wanting the flat to myself. But it had been such a luxury to have so much space and quiet, and I was enjoying the tranquillity. No Nigerian wheeler-dealers, no drug dealers, no crazy landlords, no one hammering my belongings to the wall – it was blissful.

Soon more new people were moving into the empty rooms and my quiet and blissful idyll became a thing of the past. A couple called Vinny and Trish took the two basement rooms.

Trish was a beautiful Anglo-Asian girl with a full figure and long wavy obsidian-black hair. She had studied to be an actress but was doing secretarial work in-between auditions, like most actors and actresses. I remember watching Trish put her clothes on hangers on a dress rail and thinking that I had never met anyone before who had matching coat hangers. To me, who had lived in squats where there were no wardrobes and no hangers, this was an indication of pure class.

Trish also introduced me to *You Can Heal Your Life* by Louise Hay, in which Hay lists different illnesses and the mindsets that she says create them. The author had healed herself of cancer and her story was inspiring. I looked up rheumatism, as I'd had rheumatic pains in my knees throughout my life. I was surprised to find that Hay suggests that the victim mentality attracts rheumatic pain. I was blown away, as it was certainly true for me. I had been bullied as a child, and had experienced so many other situations throughout my life in which I was a victim. I'd certainly felt like a victim with all my housing hassles over the years, along with the situations with Flick and Pongo and a whole host of other people. I bought a copy of the book and it has remained a favourite of mine for the past 25 years and counting.

One day, the housing association announced that it was going to redecorate the house. We were all thrilled as it still looked in as much of a state as it had when I'd first viewed it all those years ago. I'd completely given up hope that the builders would return from their protracted tea-and-biscuit break and finish the job. My old room had been checked for damp and was found to be 70 per cent saturated. SEVENTY PER CENT! I had slept with my poor little backcombed noggin next to a smelly wall dripping with deadly spores for years!

Chapter 17

That kind of explained the wealth of health complaints, including the respiratory problems, constant bronchitis and coughing fits, that I'd had. I must have lungs like a Victorian miner who went down t'pit every day with the amount of moulds, toxins, resins, spores and paints I've breathed in over the years.

The decorators were to decorate only the communal areas as we were responsible for decorating our own rooms. The old wooden sash windows were restored almost to their former glory, which was a blessing as it decreased the draughts. The living room was painted an interesting combination of cream, light brown and dark chocolate brown, in accordance with the original colours from the Georgian period. Funding had been provided to restore the house, but with the stipulation that it had to be as accurate to the house's original period as possible. So we now had a living room decorated in what we called 'giant cappuccino'.

The builders were as dodgy as hell and would leer at the girls in the house at every opportunity. You'd think that men of that age would be used to seeing female human beings without their Neanderthal tongues falling out the sides of their mouths, but the fact that we were human and probably had bosoms somewhere beneath our clothes was clearly too much for them. When they finally completed the work and left, not only did they leave a load of mess for us to clear up but we also found a ginormous pair of badly stained knickers hidden amongst the rubbish. I shuddered and threw them in the bin. No woman I knew would ever own, or admit to owning, such a hideous garment.

A couple of weeks later, the phone bill came and I was horrified to see an extra 30 quid on the bill – all on calls to one unknown number. Who would sit there with 30 pounds' worth of 10-pence pieces, feeding them into the phone box? I checked the phone's money box and it was 30 pounds short. I showed the bill to the other housemates and they all denied knowledge of the phone number, and then we realised that it was a sex-line number. The builders must have brought their own phone in and plugged it into our socket. If I'd thought for too long, I think I'd have come up with an answer as to what the stains were on the huge pants, but I decided not to. Columbo doesn't take every case.

During the mid-1990s, housing was in huge demand as the Conservative government had been selling off council properties and encouraging council tenants to buy the properties they were already in. The government had also failed to build new housing. The housing association properties were therefore in greater demand than ever and you could no longer refer yourself to be housed, you now had to go on the council waiting list and be referred by the local council. There was a points system and if you were a healthy, single, UK-born citizen with no kids, you stood virtually no chance of getting housed or rehoused, even if you had an Irish accent. Not to be put off, I put my name on the council list for a permanent home anyway. One day, I went to a meeting at the local council offices to find out how my application was progressing, as I'd been on the list for a few years and wondered if there was any chance of getting rehoused during my lifetime. My name was called and a man came to meet me in the reception area.

'You're not Gail Thibert!' he proclaimed accusingly when I stood up, which was news to me.

I asked him what he meant. I'd been accused of many things in my life, but being accused of not being Gail Thibert was a new one on me. I'd brought along my passport for ID, in which there was a picture of me that looked exactly like the me who was sitting in front of him, and underneath the picture was my name, which was, and still is, Gail Thibert. I assured him that I was me and that I'd been me for as long as I'd known me. Which was years. I couldn't have been more Gail Thiberty if I'd tried.

'Gail Thibert is a short, slim, blonde woman, and you're clearly none of those,' he said rudely.

All right, Columbo, you're no Nick Kamen yourself, I thought. And actually, I am a woman, so at least I'm one of those. And anyway I've got big bones. I really had no idea what in the world of shit he was talking about. The only short, slim, blonde woman I knew was... Debbie, my housemate, who admittedly had become increasingly interested in me and my lifestyle of late.

246

Chapter 17

I wondered if she had tried to impersonate me for some reason. She'd gone behind my back to get into my current house, so God knows whether she'd been trying to pass herself off as me. A law had not yet been introduced that prohibited a person from impersonating a Gail Thibert, so whoever had been impersonating me had created a precedent. As far as I know at least. There could be swarms of me out there that I don't even know about. The interviewer leaned over me in an intimidating manner, insanely refusing to believe that I was me, despite me having evidence in my possession that I really was me. No wonder I had rheumatism. Eventually, I gave up asking the council for help and asked the housing association to transfer me to a one-bedroom property. I felt I had done my time living with others. Gail Thibert – the real one – had had a-fucking-nuff.

As housing associations had become more and more in demand, there was a pressure to fill empty houses and rooms as the homeless problem continued to escalate in London, particularly in areas like King's Cross – which was still a very run-down and shabby area in the '90s. The existing tenants in the house were no longer consulted about who was going to move in with them and were forced to accept the next person on the waiting list, no matter who they were. The waiting lists gave priority to criminals just out of prison or to anybody, it seemed, who had recently been released from some kind of institution, such as recovering alcoholics and drug addicts. Of course, these people need to be homed and reintegrated into society, but they don't always make for the greatest housemates. Several of my friends were in housing association properties and I was forever hearing horror stories about some of the nightmarish individuals they had had to share with. Knives had been pulled and possessions stolen, and that's just for starters.

One friend had an alcoholic living in their basement who was either too lost to the disease or just too lazy and filthy to use the actual lavatory, and who'd taken to pissing in bottles instead. When he was finally evicted from the property, the council had to call in the blitz squad – a crack team of super-cleaners – to deal with the disgusting aftermath. A friend who had worked for the housing department of

Haringey Council told me that their blitz team had often gone into disgusting properties and that, on one occasion, one of the team had noticed that the carpet was moving beneath his feet. He peeled back the carpet and it was teeming with maggots.

We had been lucky in Wilmington Square that we hadn't had to live with anyone too crazy. Carol came to view my old room. Carol was an African woman with a sing-song voice. She had an official with her, who we found out was her key worker, which suggested that she had come from some kind of hostel or institution.

Carol was extremely neat in her appearance and much more conventional-looking than the rest of us. She was obsessively clean, tidy and meticulous; locking herself in her room most of the time. Whenever she left her room, she would lock it immediately behind her, even if she was just using the toilet next door to her. So either she was terrified of us or she was suffering with obsessive-compulsive disorder. Carol even kept her pots and pans inside her room, to make sure no one else used them. At first we thought she was being selfish; then we decided it was probably related to her obsession with germs.

Carol's OTT OCD took a toll on the rest of the house but, for some reason, she had developed a grudge against me in particular. She would vacuum her room every day without exception. And, when she did so, she repeatedly bashed the vacuum cleaner against the wall that divided our rooms. I was sure it was done deliberately to annoy me as she didn't seem to bash it so much on the other walls, although perhaps I was being paranoid.

When I was at the cooker, she would come and use the sink that was located directly next to it and spend 15 minutes washing the same plate repeatedly. And she used to sing songs about Jesus in a tuneless voice. Often she would just sing *Jesus loves me* loudly and fanatically, over and over again. Her songs were always about Jesus. Now I have nothing against Jesus, but I have to say that his fan base is full of weirdos. And I really don't think Jesus would have appreciated this singing. Her crazy behaviour seemed deliberate and vindictive. I wondered if she knew I was pagan. Perhaps she had seen me giving tarot readings in the kitchen and had labelled me a devil-worshipper.

Carol would also monopolise the bathroom, locking herself in

Chapter 17

whilst she slowly and painstakingly washed her clothes one by one in the bath rather than use the communal washing machine downstairs, which she thought was dirty and contaminated. She clearly didn't realise that the rest of the housemates washed their bottoms in the bath. We were finding Carol's behaviour increasingly crazy and unbearable. In short: she was a nut job.

The crunch finally came one day when Carol had taken forever in the bathroom, 'singing' hymns tunelessly and at the top of her voice. I asked her politely to tone it down as the bathroom was directly opposite my room. When she eventually came out, she began following me around the house and chanting that I was evil. Her lip curled into a snarl as she spat out the words. At first I laughed; I mean it was comical really. She persisted and it really started to become annoying. I went into my room and closed the door behind me. 'EVIL! EVIL! EVIL!' she chanted outside my door, like she was trying to exorcise a demon in a camp 1970s horror film of dubious quality and made on a very low budget.

Half an hour later, Carol – the mad loon – was blocking my door and showing no signs of letting up with her chanting. Frustrated, and developing a splitting headache, I picked up the phone and rang the housing association. They thought I was being petty until I held the receiver up to the door and they could hear 'Evil! Evil! Evil!' being chanted over and over again. The housing manager, trying to be reasonable, explained to me that as I was the saner one (no shit, Sherlock) it was therefore up to me to diffuse the situation. I was the object of her taunting; if I simply wasn't there, then she would stop and calm down.

I took their advice and went for a canter around town and, by the time I got back a few hours later, she had indeed calmed back down to only slightly mad. Why these poor people are allowed to fend for themselves when they obviously need to be in a more structured and secure place where they can be looked after and the rest of the populace can be kept safe from them, I'll never know. Carol was clearly at least a ha'penny short of a shilling, if not a shilling short of a shilling.

Chapter 18

The Cally Road

Despite the fact that I was a demon and, of course, not actually Gail Thibert, my housing transfer finally came up and I was offered a place just off the Cally Road. At that time, you were only allowed to refuse two council or housing association properties that you were offered, or else you were struck off the waiting list, which seems fair enough. So I decided to take the very first offer so long as it was vaguely habitable, just in case the second offer was worse, which I had heard had happened to a few people who had regretted not taking the first one and wound up in a right shithole.

The Caledonian Road, or 'the Cally' as it's affectionately known, was grubby and run-down at that time (although I'm not sure it's changed much) and is almost flanked by two prisons: Pentonville for men, and Holloway for women. However, the flat was on nearby Hartham Road in a leafy and quiet road behind Caledonian Road Tube station. The street looked almost suburban, with its imposing Victorian houses and big concrete steps.

My new studio flat had original fixtures, such as two large sash windows. Everything was clean and in good condition. And the best part was: I didn't have to share with anyone. I had my own home! I had no access to the gardens but I could open the window in the hallway and climb onto the basement flat's roof in the summer and enjoy the view. I even placed a few potted plants there, inspired by the millionaire neighbour who'd moved into the house next door. He owned the entire house and filled his property with window boxes that went through two seasonal changes. Berries and pink cyclamen brightened up the winter months and multicoloured pansies lit up in the summer sunshine. I had a plastic bucket with some shrubs in, and that was enough to make me happy.

I painted the walls blue and the skirting boards and picture rails yellow and I made curtains out of yellow chintz and painted the tiny hallway shocking pink. In the bathroom, I stencilled pink-and-blue octopuses around the bath. The kitchen was painted a bright apple green and I stencilled metallic-gold lobsters on the kitchen units because, quite simply, I bloody well could. I wanted to personalise the place. It was mine. My kitchen, my kitchen cupboards, my metallic-gold lobsters. My first permanent place all of my own that no one could take away from me – and I wanted to put my stamp all over the fucker. And I did.

Paul and I were still friends and as he was a good handyman he built a raised bed for me about five feet off the ground, so I could have separate sleeping and living areas.

Living above me was a man called Frizz, who was a black-rights campaigner and who liked to sing opera and musicals. After a while, he moved his saxophonist brother in and I could hear them both practising. They were friendly enough, and I got used to the sound of Frizz singing the same piece over and over again and going off-key at the same point over and over again. It was a vast improvement on Carol's singing, which was never on-key.

Frizz had a lot of visitors who would call for him at all times of the day and night and, after a while, I donned my Columbo mackintosh and started to suspect that he might be a drug dealer, as many of the callers would also ring my bell and then not know who they were looking for. I didn't care so long as I was left to live in peace.

I started a new job in a casino called the Royal Lion in Oxford Street, where I worked in the uniform room as a seamstress, in charge of fitting out the new recruits in smart evening wear and doing repairs and alterations to the uniforms. One of the highlights was that I also fitted the uniforms for cruise ships' on-board croupiers, which meant that one weekend I was paid to go to Southampton to fit the croupiers on-board the QE2 – which impressed my dad.

I had a room to myself on one of the upper floors of the casino and wasn't allowed onto the gaming floor for security reasons. In fact, in all my time there, I never once saw what the casino looked like.

The casino was located close to Soho and Chinatown in Central London, and we had lots of Chinese punters. Sometimes, when I was carrying uniforms in the lift, some punters would get in and demand that I give

CHAPTER 18

them random numbers for them to gamble with, which they hoped would bring them luck. It was saddening to see people so desperate to win money, and clearly addicted to gambling. The casino gave away free food and drink to keep the punters coming, so that they could take their money. They were like rats in a Skinner box, pressing levers in the hope of randomly winning a coin but invariably losing large quantities of money at a time.

Del, my new boyfriend, was a cycle courier and a drummer for Altered States and Brigandage, who Marina (whose boyfriend had nearly been defenestrated at my house party years before) played bass with. He had long dark hair and wore John Lennon glasses. My hair was also long and dark as I had grown all the dye out of it by then. The natural look! We both wore tight stretch black jeans and black leather jackets and Del would often get mistaken for a girl because of his long hair, while I would often get mistaken for a boy because I'm tall and buxom. People often did a double take when they looked at us. When I first encountered Del at the Electric Ballroom in Camden he had bought me a drink and told me he was celebrating his divorce. After a while, Del said he was bored with cycle-courier work in all weathers and I got him a job in the casino, working in the kitchens. It wasn't a great job but at least he didn't have to work in the cold and rain anymore.

When Altered States were offered some gigs in Germany, Del's supposedly ex-wife suddenly materialised from America! You can imagine how shocked I was. She went along on the Germany tour instead of me. Clearly there was still a connection between them. I was upset about becoming single again, as we had had some good times and a lot of laughs. However, I realised I was better off being single and heartbroken than staying with him. When I later heard that they had split up, I felt slightly better about the whole situation, but I was still single. Although Del continued to work in the casino, our paths rarely crossed. I reconnected with Del some 22 years later and he apologised for treating me badly back then. Apology accepted – and romance blossomed between us again in 2016.

The window of my little sewing room at work overlooked Oxford Street and I would often gaze out of the window, watching as the portrait artists set up their easels on the pavements, and quickly clearing them away when it started to rain. Buses would splash through puddles and send great waves of dirty rainwater onto the legs of pedestrians. I watched as the inhabitants of Central London went about their daily business – it was like observing bees in a hive. Being on the edge of Soho and Chinatown, I generally got to see some interesting sights. I often saw a peroxide blonde-haired woman frog-march various men to the cashpoint and then away again, with her arm firmly linked in theirs. She was obviously a sex worker, fleecing yet another unsuspecting victim who'd innocently just wanted to wank over a stripper.

I had a couple of friends who worked the sex joints in Soho and occasionally I would meet one of them for coffee and cake. Me after a hard day's sewing, her before a hard night's dancing. I was always slightly curious about the sleazy underbelly of London, and so one day she took me to the joint where she worked. Beyond the flickering neon 'LIVE BED SHOW' sign was a creaking stairwell that led down to a dodgy basement for which the words 'dingy' and 'dark' might have been invented. In one corner there was a large trunk with a cheap throw slung over it, positioned in front of a mirrored wall. I think I'd expected a bit more of a glamorous setting but everything about this set-up smacked of stomach-churning sleaze. I sat down on the trunk and asked where the bed was. 'You're sitting on it!' laughed my friend. I jumped off it immediately.

It turned out that the whole place was a scam, even though it was licensed by Westminster City Council. My friend told me that foreign tourists would enter, fooled by the signs, and, once they had entered, a tab started running. Entrance was free, but if my friend or one of the other girls sat with a punter, they were charged a hostess fee, which could be as much as £200.

The hostess's job was to encourage the punters to buy themselves a drink and one for her too. There was no alcohol licence, so the beer was alcohol-free and sold at extortionate prices. The 'cocktails' were blackcurrant cordial. The sex show was a joke as council regulations at that time prohibited the dancers from showing any bare flesh from above or below the navel apparently. So basically these punters were being stung for hundreds of

Chapter 18

quid to see a girl's navel. It would have been cheaper to go to the local swimming baths. And you'd have seen more flesh.

My friend wore tight leggings and either a crop top or bikini top and would then attempt to 'tantalise' the punters with some feeble semblance of an erotic dance. One day, when she was really bored, she told me she had started to do aerobics. Apparently, men began to walk out when she started doing star jumps.

Of course, the unsuspecting punters were then presented with ludicrous bills, which they were invariably unable to pay, for watching my mate jog on the spot wearing cheap Lycra; hence them being frogmarched to cashpoints with threats of informing the police, telling their wives that they were a bit sad or just a nice bit of violence.

I was also friendly with one of the managers at the casino. Her name was Nora and she told me she practised bodywork – a form of healing in which the therapist gently manipulates the limbs to release past trauma. Nora told me that, once they were in a relaxed state, limbs would return to the position they were in when the body was traumatised, regardless of whether the position was natural or comfortable. I imagined that I'd suddenly transmogrify into a pretzel if my limbs were encouraged to release past trauma. The theory was that, once back in the traumatised position, the limbs were able to remember the trauma and release it. The whole process sounded intriguing.

After reading Louise Hay's *You Can Heal Your Life* I was becoming more and more fascinated by natural healing methods. I decided to give Nora's treatment a try – pretzel or no pretzel – to see if I could finally sort out my dodgy knee, which still flared up from time to time and made starting the motorbike with its high kick-start increasingly painful. Nora agreed to exchange a session for a tarot card reading. The bartering system was alive and well and living in London and probably sharing a squat with no heating with a drug dealer and an assortment of fungi.

During my treatment, I confided in Nora about the little electric-blue orbs of light I had seen bouncing around the corridors of the casino, about a foot above floor level. I generally saw about 20 to 30 of these two-pound-coin-sized blue-white sparkling 'entities' at a time. They would appear suddenly as I was taking laundry from one room to another, bounce around a few feet in front of me and then just disappear. I had seen the same little luminous critters before, often appearing around people's faces while I was talking to them. Not knowing what the fuck they were, I'd always referred to them as healing fairies, as they seemed to hover around areas of the body that needed healing. I hadn't told many people about them because I thought it was only me that saw them and I didn't want to end up in the lunatic asylum. But I also confided in my friend Marina, who said that she had also seen a few and that they were called 'orbs' and were thought to be spirit energy.

When I told Nora about the orbs, she revealed that she had seen them too. The building we worked in was very old and full of all sorts of energies and she told me she had also seen leprechaun-like creatures dancing on the roulette wheel. I found the leprechauns a bit too hard to get my head around, simply because it wasn't something I had experienced myself. Little blue jumpy sparkles and scary phantoms entering me through the soles of my feet and whooshing through my body, yes. But leprechauns – ridiculous, I thought to myself. But Nora was convinced that she'd seen them.

The meals at the casino were free, which was one of the perks of the job – just as one of the non-perks was that no one was allowed out of the casino once they were inside until their shift finished, as a security precaution. One of the catering team, a young gay man called Tarquin, would always save me the best jacket potato, because he knew I was partial to a baked spud. His young assistant, who was also gay and fresh out of catering college, would also bring me a perfect cappuccino every day and stay for a chat, swapping casino gossip. In return, I would do a few little personal repairs for them, such as mending Tarquin's leather chaps. We would sometimes go for a drink together after work and Tarquin would have me in fits of laughter as he vilified the clothing choices of the general public in a superbly camp voice, reducing their sartorial choices to cheap nylon rubble with a short phrase or often just a single word.

I'd got to know a couple of the croupiers – Nell and Jack – and they invited me out one Valentine's night. After a few drinks in the pub, it was deemed a sensible idea to go on to a nightclub. I was a bit tipsy and leaned towards Jack and ended up 'accidentally' giving him a kiss. It turned out that we had both found each other attractive for a while

Chapter 18

but neither thought we stood a chance with the other. I had thought Jack was the best-looking croupier in the casino so, when we started dating, I was thrilled. We had to keep our burgeoning romance a secret though, as staff members weren't allowed to date each other.

Jack would often pop into my sewing room for a little chat and I would sometimes give him a clandestine shoulder massage. One day he came in looking really shocked. Someone had collapsed and died at his gaming table and, while medical help was sent for, the other punters had just stepped over the body, insisting that Jack should carry on running the game and placing their bets. He was sickened by their behaviour.

I worked in Oxford Circus in an era when the IRA were planting bombs, and had grown up at a Catholic school where threats were also often made to bomb the school, so that we regularly had to evacuate the building. Not that we cared much about having to stop lessons to go and stand outside. We were young and invincible and would rather stand outside having a crafty cigarette or talking about bands than be stuck in a classroom. The gravity of the situation never really made a great impression on our young minds. Sadly, it had become a regular occurrence.

Bomb threats had continued into my adult life and Central London was/is a prime target for terrorist attacks. These I took far more seriously.

Looking out of one of the windows of my sewing room one day, I saw that the police were cordoning off Oxford Street and Regent Street. One of the croupiers popped their head into my room and told me that there was a bomb alert and that everyone had been advised to stay away from the windows and not to leave the building. I joined the rest of the staff in the windowless dining room, where we waited for several hours – braced for a sudden explosion that would blow our hair and fingernails off. Thankfully, that never happened and eventually we went back to work.

I realised how terrifying it must have been for people during the Blitz, when they would have had to evacuate their homes in order to hide in bomb shelters or down in the Tube stations for hours with the threat of death above them. Not knowing if they would live or die, not knowing if they would return to a home or rubble. Terrifying.

It's horrendous what human beings put each other through. For the sake of money, or drugs, or power, or land or pride.

Word soon got around the casino that I could read fortunes. Jack asked me to read his palm as someone had read it for him years previously and had told him that he would be dead by the time he was 34. I was horrified. There is an unofficial rule amongst psychics and fortune-tellers – kind of like the Hippocratic oath, but for mediums (and larges) – that you never foretell negative events such as death when giving a reading. The effect such news can have on people can be devastating.

We were both 31 at the time, so Jack was worried that he only had a few years left to live. Moreover, all the other information the palmist had given him was accurate, so he was clearly worried that this might be true also. On the plus side, this meant that Jack had decided to live his life to the full, just in case the palmist's forecast was right. As such, he went on wild holidays such as the running of the bulls in Pamplona, Spain, where people are chased through the narrow Spanish streets by terrified cattle. There were often resulting injuries, and even deaths. Sadly, the bulls would usually suffer terribly too.

Jack and I only dated for a few months. It turned out that we weren't really suited and our work shifts often meant we could only see each other every other weekend. Jack also liked to drink heavily and used drugs regularly, whereas I was drug-free.

However, one random night in 1995, Jack persuaded me to try Ecstasy, which was the drug of choice for clubbers at the time. It was a time of raves and dance music, when Ecstasy was at the height of its popularity. As E was an amphetamine, dropping one meant that you could stay awake and dance all night, and it also made you feel very open and warm towards other people and… well… ecstatic. Lots of people raved about it but my druggy days were over and nothing other than booze appealed to me. However, Jack and I were on the way to a club one night when he talked me into taking half an E, just to see how I got on with it.

We got to the club and, an hour later when the E had had no effect on me, he gave me the other half. Jack seemed to be having an amazing time on the drug. He was smiling and dancing and laughing. I

CHAPTER 18

was still waiting to feel this incredible rush that everyone described, but nothing remotely rush-like was taking place. Jack came over and was wittering on about how confident and beautiful I looked but I had gone quiet and was beginning to shiver. Very quiet. Too quiet. And Jack became concerned, realising that I was acting way out of character. I asked if we could just go home. I wanted to feel safe and to be somewhere quiet. Jack realised that the Ecstasy was having a negative effect on me and took me straight home to his place, apologising all the way in the taxi. I was shivering so much that my teeth were chattering and continued to do so even after I'd had a hot bath and crawled under three duvets. Jack never encouraged me to take drugs again. And, not long after, we parted ways.

The casino job came to an abrupt halt one weekend when I came back late from a biker rally and went straight to work. The casino had introduced a clocking-in system using cards that noted the time you arrived and the time you left, and there was very little leeway for lateness. I clocked in on time but soon started to feel ill and so went home early, after informing the security staff that I was unwell. I put a note on my door and clocked out again. So far as I was aware, I had done nothing wrong.

I took dreams seriously and I'd recently dreamt that the security team had planted a credit card on me and then accused me of stealing it. Thinking this might be a portent I'd kept my nose very clean indeed, as I was convinced someone was trying to catch me out. Members of the security team had in fact started to visit me in my sewing room, using pretexts such as needing to borrow the iron. One of them asked me if I got bored but I said I was happy and that there was always something to do. I had recently taken on the workload of the elderly laundry man, whom they had generously sacked, although my wages had inexplicably remained the same.

The casino had launched an initiative offering a £500 incentive to anyone who could come up with ways of saving the company money. As if they weren't raking in enough money from the desperate and foolish punters who were throwing their hard-earned cash and life savings down the pan, thinking that they might get lucky and win a jackpot. Of course, it made sense to sack me too, and to save the casino my salary whilst netting the person whose suggestion it was £500.

The day after I'd gone home ill, I was summoned to the boss's office, where I was confronted with the note I had left on my door, and accused of being off the premises without permission. Occasionally, I would pop out of the casino to meet my friend who worked in nearby Soho. Sometimes I asked for permission and sometimes I didn't. I would find excuses to leave the building because I was so bored, stuck in the tiny room all day long with no one to talk to. I would say I needed a new reel of thread or needed to buy some sanitary towels. Any excuse for a change of scenery. But this time I was framed! They had been noting all the times I wasn't in my uniform room, despite there being a lack of work. I was sacked on the spot, with no verbal or written warning, given a week's notice and sent home in tears.

My good friend Sharon worked for a trade union and knew someone who could help me appeal against Royal Lion having sacked me. He said that, whilst it was a case of unfair dismissal, because I had only been in the job for 18 months I had no rights according to the law, as they could sack anyone who'd worked for less than two years, for any old flipping reason they wanted, and they knew it. I was screwed. It really was a dream come true.

Coincidentally, I had been due a share of profit-related pay from the casino, which I was due to receive in two weeks' time. What amazing timing! At the time I was sacked, my boss claimed that she wouldn't be so cruel and heartless as to prevent me from receiving the money that I would have been due two weeks later had they not fortuitously sacked me. However, I never received a penny and she later denied ever mentioning it. So clearly she was that cruel and heartless.

I fought hard for the £750 I would have been due and raised questions about the pay I had already received compared with the hours I had worked. The casino was part of a chain and other seamstresses at other locations were all paid more than me, yet they had less responsibility and worked more sociable hours.

However, Tarquin in gay-tering and I were still friends and he told me to be careful, reminding me that casinos were invariably run by gangsters, and warning me about what might happen to me if I was seen as a troublemaker. I really didn't want to end up wearing a con-

CHAPTER 18

crete overcoat, as grey has never really been my colour. At one point, I actually thought my landline was being tapped as I could hear clicking noises whenever certain friends rang me. I'm not sure whether it actually was tapped, as admittedly I'd been feeling exceptionally paranoid and anxious since being dismissed, but it was enough to push me over the edge. I suffered with anxiety and depression for months after I was fired and finally had to be prescribed temazepam from my GP just to help me sleep.

Eventually, I felt well enough to work again and got a job as a cloth cutter at a company that specialised in artists' canvases and equipment in North London.

I was working for a lovely guy called Fred, which was great fun. I enjoyed learning how to do quotes for large-scale drapes and curtains, mostly for theatres and schools. We supplied shark's-tooth scrim, huge backdrops, opulent theatrical curtains made from heavy velvet, stage skirts, etc. We also specialised in canvas and polyurethane boat covers. Fred called out the measurements and I would chalk them on the canvas, and he would then draw the final pattern freehand. He was extremely talented.

There was a vast cutting table that must have easily measured six metres by four metres and was about hip height, meaning that I had to stand on a chair to access it. We often had to stand on the table in order to manage the gigantic pieces of fabric.

I struck up a good friendship with one of the machinists, Babe, who was from Africa. Even though she was a practising Christian and I was still very much a pagan, she didn't seem to mind and didn't feel the need to follow me around the studio whilst chanting 'Evil' in a discordant voice like a crazed harpy. Admittedly, I had tried to keep quiet about my spiritual beliefs, as they had attracted so much negative attention in the past.

Meanwhile, I had been doing a few private tarot readings and had worked at a couple of psychic fairs. During one such psychic event in Camden Town Hall I met a lady from St Lucia called Genie, who had walked by while I was giving my friend Kevin a reading. (In which I predicted that he would meet someone called Catherine. Within a few weeks he met her and Kevin and Cathy have now been together for over 25 years.) Genie had picked up one of my business cards.

About a week later, Genie rang to book a reading for her friend, and then one for another friend, and another, but strangely never one for herself. Eventually, after I must have seen about 14 of her friends and family, she did book a reading for herself, which she was very happy with.

Genie was retired and was studying herbalism at the local college. She would often give me advice about which herbs to take for various ailments. Genie fascinated me. She didn't have much money and always had family worries but she had so many entertaining tales which she would recount to me about her life, which almost always made me laugh. I hated taking money off her, so we had an arrangement whereby I would swap readings for food or flowers. Anything so long as an exchange took place that didn't involve actual money.

Genie told me all about the Obeah, the religion that many St Lucians practise, which is a mix of pagan beliefs, magic and Christianity. She claimed to be a Catholic and was extremely knowledgeable about all things biblical. She would sometimes give me prayers to read that seemed to be thinly disguised spells involving candle magic, psalms and naming certain saints, and that used herbal and magical oils and incenses.

After my bike was stolen, Genie issued me with a prayer to recite out loud. She assured me that either the thief would bring the bike back and apologise, or something nasty would happen to him or he would steal again and get caught. I shuddered to think what the 'something nasty' might be, and decided against reciting the spell. I'd seen too many horror films and the thought of him being decapitated just for stealing my bike seemed a little extreme. Cutting his hands off though, that would be OK. Let the punishment fit the crime and all that.

My friendship with Genie grew over a number of years. Whilst reading her cards one day, the Magician card came up next to a romance card. Genie had been single for a long time and wondered if she would ever marry again. The cards revealed that she would in fact find romance with a grey-haired man with a grey moustache. As I looked closer at the card, I was reminded of someone I already knew.

'You know, Genie,' I said, 'I think I know who this is! I have a friend who looks just like that and who is also interested in astrology and psychic matters. And he is single too!'

CHAPTER 18

Genie giggled like a teenager and agreed to meet him. I took out my Cupid's bow, polished it and invited them both to dinner.

The man I had in mind was Buzz, whom I'd met a few months earlier. He'd picked up one of my leaflets and we'd met for a drink to discuss the possibility of joining forces to run some psychic development courses. It was while chatting to Buzz (who earned his name from his interest in aircraft) that I realised I had a past life connection with him, and that we'd known each other in what was then known as Persia. Anyway, I had visited Buzz recently and he said he was picking up the name Genie or Jen around me. I took that to be a pretty good sign that he and Genie were meant to meet. (And marry and live in marital bliss for the rest of their long and happy lives. And that it would all be because of me.)

On the evening of the date, Buzz rang me to ask if I wanted him to bring anything with him. 'Just a bottle of wine,' I suggested. 'Oh, and a tall dark handsome man,' I joked.

On the day of the dinner, I was up to my elbows in vegetarian spag bol when the phone rang.

'I've got the wine,' said Buzz. 'And now I'm off to pick up the other thing you asked for,' he said mischievously.

What other thing? I thought, racking my brain to recall our previous phone conversation. What was he talking about? 'A bottle of wine and… oh… and a tall dark handsome man!' I eventually blurted out. 'But that was a joke!'

I'd assumed that Buzz was calling my bluff but, as I went to answer the doorbell, I could see through the glass panels of the front door that he did actually have something human-shaped with him, someone who did indeed match the description of tall and dark. I opened the door warily and instantly realised that whoever he had brought with him also answered the description of handsome. Martyn had black shoulder-length hair and was dressed in jeans and a black leather biker jacket. Buzz had only gone and found me a tall dark handsome man! I must admit that I fancied him at first sight. In fact, I fancied his shadow before I'd even opened the front door. Buzz just stood there grinning mischievously, with a smug mission-accomplished glint in his eye.

After introducing everyone and opening a bottle of wine, I bumbled off nervously to hide in the kitchen while I prepared the meal.

Despite my bravado, I was still very shy and wasn't sure how to behave or what to say in front of this hot man. Eventually, Buzz came and found me.

'Aren't you going to even talk to him?' he said.

I eventually summoned up the courage to ask Martyn to come and help me in the kitchen chopping garlic and grating cheese. Not the most romantic first date, I'll grant you, but it was easier for me to talk to him whilst I had something to do with my hands. Ahem. We were soon bonding over the cheese grater. It was close to my birthday and I was having a party the next day, so I asked him if he wanted to come and he accepted. I was already imagining lots of things I could do to occupy my hands the next time we met.

Unfortunately, Genie and Buzz didn't hit it off quite so well. Genie found Buzz to be overly boastful and he found her prissy. They never met again. So much for my usually highly accurate predictions. However, Martyn came to my party the next night, and we stayed up until 5am, talking about anything and everything. I felt very comfortable with him. Eventually, one of us slipped an arm around the other and he stayed the night. Two weeks later, he moved in with me. There was something wonderfully quiet and peaceful about Martyn that I liked and that I needed in a man. He had a lovely aura like a blue flame and I instantly felt safe and reassured around him. Martyn's presence in my life was tranquillising. God knows, my life had been chaotic enough up until then. He was just what I wanted and needed.

Martyn was an out-of-work glazier, but Buzz soon found him some work at the goldsmiths he worked at in Hatton Garden, London's jewellery quarter. It was basic work that involved putting up shelves and painting the walls but, after just a few weeks, the boss asked Martyn if he would like to try casting gold. He gave it a try and it turned out it he was better at it than the boss, so soon became the casting manager in charge of an entire department. In a short while, he was earning good money and started paying half of the rent. Martyn went on to become not only my common-law husband but also the father of our son, Jack.

I lived in Hartham Road for a total of four years. It was only really designed for one person, so it was a bit of a squeeze with the two of

CHAPTER 18

us, especially after we started sharing the room with a third tenant – an industrial sewing machine that took up the same amount of space as a slightly overweight baby elephant.

I had started to create clothing again and had also taken up screen-printing again and was now making my own silkscreens. I found a studio where I could do silkscreen printing for 50p an hour and combined my interest in tarot and textiles by screen-printing large tarot designs onto plain T-shirts. I also made corsets and cloaks which I sold at pagan events and at a Halloween festival at the University of London Union. The skills I had learned whilst studying for my diploma in theatrical costume construction had come in very handy. The Halloween event was run by a witches' coven called the Crow and the Bat (not their real names) who invited me to join them; so for a couple of years I became a coven member.

I stayed at the North London warehouse for two years before deciding it was time to go back to being self-employed and more creative. It was slow going, trying to build up my self-employed work, so I also took on a part-time job as an ear-piercer at Selfridges, the famous department store near Bond Street. I looked very respectable. Yes, me, respectable! With shoulder-length natural (yes, natural!) brown (brown!) hair, scant make-up (I know!) and a white nurse's uniform that I had to wear for the job. I fibbed about my past – when I had pierced ears and noses on a dodgy piss-stained stall in Camden Market – and made out that I was a fully experienced ear-piercing entrepreneur.

During this time, Mum suffered a stroke due to stress and her lifestyle. She had always been an extremely hard worker, had smoked and drunk heavily for many years and eaten unhealthy food. She was overweight despite many attempts throughout her life to diet. And the only 'exercise' she got was playing darts. Darts players being renowned for their slim waistlines.

One day I had a phone call from my mum's lodger telling me that Mum was in hospital. She was unable to speak and her left side was affected. She couldn't walk and needed help standing, and the left-hand side of her mouth hung downwards so that she dribbled.

She was given a stent in her neck, where there had been a blockage, and was advised, of course, to give up smoking and change her diet and lifestyle. However, she took absolutely no notice and even managed to persuade one of the porters to push her wheelchair into the hospital grounds and give her a cigarette. I was appalled.

She eventually discharged herself after four months, having lied about my sister and I being at home to help her. They wouldn't have discharged her if they had known she was going back to an empty house.

Despite Mum being in a wheelchair, she was determined to walk again. And, bizarrely, it was her refusal to give up smoking that did it. No one would buy cigarettes for her, so she forced herself to stand and walk so that eventually she could go to the local newsagent to buy them herself. It took her over an hour to walk what used to take her five minutes, but she did it and was triumphant about her achievement, regardless of the fact that it was driven by the urge to indulge her addiction to nicotine. She also taught herself to write and play darts with her right hand. Stubborn mare!

A year later, she suffered a heart attack and was rushed into hospital. At 4am on the day that I was due to go and visit her, I had a phone call from my sister to say that the hospital had rung and Mum had gone into cardiac arrest again. By the time I reached the hospital, she had already passed away. A sense of peace had suddenly come over me on the way to the hospital, as if I'd sensed that she had already gone.

My mother's death was a massive turning point in my life. We had to sell her house as neither my sister nor I could afford to take it on, but that did mean that we then had the money from the house sale. Dealing with Mum's funeral and sorting out her paperwork was intensely stressful and took a year to complete. I had.lived the best part of 12 years in that house in Morden, from the ages of nine to 21 (if you count the couple of times I moved back), as it was the place I always went back to when my other housing options didn't work out, usually using a porter's trolley to transport my belongings.

Now my mum was gone and the house was gone too. Nothing prepares you for losing a parent. We weren't a terribly close family but, in a way, I think that makes a parent departing this mortal coil almost worse. You dwell on how your relationship should or could have been. What you could have done better. And I did love my mother.

CHAPTER 18

However, the money that I received from the sale of her house meant that I was able to put a deposit down on my very own property and move out of London. So while I had to say goodbye to my mother, I was also, because of her, able to say goodbye to the stresses of living in London and in temporary housing for good.

Thank you, Mum.

As my sister and I and also my dad (whom she had finally divorced several years previously) packed up and redistributed Mum's belongings, waves of sadness flooded over me. However, I also remembered some of the funny times: like her reaction to my blue hair when I was just 16, being introduced to my spiky-haired penfriends Flick, Angel and Cindy and not batting an eyelid at Sebastian's red hair or black nail polish.

How different my life would have been had I not slipped a small classified advert and cheque into an envelope one afternoon in 1983 and sent it to *Sounds*...

**BORED LONDON PUNKETTE (18)
SEEKS WEIRD OR INTERESTING PEOPLE
FOR FRIENDSHIP AND GIGS
REPLY TO BOX NO 13561**

Acknowledgements

Big thanks to the following people for support and creativity:

The Epping Forest Writers Group, who got me started on this journey and had to endure some of my rather shocking life stories (which I eventually toned down a tad – just a tad, mind): Peter Relph, Mo Woods, Midge Venables, Murielle Good, Mike Pugh, Ray Sleep, Carole Segal, Sheila Horsham, Christine Ives, Moira Vallane, Graham Childs, Jenny Hart, Linda Seago/Hadfield, Kim Sinclair, etc.

Gerard Evans (Flowers in the Dustbin), Sharon Brown and Gregg Bull for being the first people to read my manuscript and see the potential, and for wading through pages and pages and pages… oh and more pages… Especially Sharon for finding Unbound for me and manning my Twitter account and co-hosting the Soap the Stamps Facebook page (SoapthestampsJumpthetube) and making the first promo video.

Sarah and Glenn Noble from Sarah Pink's Gravediggers for helping record the backing track (thanks to Andy Norie-Rolfe for the guitar-playing) and for the film footage yet to be used.

A massive thank you to Michael Muldoon for the first edits and rewrites and for making sense of my writing and saying my words better and making them more humorous than I ever could, without losing my style and intention.

And to Steve Watson for the original cover design and artwork.

Thanks to the following people for letting me keep their real names:

The original Lost Cherrees – Steve, Sian, Bev, Deb, Andy and Nuts.

Thanks also to Mary, Tony, Saucy Jon, Nic and Sean (the Totten-ham crew – 'we survived "Nam", Totten-Nam, together').

Simon, Tom Vague and Dev (the Kyverdale Road gang).

Nigel, Sebastian and Steve C.

Paul, Chris, Veg and Julie (WAGTEY and Hagar the Womb).

Yasmin, Paul (aka Paulo, the 'o' added so as to not confuse him with Paul WAGTEY), Ellen and the Paros lot.

Lisa, Dave and George (from Adventures in Colour) for use of their real names and for permission to use song lyrics from 'Adventures in Colour'.

Also Sharon, Marina and Bill Grey (lifelong friends).

To Des Connolly for believing in me and supporting this project.

And the two Keiths – Keith Goldhanger Chapman and Keith Bailey (Here and Now).

To all the punks, bikers, witches and goths – for being punks, bikers, witches and goths.

To anyone who ever started a band or made their own clothes or squatted.

And to Unbound for making it all happen!

Finally, to those who never made it: RIP Rupert, Pus, Mal, Fiona Fallover, Nogbad, Gay Steve, Kev, Paco from Conflict and many more.

Patrons

Melissa Abs
Karen Amsden
Amy Appleby
Caroline Tropicalbird Artist
Riff Atta
Nicola Barrett
Mary Barrett
Rachel Bass
Belle Benfield
Natalie Brett
Paola Camacho
Karen Challinor
Giles Coe
Steven Corr
Kevin Currie
Caroline Dobson
Gerard Evans
Laura Evans
Pawla Flaming
Sarah Forsdyke
Alice Frankreiter
Kathy Freeman
Juliette Gilbert
Brian Gilvary
Kim J Griffin
Lucinda Grove
Ruth Hagar
Svenny Hoo Har
Daniel Jervis
Catherine Keevil
Emma Kiersey
Chris Knowles

Simon Leadbeater
David Leverno
Melanie Maddison
Jessica Martin
Elaine McDonald
Derek McGillivray
Carlo Navato
Dave Reeves
Shea Refuse
Tara Rez
Vicky Ridley
Angie Runagall
Anita Schäffer-Szász
Kristina-Rose Sears
Jane Shann
Barbara Stefanelli
Barbara Ulargiu
Sig Waller
Sherry Warrick
Pauline Wing